CONTROL AND DISCIPLINE IN SCHOOLS:
PERSPECTIVES AND APPROACHES

J. W. **Docking** is Principal Lecturer in Education at the Roehampton Institute of Higher Education, London. He began his teaching career at a comprehensive school in Yorkshire, and was Head of History at a comprehensive school in Coventry before taking up his appointment as Lecturer in Education at Whitelands College, London. His publications include *Victorian Schools and Scholars, Men and Machines*, and various articles on control and discipline in schools. His doctoral thesis in psychology was a developmental study of the attribution of personal responsibility.

CONTROL AND DISCIPLINE IN SCHOOLS: PERSPECTIVES AND APPROACHES

Second Edition

J. W. DOCKING

P·C·P
Paul Chapman
Publishing Ltd

Copyright © 1987 J. W. Docking
All rights reserved

First published 1987 by
Harper & Row Ltd

Reprinted in this edition by
Paul Chapman Publishing Ltd
144 Liverpool Road
London N1 1LA

No part of this publication may be reproduced, stored in a retrieval system, or transmitted, in any form or by any means, electronic, mechanical, photocopying, recording or otherwise, without the prior permission of Paul Chapman Publishing Ltd.

British Library Cataloguing in Publication Data
Docking, J. W.
　Control and discipline in schools:
　perspectives and approaches. — 2nd ed.
　1. School discipline — Great Britain
　I. Title
　371.5'0941　　　LB3012

ISBN 1 85396 156 6

Typeset by Burns & Smith, Derby
Printed and bound by Athenaeum Press Ltd, Newcastle upon Tyne.

A B C D E F G H I   8 7 6 5 4 3 2 1 0

CONTENTS

Acknowledgements viii
Preface to First Edition ix
Preface to Second Edition xiii

1 INTRODUCTION: THE PROBLEM OF SCHOOL 1
BEHAVIOUR AND DISCIPLINE
   Further reading 10

2 ACCOUNTING FOR CHILDREN'S BEHAVIOUR: 12
I. INFLUENCES OUTSIDE THE SCHOOL
   Problems in explaining unacceptable behaviour 12
   Factors within the child 14
   Factors in the home 17
   Factors in society 23
   The physical environment 26
   Some implications for teachers 27
   Further reading 29

3 ACCOUNTING FOR CHILDREN'S BEHAVIOUR: 30
II. THE IMPACT OF THE SCHOOL
   Research problems 31
   Findings from school effectiveness studies 33
   Learning difficulties and curriculum opportunities 39
   Adjustment to school 41
   The interaction of home and school influences 43
   Further reading 44

4	THE PLACE OF DISCIPLINE IN SCHOOL	45
	(1) 'Society depends upon a disciplined community'	46
	(2) 'Children need discipline for their own good'	50
	(3) 'You can't teach without good discipline'	51
	(4) 'Discipline is educative'	53
	Further reading	57
5	TEACHER–PUPIL RELATIONSHIPS: PERCEPTIONS AND EXPECTATIONS	58
	The meaning of relationships in school	58
	Teachers' judgements of pupils	60
	Pupils' judgements of teachers	71
	Further reading	79
6	THE MANAGEMENT OF PUPIL BEHAVIOUR	81
	The significance of the class as a group	82
	The significance of verbal and non-verbal communication	84
	First encounters with a class	86
	Classroom management skills	90
	Seating arrangements	95
	A whole-school policy for the management of behaviour	96
	Further reading	98
7	PRAISE AND REWARDS	99
	Rewards and intrinsic interest	100
	The effects of praise	102
	Behaviour modification	104
	Further reading	113
8	PUNISHMENT IN SCHOOL	115
	Punishment as a means of social control	115
	Corporal punishment	123
	Can punishment be educative?	129
	Further reading	136
9	PASTORAL CARE AND SOCIAL CONTROL	137
	The concept of pastoral care	137
	Pastoral care and school discipline	139
	Pastoral systems and 'troubleshooting'	141
	The pastoral curriculum	142
	Counselling in schools	145
	Further reading	149

10	BEYOND THE SCHOOL'S RESOURCES?	150
	Welfare and psychological services	150
	Suspension and exclusion	154
	Off-site support units	157
	Alternatives to off-site units	162
	Further reading	166
	References and Author Index	168
	Subject Index	189

ACKNOWLEDGEMENTS

I would like to record my grateful thanks to my wife, Anne, Paul Brannan and Ted Fisk, who read the whole manuscript and made many valuable comments that prompted me to re-write parts of the text.

I wish to acknowledge permission to quote extracts from the following books: J. Plamenatz, 'Responsibility and Punishment', in P. Laslett and W. C. Runciman (eds.) *Philosophy, Politics and Society*, third series (Blackwell, Oxford); R. Best, P. Ribbins, C. Jarvis and D. Oddy, *Education and Care* (Heinemann Educational Books, London, 1983); D. H. Lawrence (1915) *The Rainbow*, by permission of Laurence Pollinger Ltd, the Estate of Mrs Frieda Lawrence Ravagli, London, and Viking Penguin Inc., New York; C. Lacey, *Hightown Grammar* (Manchester University Press, 1970); N. Otty, *Learner Teacher* (Penguin Books, Harmondsworth, 1972, reprinted 1983 by Bristol Classical Press); D. H. Hargreaves, *The Challenge of the Comprehensive School (1982)* and *Interpersonal Relations and Education* (1975); D. H. Hargreaves, S. Hester and F. J. Mellor, *Deviance in Classrooms* (Routledge & Kegan Paul, London, 1975). The extract from the article by J. W. Docking in *Early Child Development and Care*, Vol. 8, is reprinted by permission of the publishers, Gordon & Breach Science Publishers Inc.

PREFACE TO FIRST EDITION

Little can be said with confidence about the subject of children's behaviour in schools today. But two things are certain: there is no shortage of opinion, and the literature is profuse. Equally clear, at least in the English-speaking world, is that there is no consensus view, but rather a variety of perspectives and approaches. Some consider this a matter for regret, others a cause for rejoicing. Whatever view is taken, all who are professionally concerned with children's behaviour in schools need to have some understanding of the various positions that are taken and some guidance concerning appropriate action.

In the numerous research studies and the literature concerning theories of children's behaviour, the emphasis is variously placed. It can be on emotional deprivation in early childhood, on the child's inability to direct his behaviour in a rational way, on the way environmental factors shape behaviour patterns, on the way children model their behaviour on those of others, on hereditary influences, on the development of adolescent 'identity crisis' and delinquent subculture, or on the antecedents of self-esteem. The theories in turn have generated a proliferation of prescriptions, some based on welfare, some on therapy, some on rewards, some on punishment, some on societal change, some on education. Parallel to these studies are writings concerned with the concepts of order, control, discipline, punishment, deviance, etc., demonstrating how statements concerning order in schools reflect fundamental values and different sets of assumptions relating to the purpose of schools, the education system, and what should characterize 'disciplined behaviour'.

In recent years, there has been rather less concentration on factors that lie outside the school and more on the way school experiences themselves can promote perceptions of authority and how these can, in some cases, precipitate behaviour problems. This shift of emphasis suggests that responsibility for changing pupil behaviour in schools lies to some extent in the hands of teachers and those concerned with the organization of schools. But the controversy goes further than this. Some see the need for a new conception of schooling that embodies a more 'appropriate' curriculum, a greater emphasis on pastoral care and counselling, and a fundamental change of outlook in the way some teachers view their relationships with pupils, particularly with working-class adolescents. Some see the answer in terms of modifying children's behaviour 'scientifically' by systematically rewarding approved behaviour, while others would prefer to rely more on the 'short, sharp shock' as a consequence of unacceptable behaviour. Some see the problem as essentially one that demands greater skills in classroom management. Some see it partly in terms of special provision for pupils whose behaviour is disruptive in mainstream schooling.

This book is written in the belief that, complex as all these issues and problems are, it is no solution to fall back unthinkingly on traditional tactics that 'worked' in the past; nor is it sufficient to adopt a simple pragmatic approach, utilizing whatever procedure seems to 'work best' in particular circumstances. For both these approaches avoid the more arduous but educationally necessary exercise of formulating the criteria by which what 'works best' is to be judged; and both approaches, however 'effective' their short-term impact, can lead easily to the development of unproductive teacher–pupil relationships which might prove difficult to put right later on. Any teacher who takes seriously the education of children must be prepared to come to terms with the way his or her own behaviour can affect the pupils' behaviour and with the possibility that behaviour problems in schools might be minimized both indirectly, through greater understanding of their nature and origin, and directly, through the adoption of more appropriate teaching arrangements.

I have therefore attempted in this book to map out some of the central issues concerning control and discipline in school and to bring together a range of studies that bear upon these issues and that relate to the difficult practical problems facing teachers and others concerned with children's behaviour in schools. I hope the book will therefore be helpful in bringing a variety of perspectives, arguments, ideas, evidence, and practical approaches to the attention of students, teachers, and other readers who are endeavouring to formulate or to reappraise their own beliefs about appropriate and effective ways of dealing with children in school.

Jim Docking
Whitelands College
Roehampton Institute of Higher Education
January 1980

PREFACE TO SECOND EDITION

In order to incorporate recent evidence and ideas concerning problems of control and discipline in schools, this book has been restructured and largely re-written. For reasons of space, some material in the first edition has had to be jettisoned, but it is hoped that any disadvantages this brings are outweighed by the inclusion of new material. There are now separate chapters on praise and rewards, classroom management skills, pastoral care, and problems of dealing with pupils whose antisocial behaviour presents a continuing problem. Suggestions for further reading have also been added at the end of each chapter.

Although attention is given to background factors in explaining the aetiology of classroom behaviour, the main emphasis, as before, is on the role of the school. Special consideration is given to ways in which disruptive behaviour can be prevented through improving the quality of teacher–pupil relationships by changing teachers' perceptions (especially in relation to pupils from working-class homes and ethnic minority groups), attending to classroom management skills and teacher actions, reconsidering features of school organization, and developing support for teachers.

Jim Docking
March 1987

1
INTRODUCTION: THE PROBLEM OF SCHOOL BEHAVIOUR AND DISCIPLINE

'Oh, you have to keep order if you want to teach,' said Miss Harby, hard, superior, trite.
Ursula did not answer. She felt non-valid before them.
'If you want to be let to *live*, you have,' said Mr. Brunt.
'Well, if you can't keep order, what good *are* you?' said Miss Harby.
'An' you've got to do it by yourself' – his voice rose like the bitter cry of the prophets. 'You'll get no *help* from anybody.'
(D. H. Lawrence, *The Rainbow*).

Probably nowhere in English literature is there a more faithful and perceptive account of the problems involved in keeping class order than in Chapter 13 of *The Rainbow*, in which a young teacher, Ursula Brangwen, tries to cope with her class of fifty-five eleven-year-olds in the Board school of a poor quarter in a Midlands town at the beginning of the century.

Ursula approaches her first post with passionate feelings about the significance of her role in establishing pupil–teacher relationships:

> as a teacher, she would be in authority. And it was all unknown. She was excited. ... She dreamed how she would make the little ugly children love her. She would be so *personal*. Teachers were always so hard and impersonal. There was no vivid relationship. She would make everything personal and vivid, she would give herself.

Then comes the realization that her dream is incompatible with the reality. In wanting to be 'the beloved teacher bringing light and joy to her children' she approaches the class with generosity and considerateness 'making the whole business personal, and using no compulsion'; but, in doing so, 'she was offering to the class a relationship which only one or two of the children were sensitive enough to appreciate'. She does not foresee 'what host she was gathering against herself by her superior tolerance, her kindness, and her *laisser-aller*'. She finds her class hostile and jeering, 'depending on her for command' while, paradoxically, 'command it hated and resented'.

Kindness seems counter-productive, yet she cannot help but resent the advice received from another teacher to 'get a bit tighter hand' over her class. She suspects the motives behind the head's interventions, which she finds demoralizing: 'He began to persecute her because she could not keep her class in proper condition, because her class was the weak link in the chain which made up the school.' His vicious caning of one of her pupils distresses her because she thinks that the boy's suffering was a direct consequence of her inability to keep order.

Then, resigned to imposing her will on the children, she is alarmed to find that this involves an abnegation of her personal self. Painfully, she feels she must abandon her dream 'to become the first wise teacher by making the whole business personal'. Instead, she must be 'nothing but Standard Five teacher. Ursula Brangwen must be excluded.' The tragedy is that, in shedding her own personal identity, she loses sight of the children as individuals: 'She saw no children, only the task that was to be done.' Ursula had gone 'open and warm to give herself to the children' but had found that she 'as teacher must bring them all, as scholars, into subjection'. Determined to make an example of one boy whose 'spirit infected them all', she canes him relentlessly, but succeeds only in stimulating class excitement and tension, while she herself feels upset and degraded.

Eventually Ursula finds that by being brutal and resorting to physical punishment she can establish herself – but at a price: for she is reduced to 'a hard, insentient thing' while the children are 'broken and desolate'. In winning, she has lost: 'She would rather bear all their insults and insolences a thousand times than reduce herself and them to this.' She does find 'a certain amount of pleasure in the sheer oblivion of teaching, so much work to do, so many children to see after, so much to be done, that one's self is forgotten'; yet class teaching had become an 'exhausting, wearying strain, always unnatural'. In despair she asks herself why she has become a schoolteacher.

Ursula Brangwen's experiences and encounters, thoughts and emotions, hopes and frustrations, all bear a striking resemblance to those of many young teachers in schools today. In their analysis of the transcripts of tape-recorded conversations with probationary teachers just a decade ago, Hannam, Smyth and Stephenson (1976) showed how in the first year of teaching there is still the erosion of ideals, rejection by children who see in the young teacher an opportunity to attack what they dislike about school in general, and encounters with individuals 'fighting each other for the teacher's dominance, cheered on by the rest from a safe distance' (p. 111). Of course much has changed. Yet many of the issues Lawrence describes – particularly the problems of teacher–pupil relationships, relationships between new and established staff, and punishment – are still with us. There is a striking similarity between the ways D. H. Lawrence and Hannam, Smyth and Stephenson (1976) depict the probationer's predicament:

> In some ways he represents a threat to the school: he is an unknown quantity, possibly a weak link in the chain of good order and discipline, and he will be watched very carefully.
>
> (Hannam, Smyth and Stephenson, 1976, p. 10)

> He began to persecute her because she could not keep her class in proper condition, because her class was the weak link in the chain which made up the school.
>
> (Lawrence, p. 385, Penguin ed.)

If the class control problems depicted by Lawrence are typical of the times – and the historical evidence suggests this is so (see Humphries, 1981) – there is reason to be cautious in accepting the view that standards of discipline in school have seriously deteriorated during this century. However, many teachers, judging from reports recently issued by the unions (e.g. AMMA, 1984; NAS/UWT, 1985; PAT, 1985) certainly believe that violent behaviour and major incidents of disruption in school are prevalent and are becoming worse.

Whether this is really so or is more a symptom of belief in 'the good old days' is difficult to say, not least because the evidence produced since the 1970s is conflicting. Lowenstein (1972), on the basis of 1,940 replies to a questionnaire distributed nationally to 13,500 schools, concluded that 'the amount of varied violence both in secondary and primary schools is much larger than might have been anticipated from the occasional press report, etc.' (p. 25). In 1973, Rhodes Boyson, the prominent Conservative politician and ex-headmaster, confirmed these claims when he wrote: 'England is not as far from America's Blackboard Jungle as some people would like to think and the doubt whether local education authorities will support firm action to restrain wreckers daily brings it nearer' (Boyson, 1973, p. 97). Contrast these opinions with the evidence produced in a study of twelve inner-London secondary schools over a period of twelve weeks by Michael Rutter *et al.* (1979): 'While some teachers experienced difficulties with some of their classes, the 'blackboard jungle' image of city schools was definitely not the predominant impression which emerged from our observations' (p. 65). A similar conclusion was reached by Her Majesty's Inspectors (HMI, 1979), who found 'the great majority' of the 384 secondary schools surveyed to be 'orderly communities'; indiscipline was considered to be a 'considerable' problem in only 6 per cent of schools, and a 'serious problem' in less than 1 per cent.

Consensus is also lacking in the more recent reports. In a document called *Pupil Violence and Serious Disorder in Schools*, issued in 1985, the National Association of Schoolmasters/Union of Women Teachers claimed that comments received from 3,910 members justified the belief that violence between pupils in some schools approached 'open gang warfare'; that almost one in five teachers had experienced violence 'resulting in serious injury' on one or more occasions in the first six months of the school year; that almost one in four teachers had been threatened with violence themselves; that nearly one in ten had suffered an attempted attack from a pupil, almost half the incidents involving the use of a weapon. Yet in a survey by Dierenfield (1982), covering 465 comprehensive school teachers in 41 local education authorities, no respondent regarded disruption in his or her school to be 'totally out of hand', only 3.6 per cent said it was a 'severe situation', while over two-thirds reported the position as 'a problem but one with which it is possible to cope'.

In the recent London junior school project (ILEA, 1986a), the percentage of pupils who were, at any one time, assessed as disturbed on a scale which measured aggression fluctuated between 3.9 and 6.1. Teachers viewed less than 10 per cent of pupils to be disobedient or spiteful towards other children; by contrast, more than three-quarters were judged to be cooperative. The same study, however, revealed that the pupils had less favourable self-impressions, just over half seeing themselves as generally doing what they were told!

Lawrence, Steed and Young (1984b) collected perceptions of disruptive behaviour from more than one hundred education lecturers, educational psychologists, heads of special schools and researchers in six European countries (Austria, Belgium, Denmark, France, West Germany and Switzerland). Replies certainly revealed a general belief in a growth in disruptive acts of one kind or another. However, except in France, physical violence towards teachers was seen as the least problem; and 'difficult

Introduction 5

schools' as distinct from 'difficult classes' received a low rating. The main sorts of incidents causing general concern were physical violence between children, truancy and disobedience. However, even here opinion varied considerably, even within the same localities, and some respondents commented that beliefs in an increase in disruption may not be well-founded.

That the evidence concerning serious disruption is conflicting should not be a matter of surprise since there are many problems in producing valid and reliable data on this matter. The general difficulties in assessing children's behaviour are discussed at the beginning of Chapters 2 and 3. As regards the surveys based on teachers' self-reports, confidence in the claims made by teachers depends partly on how far you believe that consensus exists among respondents about what counts as violent or disruptive behaviour and that teachers who have experienced some frightening incidents are not exaggerating. For instance, was the Birmingham teacher who stated to the NAS/UWT (1985) inquiry 'I have witnessed *literally thousands* of examples of pupil to pupil violence ranging from shooting to knifing and gang warfare' (p. 4, emphasis added) perhaps guilty of dramatization? In this context, it is worth noting the contrast between these sorts of claims and the official statistics on juvenile delinquency. Between 1980 and 1985, the total number of proceedings for indictable and summary offences against those between ten and sixteen years fell by 32 per cent from 139,000 to 94,000 (Home Office, 1985).

Another factor concerns the methodology employed and the basis on which results are interpreted. Claims are sometimes made on the basis of very small returns. Lowenstein's (1972) report, mentioned earlier, was based on replies received from only 10 per cent of the primary schools surveyed and 22 per cent of the secondary schools; his 1975 follow-up report was based on only 5 per cent of primary schools, 15 per cent of middle schools, and 18 per cent of secondary schools. According to a recent report by the Assistant Masters and Mistresses Association (AMMA) (1984) on behaviour problems at infant and junior levels, three-quarters of the responding schools believed that there had been a 'marked deterioration' in young children's conduct and their social training over the last five years. Yet these conclusions were based on a response rate of only 31.2 per cent. It is quite possible that the large majority of schools who ignore questionnaires in national surveys are not sufficiently concerned about the problem to reply. Alternatively, the absence of respectable returns might be because teachers are reluctant to disclose information that might adversely reflect upon their professional competence – in which case the situation could be even worse than that reported. We just do not know. As regards the AMMA survey, it must also be queried whether teachers can reliably recall what children were like five years previously.

Finally, could it be that part of the explanation for reports of an escalation in serious behavioural incidents is that teachers' attitudes are hardening? This possibility was raised in the Pack Report (SED, 1977) on indiscipline in Scottish schools. It received some credence between September and December 1985 when Poundswick High School in Manchester virtually ground to a halt because most of the staff took action in sympathy with eight of their colleagues who, far from being supported by the city council, had been suspended for refusing to teach five boys who had been found guilty of drawing racist and obscene graffiti on the school walls.

Although serious incidents, such as physical assaults on teachers, are probably rare events in schools, general class control problems such as boisterousness, inattentiveness, noise, cheekiness, sullenness, disobedience and bad language are clearly matters that do bother large numbers of teachers. In replies to a questionnaire circulated to junior school teachers in Wolverhampton and Bilston by Merrett and Wheldall (1984), 62 per cent of the 119 (60 per cent) who replied answered 'Yes' to the question 'Do you feel that you are spending more time dealing with problems of behaviour than you ought?' Apart from non-attendance, the behaviours that caused the greatest concern were 'talking', 'non-attending and disobeying' and 'disturbing others'. Similar findings have emerged in recent small scale but in-depth studies of London secondary schools (Denscombe, 1984; Steed, 1985). Steed found that teachers were concerned mainly about 'innumerable acts of pupils, whether deliberate or accidental, which indicate inattentiveness, unwillingness or inability to learn in the way the teachers want' (p. 5). Thus, although misbehaviour in schools today may not, on analysis, be as serious as is sometimes made out, as far as violence to teachers is concerned, it is serious in the sense that incidents often insignificant in themselves are sufficiently frequent to cause many teachers concern.

It is also clear that disruptive behaviour is a major source of stress. Kloska and Ramasut (1985) found that 'pupils' indiscipline' and 'lack of consensus on discipline by staff' ranked third and fourth respectively out of eleven sources of stress that were presented to sixty-four comprehensive school teachers in one city. In a study based on the self-reports of over 700 teachers in mixed comprehensive schools in England (Kyriacou, 1980) it was found that the proportion of teachers experiencing occupational stress (in which the dominant feeling was that of being very tense) was in the region of 20–30 per cent, and that 'pupil misbehaviour' (along with 'poor work conditions', 'time pressures' and 'poor school ethos') was a principal contributing factor. Interestingly, stress was not related to sex, qualification, age, length of service or position held in the school (though, of course, teachers who experience stress may be likely to leave the profession). However, it was related to external locus of control, i.e. a tendency to believe that events in your life are largely outside your control. This led Kyriacou to conclude that stress arises from perceptions of threat, and that teachers who experience stress are prone to perceiving their situation as threatening.

Part of the problem here, no doubt, is that pupils who are disruptive are bored and frustrated in a system they believe has little to offer them and that denies them status. Teachers in turn feel threatened by the pupils' negative response to their endeavours, over-react, and then find that this has exacerbated the situation. Steed (1985) comments from observations in two London schools that aggression against teachers 'is often the reactive response by pupils to what they perceive as inappropriate, unfair or aggressive behaviour of the teacher initially' (p. 5). Again, Antcliffe (1986), from his work as a support teacher working with disaffected pupils in Nottinghamshire, suggests that a good deal of classroom disruption and teacher stress arises because some teachers misrepresent relatively minor but regular incidents of misbehaviour as evidence of personal maliciousness; this belief in turn is communicated to the pupil, bringing about further disruption. It may be, therefore, that one way of relieving stress in teachers is to help them develop more appropriate understandings of disaffected pupils. The Hargreaves Committee on secondary education (ILEA, 1984), recognizing that 'the response of punishment and rejection tends to make pupils worse, not better', was quite clear about this: 'The most urgent need, we believe, is to change the way we perceive these pupils' (paras. 3.16.2/3). This is a matter we take up in Chapter 5.

Teachers also need help in planning and organizing lessons so that classes are less likely to get out of hand (see Chapter 6). Denscombe (1984) concluded from his observations and interviews with staff in two London comprehensive schools that referrals to heads of houses (which tended to come mainly from young, inexperienced teachers) were regarded by the senior staff 'as problems of teacher control rather than problems of particular pupils. ... the problem, in other words, was seen as the teacher not the pupil' (p. 146). Teachers who have learned the skills of effective classroom management should be less susceptible to stress since, through preventative strategies, they are able to remove some of the occasion for confrontation and disruption. Being more in control of the situation, they have less need to worry about how to cope with behaviour problems when they arise.

Teachers are also more likely to feel competent in potentially threatening situations if they know that they are not themselves victims of a closed system, that they can influence policy that affects their work situation (Dunham, 1981). Additionally, according to findings by Phillips and Whitfield (1980), teachers feel a need to discuss their professional problems in confidence with someone in authority, but find that this kind of opportunity is rarely afforded in schools. It is probably true to say that we often seem more concerned to provide support for disaffected pupils directly (e.g. through sanctions, counselling, therapy, referral to special units) than indirectly by giving the kind of support to teachers that will enable them to develop more positive relationships with these children. As Hargreaves (1978, p. 541) has pointed out, 'Teachers bear their stress in painful isolation'.

The next two chapters of this book deal with the problem of explaining children's behaviour in school. Chapter 2 deals with factors in the child, his home and the general environment; Chapter 3 shifts the focus to features of the school situation itself. The general argument is that (a) factors outside the immediate control of the school (such as quality of upbringing in the home) are very important in influencing children's behaviour in and out of school, but (b) school factors are also highly influential, sometimes even more so. The appropriate approach, then, is one that tries to understand not only the child himself and his background but also the impact of the institutional setting in which the child functions.

It seems unhelpful to represent misbehaviour in schools in terms of 'difficult pupils' who come from 'problem families'. This simply absolves schools of their responsibility, and, in any case, oversimplifies the aetiology of the problem. If instead, we conceptualize the issue in terms of the *behaviour* rather than the person, then we can appreciate more readily how that behaviour is affected by a range of interrelated factors which include those in the school. The question we must ask is 'What are the various features of a school situation that maintain, and even generate, unacceptable behaviour, and how can these be suitably changed?' Needless to say, co-operation with the family is of the greatest importance – but this will be more effective if it is part of a general strategy that addresses the issues relating directly to the context in which the problem behaviour is manifest.

One of the most interesting findings that emerged in both the London secondary school study by Rutter *et al.* (1979) and the Junior School Project (ILEA, 1986a) was that pupil behaviour and work was affected by the school *as an institution*, and not only by individual factors. Thus the common-sense belief, that 'school climate' or 'ethos' – the 'feel' of the place – is important was empirically verified. A piecemeal consideration of school factors, focusing on only one element in the situation (e.g. sanctions whilst ignoring teacher–pupil relationships; or pastoral care whilst ignoring the curriculum) is therefore unlikely to be effective since this fails to recognize their combined influence and interrelatedness. Similarly, piecemeal action by individual teachers is unlikely to be as effective as concerted 'whole school' efforts planned by the staff as a team.

The kind of strategy just outlined involves what is sometimes called a 'systemic approach'. This assumes that behaviour can be effectively changed only by recognizing that the individual behaves the way he does because he exists in a 'system', or rather a series of systems, such as the family, neighbourhood, and school. A system comprises a complex network of interacting elements. These elements can be regarded as any aspects of the situation: in a school this clearly includes the individual and other people, but also, for instance, customs, roles, procedures, structures, relationships. Thus, while pupils and teachers are clearly part of the school system, so also is the procedure for registration, the grouping system, the school rules, rewards and punishments, the curriculum, the buildings, the timetable, the style of staff management, teacher–pupil relationships, and so on.

A systemic approach to behavioural change therefore involves looking at the whole system in which the individual operates. Individual treatment is not inconsistent with a systemic approach since the individual is an element in the system. However, there is a real sense in which one cannot properly attend to individual behaviour while ignoring the context in which the behaviour is manifest. It is also important to appreciate that the components of a system interact, so that by changing one component the others are affected. For instance, changing the lengths of lessons will affect curriculum opportunities and teacher–pupil relationships. Further, each system is unique. What works in one school may not work in another; what works for one teacher may not work for another; and the same teacher may find that a lesson that is successful with one class may not go down at all well with another in the same age-band. This has the important practical implication that, because each aspect of the 'system' interacts with others, any changes must be carefully monitored to ensure the system as a whole is working well. Of course, this does not mean that no general guidelines can be suggested; but it does mean, if change is to be effective, that the *interpretation* of these guidelines has to be varied according to the particular make-up of the school system.

In talking of dealing 'effectively' with behaviour problems, it is important to be clear about the criteria by which such effectiveness should be judged. Is it in terms of social training? the happiness of the individual pupil? an orderly classroom? educative learning? These questions are considered in Chapter 4, which consists of a discussion about the different senses in which 'discipline' is used. This is important, since different constructions of the concept will affect the kind of action taken. For instance, while it is obviously very important to attend to discipline in the sense of class control ('You have to keep order if you want to teach', as Miss Harby advised Ursula Brangwen), this in itself will do nothing to provide discipline in the educative sense, by which children come to think in a more 'disciplined way' about their behaviour and curriculum activities. Moreover, some styles of classroom control are more likely than others to lead to educational outcomes.

In Chapter 5, the issue that concerned Ursula Brangwen most of all, the quality of teacher–pupil relationships, is explored in some detail. Following a discussion of the concept of 'relationships', attention is given to evidence and argument concerning the way teachers and pupils perceive and judge each other. It is important to address this issue because interpersonal perceptions materially affect relationships, and these in turn affect the disciplinary situation.

In the remaining chapters, the issues discussed above – accounting for behaviour problems in school, the criteria of 'effective' school discipline, and factors affecting the quality of teacher–pupil relationships – are used to evaluate particular classroom strategies and kinds of provision for coping with behaviour problems. The effects of different kinds of classroom management strategies, including those used when meeting a class for the first time, are discussed in Chapter 6; the significance of praise and rewards is considered in Chapter 7, which also includes an appraisal of behaviour modification techniques; the role of punishment and its consequences are the subject of Chapter 8; the compatibility of pastoral care and discipline responsibilities is considered in Chapter 9; finally, support services, suspension and exclusion from schools, and the kind of arrangements appropriate for supporting pupils whose disaffection has reached 'crisis' proportions, are discussed in Chapter 10.

FURTHER READING

Cohen, L. and Cohen, A. (1987) *Disruptive Behaviour: A Sourcebook for Teachers*, Harper & Row, London.
(A collection of recent papers arranged in three sections concerning defining, understanding and coping with disruptive behaviour. A useful companion to this book.)

Grunsell, R. (1985) *Finding Answers to Disruption: Discussion Exercises for Secondary Teachers*, School Curriculum Development Committee/Longman, York.
(Helpful material for in-service courses.)

2
ACCOUNTING FOR CHILDREN'S BEHAVIOUR: I. – INFLUENCES OUTSIDE THE SCHOOL

When we ask 'Why are some children difficult to control in school?' we are really concerned with two questions:

(1) How can behaviour problems in school be explained in terms of factors that lie beyond the school's immediate control, such as factors within the child, in the family, or the social and physical environment?
(2) What is there specifically about a school situation that precipitates or promotes unacceptable behaviour in some children?

This chapter is concerned with the first of these questions. The more specific school-based factors will be considered in Chapter 3 and succeeding chapters.

PROBLEMS IN EXPLAINING UNACCEPTABLE BEHAVIOUR

Research findings do not enable us to offer definitive causal accounts of behaviour problems in children. There are several reasons for this. To begin with, there is no agreed definition of 'unacceptable behaviour'. As Chazan and Laing (1982, p. 79) have pointed out, 'Different people have different degrees of tolerance as far as children's behaviour is concerned, and what is a significant problem to one may be acceptable conduct to another'.

Secondly, even when 'unacceptable behaviour' is carefully defined, there is no objective way of identifying children who come within the definition. Various checklists have been developed to make assessment less subjective. Examples are the Bristol Social Adjustment Guides (Stott, 1974, 1979), the 'Child at School' schedule (Kysel et al., 1983), the Children's Behaviour Questionnaire (Rutter, 1967) and the Swansea Behaviour Checklist (Chazan et al., 1983). However, the assessment of an individual child will depend somewhat on the particular measure used. For instance, McMichael (1981) has shown that consistently more children are categorized as 'antisocial' on the Children's Behaviour Questionnaire than as 'overreactive' on the Bristol scale. Similarly, the lack of a universal definition of the term 'maladjustment' has led Norman Tutt (1983, p. 13) to comment: 'to the question "What is maladjustment?", we should firstly admit our ignorance and state clearly "maladjustment" is what professional assessors say it is! It is not a clearly defined concept which can be accurately tested.'

Another illustration of the subjectivity of behavioural assessment comes from a recent study by Gilmore et al. (1985). In an attempt to identify which children in a sample of 8- to 9-year-olds were presenting aggressive behaviour, the teachers and children were asked to complete questionnaires. Teachers commented on the children, who in turn were asked to comment on themselves and each other. The results showed little agreement between the various assessing groups as to which children were the most aggressive. Children who saw themselves as aggressive were not necessarily seen as such by other children or by their teachers, while children who were seen as aggressive by other children were often unaware of these tendencies or unwilling to admit them.

In the third place, behaviour problems are to some extent situationally specific. Because a child's behaviour will vary somewhat according to where he is and who he is with, teachers and parents (and teachers between them) do not always 'see' the same child. Mitchell and Shepherd (1966) found remarkably little overlap between children who were a problem at school and at home. In a recent study of about one thousand seven-year-olds in New Zealand, McGee, Silva and Williams (1984) found that parents were twice as likely as teachers to identify children as 'neurotic' or as 'antisocial'. One wonders whether this is because children really do behave very differently at school, or because teachers are more accepting of extreme forms of behaviour.

A fourth difficulty in establishing the causes of behaviour in children relates to the large number of associated variables. As we shall see in this chapter, those which have been investigated include various factors within the child, home circumstances and upbringing practices, cultural and subcultural influences, the physical environment, and the impact of mass media. Yet any factor, or cluster of factors, will at best be only moderately correlated with the incidence of unacceptable or problem behaviour. In a recent study on the roots of delinquency, West (1982, p. 129) has commented on 'the enormous margin of unexplained variation left over in every prediction exercise'.

Fifthly, it is important to appreciate that the establishment of a correlation between a behaviour pattern and a factor does not constitute proof of a causal relationship. An example should clarify this point. Several studies have pointed to a statistical link between watching violence on television and committing violent acts (e.g. Halloran, Brown and Chaney, 1970; Belson, 1978). However, it would be wrong to conclude that violence is necessarily caused by observing such behaviour on film. The direction of cause and effect could be the other way round: as Marsh (1979) points out, it could be that it is a propensity to be violent that makes some people watch violence on TV. Or maybe there is no direct causal link: a third factor, perhaps certain kinds of parental upbringing practices, could be responsible for both watching violence and being violent. In short, statistical explanations are not causal explanations: they indicate certain possibilities, but they do not by themselves mean that one factor is the cause and the other the effect. None the less, because correlations constitute possible explanations, the evidence may constitute grounds for social action (e.g. provision of support services for parents, or reducing the prevalence of violence on television).

Finally, there is the problem of interpreting research findings in terms of a theory of human behaviour. Problem behaviour may be construed as, for instance, a consequence of a disturbance or instability emanating from within the child and rooted in the experiences of infancy (psychodynamic theory); or as a misconstruction the child puts upon experiences as a result of being faced with unpredictable responses (cognitive developmental theory); or as the result of social reinforcement and environmental contingencies (learning theory); or as a consequence of modelling the observed behaviour of respected others (social learning theory); or as reflecting negative personal evaluations (self theory); or as arising from negative labelling (labelling theory); or in terms of the incompatibility of group cultures (subcultural theories). In this extraordinarily complex matter of trying to account for unacceptable social behaviour, it is probable that no one theory provides a complete explanation.

FACTORS WITHIN THE CHILD

One possible reason for disruptive behaviour in school is that the pupils concerned have some deficiency that is the source of the behaviour problem. For instance, it is usual to refer to 'disruptive *pupils*' who are 'disturbed' or suffer from conduct 'disorders'. The latter term is officially used to denote continuing abnormal behaviour that attracts social disapproval. Examples are lying, stealing, bullying, defiance of authority, and destruction of other people's belongings. However, as Rutter (1975) points out, disorders of any kind do not constitute diseases or illnesses; they may be situationally specific, and their diagnosis is not an objective matter since it depends upon social norms. Although factors such as sex, congenital impairment and temperament are linked with conduct disorders, it is best to 'say the problem lies in the interaction between a child and his environment, and not just within the child himself' (Rutter, 1975, p. 18).

There is abundant evidence which reveals sex differences in the incidence of aggression and conduct disorders (e.g. Rutter, 1970; Chazan and Jackson, 1971, 1974; Davie, Butler and Goldstein, 1972; Kagan, 1979; McGee, Silva and Williams, 1984; ILEA, 1986a). Boys appear to be more vulnerable than girls to various psychological stresses, and reveal greater verbal and physical aggression from the pre-school years. This seems to apply cross-culturally and also to subhuman primates. The ratio of boys to girls in off-site units for disaffected pupils is about 2 : 1 (ILEA, 1985). However, the existence of sex differences does not mean that they are necessarily biologically rooted; they may simply be a response to prevailing social conditions.

Some childhood behaviour problems are associated with various physical weaknesses that may have a congenital origin. In a study of thirty-three troublesome children, Denis Stott (1966) found that in twenty-six cases there were symptoms of somatic–neural impairment, such as epilepsy, squint, defective speech, or enuresis. Stott concluded, however, that impairment did not cause behaviour problems directly; rather it made the children more susceptible to stress, which in turn induced the behaviour problems. In the recent Cambridge Study of 400 males from age eight to twenty-five (West, 1982), no significant association was found between delinquency and illness or impairment in early life. Again, from the work of Sula Wolff (1967), who compared one hundred primary schoolchildren who had adverse obstetric histories with an equal number of 'normal' children, it would seem that children who have sustained damage at birth constitute only a minority of those who present behaviour problems.

Another possibility is that extreme forms of antisocial behaviour are genetically determined. Some students of criminality (e.g. West, 1982) have suggested a high frequency of social maladjustment amongst the offenders' parents. However, this correlation does not necessarily mean that criminal tendencies are inherited. An alternative interpretation is that the children come to behave abnormally as a consequence of the abnormal ways in which their parents behave towards them. Most studies in genetic influences have involved comparisons between identical (monozygotic) twins, who have identical genotypes because they originate from one egg, and fraternal (dizygotic) twins, who originate from two separate eggs. In a review of this research, Rutter and Madge (1976) suggested that heredity plays a substantial part in determining temperamental features, but that delinquent behaviour is not inherited directly. Rather it is that differences in temperament render some children more susceptible to stress, which might precipitate deviant behaviour.

Another way of studying the contributions of heredity and environment is to investigate subjects who have been separated from their parents at an early age. Since adopted children are not brought up by their biological parents, or only for a short time, the influence of the biological childhood environment can be virtually eliminated. From the findings of recent studies in Sweden, adoption appears to be fairly effective in the prevention of social maladjustment among children whose biological parents had criminal tendencies (Bohman, 1981). This again points to the significance of the social environment rather than genetic influences.

Eysenck (1975, 1977, 1979) argues that antisocial and violent conduct are genetically determined in so far as personality differences have a genetic origin. According to Eysenck, introversion is produced by high arousal levels in the cortex of the brain, and that arousal helps a person to learn from conditioned responses. Because extroverts tend to have low levels of arousal, they tend to seek sensation and have a lower resistance to temptation. Consequently 'extroverts need a firmer, more consistent type of upbringing in order to produce the same effect that in an introvert would be produced by a more lenient and possibly less consistent kind of upbringing' (Eysenck, 1975, p. 201).

Yet Eysenck's claim that delinquents are more likely to be extrovert is controversial. Farrington, Biron and Leblanc (1982) found no association between juvenile delinquency and either extroversion or neuroticism. Correlations between delinquency and Eysenck's scale for psychoticism appear stronger (Emler, 1983). Psychotics include individuals who are insensitive, sensation-seeking, foolhardy, and enjoy upsetting others. Although personality traits may not be directly linked to delinquency, a child's temperament is important in modifying responses to deprivation and disadvantage. Rutter (1979) has reported evidence to show that adverse temperamental features, such as low malleability or negative mood, are more likely to bring on parental criticism and thus help to foster family discord; conversely, a child's positive temperamental features can help to protect him from disharmony at home.

In short, the view that continuing antisocial behaviour is *determined* by factors within the child seems unlikely. At the same time, the evidence does suggest that certain factors such as congenital impairment and personality make children particularly susceptible to stress, vulnerable to undesirable social influences and likely to foment conflict in the family, which in turn helps to maintain the problem.

FACTORS IN THE HOME
Early childhood attachments

Of all the factors associated with behaviour difficulties, the 'psychopathic child syndrome' has been considered the most significant in its long-lasting effects. Aggressive or antisocial behaviour, and the inability of the child to establish a lasting relationship with an adult, has been attributed by John Bowlby to 'maternal deprivation' resulting from a separation of mother and child. In his account of a *psychodynamic theory*, developed from the work of Freud, Bowlby (1953, p. 13) argued that 'what is believed to be essential for mental health is that an infant and young child should experience a warm, intimate, and continuous relationship with his mother (or permanent mother-substitute – one person who steadily mothers him) in which both find satisfaction and enjoyment'. Bowlby drew this evidence from studies involving direct observation of children in institutions, hospitals and foster homes, together with investigations into the early histories of adolescents and adults who had developed psychological illnesses. From a vast range of such studies, he developed the concept of 'affectionless character', typified by superficial relationships, an uncaring attitude for others, regular stealing and lack of concentration. These characteristics were thought to be the result of inopportunity to form a bond of attachment to a mother figure during infancy. If the bonding process is disturbed by separation from the mother after the first six months or so (when the child begins to differentiate other adults from his mother), adverse consequences for stable personality development are likely to follow. Bowlby's later work widened his concern with the effects of maternal discontinuity to include other pathogenic patterns of parental behaviour, such as persistent unresponsiveness to the child or threats of abandonment (Bowlby, 1979).

From extensive reviews of the literature in this field, Michael Rutter (1981) has modified Bowlby's view in a number of respects. While the development of attachments in early childhood appears to be the most crucial variable in preventing later antisocial behaviour, the bond does not need to be with a mother, a female, or even with an adult. Nor does separation from the mother necessarily disrupt the bond since the quality of relationship may be continued with another person. Further, bonds developed with the father, brother or sister, teacher and other figures are each important in the child's emotional development. It is distorted relationships with the child, rather than weak bonds, that Rutter sees as responsible for antisocial behaviour — and the middle years of childhood, as well as infancy, can be important here. Further, improvement in relationships with adults in middle or later childhood, as well as a supportive school environment, can lead to marked social and behavioural improvement.

All this more recent evidence gives grounds for being more optimistic about the chances of child care work preventing emotional instability in later childhood. At the same time, an overemphasis on the psychodynamic model of human behaviour, with its focus on inherent pathology, may encourage teachers to believe that they can do little to help children whose behaviour is seriously unacceptable since they lack the special skills only trained professionals can provide. It may also encourage the belief that, because behaviour is a symptom of an unconscious process, the child cannot have conscious control over his own behaviour.

Child-rearing practices

Many studies have produced evidence to demonstrate how children's conduct is related to the ways their parents respond to them and control their behaviour. For instance, from the work of Robert Hinde and Alison Tamplin (1983), it would seem that hostility to adults and peers among preschool children is associated with infrequent positive or neutral parent–child interaction. Where such interactions are frequent, the young child is more likely to be friendly and co-operative. More important, however, is the quality rather than the frequency of parental response. French and Waas (1985) concluded from their study of 870 8- to 11-year-olds that it was rejected rather than neglected children who tended to exhibit behaviour problems. The Cambridge longitudinal study showed that delinquents differ from non-delinquents in having experienced cold, harsh parents (West, 1982). Again, Lefkowitz et al. (1977) found from a ten-year longitudinal study of over 800 children that the least violent boys were those whose parents were moderately punitive towards aggression, whereas the most violent boys were those whose parents were permissive or harshly punitive. A similar finding emerged from an investigation into a sample of 570 German families (Engfer and Schneewind, 1982) in which conduct disorder and personality problems such as anxiety were related to harsh punishment and the child's perception of rejection.

These findings are consistent with those of Hoffman (1970), who argued that the degree of arousal in parental control affects the ability of children to show concern for others and to modify their interpersonal judgements according to extenuating circumstances. When the level of arousal is optimal, the child attends to the meaning of punishment; when it is too much, the child becomes more concerned with avoiding punishment than with thinking about the effects of his behaviour on others. According to Hoffman, 12-year-old children who show concern for others tend to have parents who express affection most frequently, vary their means of control according to the situation, and suggest means of reparation whenever possible. Similar findings with respect to 3- to 6-year-olds have been reported by Sparks *et al.* (1984).

Rutter (1975; Rutter and Giller, 1983), referring to the research of Jenkins (1973) and other writers, has outlined the nature of the relationship between child-rearing practices and different sorts of behaviour problems. 'Socialized delinquency', in which relationships with peers are adequate, is associated with parental neglect rather than rejection – i.e. the absence of behavioural standards or the presence of inappropriate standards. The remedy would therefore seem to lie in social education, rather than in psychiatric treatment, in developing a coherent set of values and a sense of social responsibility. On the other hand, 'unsocialized aggression', which involves general unpopularity and often malicious tendencies, is more likely to be associated with a punitive home background, broken homes, family hostility and maternal rejection. Rutter's view here is that treatment methods are less likely to be satisfactory than attempts to provide better family relationships to reduce stress and provide a consistent and reasonable pattern of discipline – though such intervention is difficult when the family is unprepared to change the situation. At the same time, Rutter and Giller (1983) have suggested that, as far as juvenile delinquency is concerned, quality of parental supervision (e.g. rules about where the child is going or when he must be home) may be even more important than parental punishment styles. Results from a recent national survey of young teenagers and their parents (Riley and Shaw, 1985) support this view (especially in the case of girls). Children who perceive their parents to be concerned about where they are going, who they are with, and what they are doing, are more likely to share with them their life outside the home. This in turn gives parents the opportunity to influence their children's behaviour.

The significance of a predictable social environment that enables children to develop stable and purposeful behaviour is emphasized in *cognitive developmental theory* (Piaget, 1953). This theory points to the importance of conceptual growth – how the growing child consciously construes experience – rather than the impact of unconscious forces rooted in childhood.

Wall (1973) has outlined a model on Piagetian lines as a way of helping us to understand how social maladaption can develop. From early infancy, a child tries to construct a 'map' of his experience with himself as a reference point. This 'map' enables him to make sense not only of the physical world but also the world of human interaction. With increasing social experience, the child's 'map' changes, enabling him to make increasingly accurate predictions about social intercourse. However, if the child is faced constantly with unpredictable responses, then, in Piagetian terms, the assimilations into his existing cognitive schemes will become increasingly idiosyncratic. He is then forced to distort experience to fit his cognitive schemes rather than to modify them to accommodate change. In this way Wall explains that an adult not 'getting through' to a child is symptomatic of their two 'maps' not coinciding. The child has constructed his 'map' in an environment so far removed from the adult's that he cannot bridge the two, and he therefore experiences a feeling of rejection. Additionally, the child's environment in infancy may have been so lacking in stimuli that his capacity to learn is impaired, so making it difficult for him to adjust in relation to others. As Wall points out, intellectual growth conducive to social adjustment will be fostered in a home environment in which the rules are not only consistent and non-arbitrary but are explained and allow scope for genuine choices that help children to predict the consequences of their actions.

Learning theory, which is associated with the work of B. F. Skinner, helps us to see how children's unacceptable behaviour can be unwittingly reinforced by parents and others. This is particularly likely to happen when children misbehave to get attention. Suppose a mother finds the conduct of her young child unacceptable. In trying to placate him by giving sweets, toys or money, she is unintentionally rewarding the child for behaving badly. The child's unwanted behavioural tendencies are thus effectively strengthened through a process of instrumental conditioning. At first, the parent or teacher may ignore the attention-seeking behaviour. The child then intensifies his actions as his first attempts go unheeded. As the conduct becomes more and more aggravating, the adult gives way. The child thus learns that adults can be controlled through coercion! At the same time, it is no solution for adults to react by punishing because the punishment can act as a reinforcer of the unwanted behaviour in representing success in getting noticed. One study (Patterson *et al.*, 1967) has shown that no less than 80 per cent of aggressive acts in nursery schools lead to favourable consequences for the child in that they 'pay off' in some way. Learning theorists would therefore hold that it is best to ignore undesired behaviour whilst also rewarding behaviour that is wanted.

Learning theory can be contrasted with the earlier theories reviewed. According to Skinner (1973, p. 211), 'A person does not act upon the world, the world acts upon him.' On this view, unconscious psychic forces (as in psychodynamic theory), or how a person construes the situation (as in cognitive-developmental theory), is of no value in understanding or trying to modify the way a person acts; rather, human behaviour is considered to be shaped solely by environmental contingencies.

However, children also appear to learn socially undesirable behaviours through experiencing similar behaviours in others, either directly, or indirectly through observation; and they may sometimes do so even if they do not find the experiences immediately rewarding. For instance, children can develop aggressive tendencies, not only as a result of regularly experiencing harsh punishment themselves, but vicariously through witnessing such treatment to others.

This idea that adults act as powerful *models* for children to imitate is central to the *social learning theory* of Albert Bandura, who rejects both psychodynamic explanations and Skinnerian mechanistic accounts as too limiting: 'In the social learning view, people are neither driven by inner forces nor buffeted by environmental stimuli. Rather, psychological function is explained in terms of a continuous reciprocal interaction of personal and environmental determinants' (Bandura, 1977, pp. 11-12). Because Bandura gives a significant role to personal factors, the perceptions the child has of the adult affect the likelihood of the adult's behaviour being copied. If the child identifies with the adult, perhaps admiring his aggressive power, imitation will be more probable. Fortunately, children also learn socially non-violent ways of resolving conflict from being with adults they like and who represent good behaviour models.

Parents and other significant adults are also important for the way they affect a child's self-picture, which in turn affects behaviour. The work of Stanley Coopersmith on the antecedents of self-esteem has shown that children are more likely to develop feelings of worth if the parents impose reasonable limits on behaviour. According to this *self-theory*, children who value themselves highly tend to be those whose parents have definite values but who do not enforce their beliefs punitively. Provided that the limits of behaviour are rational and appropriate to the age of the child, their enforcement 'gives the child a sense that norms are real and significant, contributes to self-definition, and increases the likelihood that the child will believe that a sense of reality is attainable' (Coopersmith, 1967, p. 238). This has behavioural implications, since a child who develops high self-esteem will feel less need to put up defensive reactions, and will feel capable of coping with adversity without hostility.

Carl Rogers (1951) suggested a theory of self that could account for maladjustment partly in terms of the child's perception of the evaluation parents and other significant adults have of him. The emphasis is not only on the significance of parental affection but on the regard the parents have for the young child as a person of worth. Maladjustment can thus arise when the child senses an unbridgeable gap between his real self-image and his social self-image (i.e. himself as seen by others), so that he has difficulty in developing a positive concept of himself. As a consequence, there is an impulsion to take on defensive attitudes. The Rogerian model of behaviour therefore sees the child neither as the victim of pathological disturbance (as in psychodynamic theory) nor environmental influences (as in learning theory). Rather the child is seen as a purposeful being who modifies his behaviour in the light of his self-picture and perception of how others feel towards him. From the school's point of view, this theory is important for its emphasis on a social environment that encourages children to express their individual views without fear of rejection.

The significance of the evaluations we believe others have of us is also central to *labelling theory*, according to which we adapt our behaviour to fit the 'label' other people give us. Children are frequently stereotyped by parents and others and consequently come to see themselves as exceptional in some way. This can be beneficial to their personal adjustment if the label is positive (e.g. 'You're good at making friends easily') but can contribute to maladaption if the label is negative (e.g. 'That's just the sort of behaviour I'd expect from a naughty boy like you'). Since the labelling of children has been studied mainly in school settings, further discussion of its impact will be deferred until Chapter 5.

One-parent families and broken homes

Data from the National Child Development Study (Davie, Butler and Goldstein, 1972) revealed that four out of ten parents believed that their child's maladjusted behaviour could be attributed to loss of father or mother. It may be, however, that the single parent is too ready to attribute adolescent behaviour problems to family situations (Ferri, 1975). The National Child Development Study data (Davie, Butler and Goldstein,

1972) and a recent report on disruption in London schools (Mortimore et al., 1983) show that children from one-parent families are no more likely to be a behaviour problem than those from two-parent families once economic circumstances have been taken into account. Similarly, evidence from a recent national survey (Riley and Shaw, 1985) shows that one-parent families do not contribute disproportionately to delinquency rates. As regards the effects of divorce, Rutter and Giller (1983) argue that it is the family discord, rather than the separation from parents, which seems to be associated with conduct disturbances, and divorce does not necessarily bring such discord to an end. The same authors suggest that behaviour problems are not necessarily associated with the mother working, or the child in day care: indeed children might thereby be protected from their mother's depression, which can be a consequence of unrelieved childrearing.

FACTORS IN SOCIETY

Cultural and subcultural differences

Data from various large-scale studies in both Britain (e.g. Davie, Butler and Goldstein, 1972; ILEA, 1986a) and the USA (e.g. Lefkowitz, 1977) have demonstrated that children from working-class homes are more likely than those from professional homes to show aggressive behaviour. These findings may indicate that aggression is more acceptable in a working-class environment. The Newsons (1963), for instance, found that 'hitting back' was more likely to be sanctioned by working-class than by middle-class mothers.

Albert Cohen (1956) suggested that young delinquents who come from homes of manual workers find that they cannot succeed in terms of the school's middle-class values, such as ambition, planning, control of physical aggression, deferred gratification and the cultivation of manners. Their delinquency can therefore be seen as a reaction against middle-class criteria of status and power. By way of demonstrating a rejection of these criteria, pleasure-seeking and vandalism are taken on as virtues. An alternative explanation for delinquent behaviour in terms of subcultural differences is that of W. B. Miller (1958). Miller saw juvenile delinquency not as a reaction to middle-class values, but as an acting out of genuine working-class traditions, such as those of toughness, masculinity and searching for excitement as a relief from dull routine. According to this view, some working-class adolescents see the values upheld by schools as contradicting their own class values, and they therefore turn to the gang as their reference group. Paul Willis (1977), writing from a Marxist perspective, sees counter-school cultures as a manifestation of working-class culture generally. He argues that nothing schools do to cope with their 'disruptive minority' will deal with entrenched attitudes in pupils' social class roots. However, although the school in which Willis based his conclusions had an exclusively working-class intake, it contained conformists as well as the 'lads' who resisted authority. Moreover, as we shall see in the next chapter, schools vary considerably in the response they elicit from working-class pupils.

Ethnic differences

Many teachers undoubtedly consider children from some racial groups to be easier to control than others. In particular, teachers sometimes report the behaviour of Afro-Caribbean children to be more disruptive than that of whites or Asians (Giles, 1977; Bagley, 1982; Taylor, 1983; Swann Report, 1985). However as we shall see in Chapter 5, this may be a response to the school situation rather than a 'problem' in the children. Earls and Richman (1980) found no evidence of differences in the behaviour adjustment of black and white children of pre-school age. Interviews conducted by Rutter *et al.* (1974) showed that many of the behaviour problems exhibited at school by Afro-Caribbeans, according to their teachers, were not evident in the home, according to their parents; nor were they accompanied by difficulties in peer relationships at school. In another study (Rutter *et al.*, 1975), behaviour problems amongst black children in school were found to be associated with economic disadvantage and adverse family circumstances, which are sometimes more prevalent in black communities.

Findings from the London junior school study (ILEA, 1986a) suggested that the higher incidence of behaviour difficulties amongst Afro-Caribbean children in school (as assessed by their teachers) was due in part to the fact that these pupils also had lower scores in reading, which in turn was linked to poorer behaviour. Once reading attainment was taken into account, the relationship between race and behaviour disappeared.

Effects of mass media

We saw earlier that, in social learning theory, emphasis is placed on the way children model their behaviour on others. A number of studies have shown how young children and adolescents imitate aggressive behaviour they see on film, even if this is in cartoon form, and that the effects of such observational learning can still be seen a week or more later (Bandura, Ross and Ross, 1961; Kniveton, 1973; Berkowitz et al., 1978).

Aggressive and delinquent behaviour is sometimes considered to be a consequence of watching violence on television. It is evident, however, that such exposure does not produce antisocial behaviour in us all. Halloran et al. (1970) concluded that delinquents did not watch more television violence; rather, they took a disproportionate interest in exciting programmes. The researchers formed the view that delinquents seem more prone than others to rationalize their violent acts by reference to television: if people behave aggressively and destructively on the box, it's OK to behave likewise in real life. The majority of the probationers studied were found to come from disorganized working-class families, so that the association between television and delinquency could be explained partly in terms of social background and mode of parental control. Other evidence, however, suggests that TV violence is more directly linked to aggression in society. For instance, Belson (1978), after controlling for various background factors that are associated with violence, concluded that high exposure to television was linked to the use of violence amongst adolescent boys in London. Eysenck and Nias (1978) concluded from their comprehensive review of research on the effects of violence that 'aggressive acts new to the subject's repertoire of responses, as well as acts already established, can be evoked by the viewing of violent scenes portrayed on film, T.V. or in the theatre' (p. 252). The authors believe that the evidence is sufficiently strong to warrant measures to reduce the amount of violence in entertainment, particularly television. In a comparable American review of studies, the National Institute of Mental Health (1982) also came to the conclusion that the evidence accumulated in the 1970s shows clearly that television and aggression are positively correlated in children.

Why might TV be associated with behaviour problems? As we saw earlier, according to Bandura's social learning theory, children may learn to act aggressively as a consequence of modelling their behaviour on those they observe. Another possibility is that repeated exposure to violence blunts our sensibilities and sense of compassion, or weakens our propensity to inhibit and constrain our baser tendencies (Berkowitz, 1962; Belson, 1978). Thirdly, exposure to filmed violence may have a psychologically arousing effect, satisfying the viewer's urge for an 'adrenalin high' (e.g. Tannenbaum, 1980); this is sometimes countered by the argument that watching TV violence has a cathartic effect in reducing aggressive feelings (Feshback and Singer, 1971). Fourthly, constant watching of TV may have adverse effects on family life, reducing the chances of family talk, playing games and other events that help in the child's character formation (Bronfenbrenner, 1976). Finally, one's own aggression towards those we do not like may seem 'justified' when it is the 'bad person' in a film who gets beaten up (Berkowitz et al., 1978).

Gunter (1981) has warned against the dangers of making a scapegoat of television violence, distracting attention away from underlying disturbances and social problems in contemporary society. Gunter (1981, 1984) has also pointed to experiments that demonstrate the pro-social influences of watching examples of good behaviour on television. Thus, although exposure to violence on television, videos or in the cinema may contribute to aggression in society, it is also possible that the pro-social content of many popular programmes helps to counteract the antisocial content.

THE PHYSICAL ENVIRONMENT

Violence and aggression in inner-city areas have sometimes been attributed to overcrowding. Claire Russell and W. M. S. Russell (1979) draw an analogy between animals such as chimpanzees, which are known to be peaceful in the wild but become aggressive in zoos, and human beings who live in high density stress-inducing inner-city environments. When individuals have insufficient social space and cannot escape, their frustration easily turns to violence. Sollenberger (1968), however, has commented on the relative absence of juvenile delinquency in Chinatown, New York, despite the high-density living. As a result of participant observation for seven weeks and extensive interviews with mothers, Sollenberger concluded that the low delinquency rate was due to an abundance of nurture and protection during early childhood so that a reservoir of security and trust was built up. Freedman (1975) has demonstrated that crowded living conditions do not directly produce antisocial behaviour, but may serve to intensify a person's typical reaction to a situation. Thus those who would ordinarily be aggressive will react even more aggressively in overcrowded conditions.

Some findings have pointed to the possible effects that even low levels of lead in the blood have on intellectual ability and behaviour (Yule et al., 1984). The two major sources of lead found in the blood are diet (especially from water in areas with lead piping) and emission from motor vehicle exhausts. Food additives and diet deficiencies have also been suggested as a cause of hyperactivity (Feingold, 1975; Weiss, 1982), symptoms of which include excitability, destructiveness and unpredictable temperament. Particularly harmful are synthetic yellow dyes, such as tartrazine (E102), often contained in cakes, sweets and crisps. Because young children are small, the toxic concentration in their bodies makes them especially vulnerable to harmful food substances.

SOME IMPLICATIONS FOR TEACHERS

Given the vast range of outside-school factors that are associated with behaviour problems in children, what might be the implications for teachers? First of all, it is clear that, just as no one theory offers a sufficient explanation, so no one explanation can form a sufficient basis for a remedy. The implication of psychodynamic theory, with its emphasis on a disordered mind, is that psychotherapeutic treatment is a suitable response to the problem. Cognitive-developmental explanations point more to social education than therapy. Learning theory suggests that attempts should be made, through a programme of behaviour modification, to reverse the unfortunate effects of previous environmental factors in order to reshape patterns of conduct through reinforcement of socially approved responses. In social learning theory, the role of the adult in setting a model for good behaviour, as well as reinforcement, will be regarded as important. Subcultural theories of deviance draw attention to the influence of middle-class culture and raise questions concerning the need for changes in institutional structures. Labelling theory suggests the need to be sensitive to the consequences of persistent public evaluation and the circumstances in which children are perceived negatively or positively. In our present state of knowledge, however, it is probably best to regard each sort of explanation as having something to offer, though some may appear more useful than others in predicting behaviour problems and pointing to possible ways of changing the behaviour.

Since the evidence increasingly suggests that the effects of early experience and other factors are reversible, at least to some extent, some form of social intervention is desirable in certain cases. Maurice Chazan argues that children who present many or extreme behaviour problems should be regarded as 'at risk' and therefore in need of help of one kind or another: 'There are many "at risk" situations which are only too painfully obvious at an early age, and which cry out for action which may minimize their effects' (Chazan, 1976, p. 36). In his respect, teachers have an important role to play.

Chazan (1976) has recognized three important problems (other than those of assessment) that are associated with the early identification of behaviour disorder. First of all, since almost all young children display some behaviour problems, 'no child should be considered a problem unless the frequency and/or intensity of these reactions interfere with effective functioning or the enjoyment of normal social interaction' (ibid., p. 37). To this could be added the evidence in research literature reviewed by Topping (1983), that about one-third of children identified as presenting behaviour problems demonstrate 'spontaneous remission' – i.e. their behaviour improves irrespective of any treatment or special provision. A second problem arises from the fact that intervention involves the invasion of privacy. Fortunately, most parents are strongly motivated to do what is necessary in the interests of their child's welfare. None the less, care must be taken to preserve the dignity of the family, who might resent interference, however well-intentioned. Thirdly, it is important to appreciate the potentially labelling effect of such terms as 'maladjustment' or 'disturbed'. If teachers were to take on rigid attitudes towards children assessed as a behaviour 'problem', the potentially remedial effects of intervention would be undermined. Chazan (1976) therefore emphasizes the importance of including statements of a positive nature in any assessment procedure.

Chazan and his colleagues (1983) have produced a handbook to help teachers involved with young children presenting behavioural difficulties. Guidance is given for the recognition of behaviour problems (using the Swansea Behaviour Checklist), assessment and record-keeping, working with parents, classroom activities and special approaches. The book covers shyness and immaturity as well as restlessness and aggression.

In this chapter we have considered the view that disruptive behaviour in school might be interpreted in terms of the personal characteristics of children, the influence of the home and other background factors. However, there is more to the aetiology of classroom conduct than this, since the impact of the school situation, in which the problem behaviour is manifest, is crucial. Certainly background factors cannot be discounted in explanations of children's behaviour at school. For instance, the marked variations in aggression among children admitted to nursery school indicate that such tendencies must at least sometimes be a consequence of factors in the children or their home or both (Manning, Heron and Marshall, 1978). None the less, as we shall see in later chapters, schools and teachers do play a significant part in maintaining or controlling antisocial tendencies at all age levels, and in some cases may even unintentionally promote the very behaviour they deplore.

Emler (1983) has argued that it is a mistake to interpret deviant behaviour simply in terms of individual personality characteristics since this ignores the relationship between the deviant person and his audience. Emler suggests that deviance should be seen as the consequence of the frustrated attempts of some individuals to present themselves to their audience by conventional means. This is because some people, in their attempts to manage their social reputation, feel that they have more to gain by deviating from conventional standards than by upholding them. On the basis of this argument, we might suppose that an environment that helps children to feel they matter as individuals, and that each has something important to contribute to the community, is more likely to elicit co-operative behaviour than one in which some individuals find it difficult to achieve recognition of their worth. Hence, however important individual characteristics and background factors may be in generating behaviour problems in school, the quality of the school environment can also make a difference since this will make it more or less possible for pupils to gain status without resorting to deviant behaviour. For teachers, this means being prepared to change one's perceptions of children whose behaviour is disruptive, and looking at ways in which the curriculum, classroom arrangements and school organization should be changed to provide an ethos in which pupils feel they can achieve a positive social identity by behaving co-operatively. These are issues that we address in the next chapter and in later sections of this book.

FURTHER READING

Davie, R., Butler, N. and Goldstein, H. (1972) *From Birth to Seven*, Longman, London.

Fogelman, K. (1983) *Growing up in Britain*, Macmillan, London.

(The above two publications report the detailed findings of the National Child Development Study, a long-term investigation of all people born between 3 and 9 March 1958.)

West, D. J. (1982) *Delinquency: Its Roots, Careers and Prospects*, Heinemann, London.

(The Cambridge Study of delinquency, which followed 400 schoolboys from the age of eight to twenty-five.)

Willis, P. E. (1977) *Learning to Labour*, Saxon House, Farnborough.

Together with: Cultural production and theories of reproduction, in L. Barton and S. Walker (eds.) *Race, Class and Education*, Croom Helm, London, 1983.

(A study of the notion of cultural production.)

3
ACCOUNTING FOR CHILDREN'S BEHAVIOUR:
II. – THE IMPACT OF THE SCHOOL

In the last chapter we saw how children's behaviour can be affected by many factors that lie outside the school's immediate control. Some of these factors are 'within' the child, some are associated with experiences in infancy and styles of upbringing, some are related to societal and cultural influences and some involve the physical environment and social disadvantage.

We also noted, however, that children's behaviour varies according to the circumstances in which they are placed. It is because behaviour is, to some extent, context-related that classroom control problems cannot be understood by focusing on the child and his background alone. However important the home and other outside-school factors may be in predisposing children to behave in certain ways, the potentiality of the school to maintain, ameliorate, or even generate behaviour patterns should not be ignored. As was argued in Chapter 1, the individual exists in a 'system', such as the family, neighbourhood and school. Individual behaviour cannot therefore be understood properly without reference to the whole system in which the behaviour is manifest. Features of the school system that are likely to affect behaviour include the kinds of expectations and perceptions teachers have of their pupils, the nature of the curriculum, the style of classroom management and organizational aspects. On the basis of these arguments, the school, along with parents and society, must share the responsibility for the development of acceptable social behaviour in its pupils.

Yet the view that indiscipline in schools is essentially the responsibility of parents and society, rather than one that is shared with the school, is strongly held by some teachers. A recent teachers' union report (NAS/UWT, 1981), after blaming society for the 'retreat from authority', places the main responsibility for disruption in school on the offenders' parents. 'Sterner measures' are recommended against those parents 'whose abdication of parental responsibility leads often to pupils' repeated non-cooperation', and the report suggests that 'it might be helpful to resort to requiring parents/pupils to appear before tribunals of Government and/or LEAs'.

From the research evidence to be reviewed in this chapter, it would appear that some schools appear to be noticeably more successful than others in exerting a positive influence on the way their pupils behave. Moreover, from recent investigations, we are beginning to identify the characteristics that distinguish these schools. The findings from these studies provide an important corrective to the view that behaviour problems are located exclusively in the child, his upbringing and his culture. Indeed, the idea that the child has a 'deficit' is likely to make the problem irremediable because it is assumed that the school lacks the power to change the behaviour. Further, too much emphasis on the child's general malfunctioning may actually create problems since the context in which 'misbehaviour' arises will be overlooked, and attention will not be given to changing those characteristics of the school situation that might lead to improvement in behaviour.

RESEARCH PROBLEMS

It is not easy to estimate the effects of schools on children's behaviour. One fundamental problem, which was raised in Chapter 1, concerns the concept of 'disruptive behaviour'. As Galloway *et al.* (1982, p. xv) have pointed out, 'behaviour at school does not fall into neat groups of normal and disruptive' but 'consists of a continuum, from extremely cooperative to totally unacceptable'. Moreover 'few children consistently occupy the same position on the continuum; their behaviour changes as their teachers, their age and their family circumstances change' (ibid., p. xv). Problems of definition are also bedevilled by problems of values. Wedge and Prosser (1973, p. 51) have put it this way: 'When, for example, does politeness become fawning, independence become selfishness, shyness become withdrawal, or non-conformity become hostility?' Use of the term 'disruptive *pupil*' suggests that the causes of classroom control problems are located exclusively in the child, rather than shared with the environment. It is preferable, therefore, to think in terms of 'disruptive *behaviour*' since this leaves open questions of causality. The definition adopted by Mortimore *et al.* (1983) illustrates this point: disruptive behaviour is 'any act which interferes with the learning, development, or happiness of a pupil or his peers, or with the teacher's attempts to foster these processes or feelings' (p. 1).

A further research problem relates to the number of school factors that might have an influence on pupil behaviour. How do you decide which ones to look for? It is tempting to concentrate on those that are most easily measurable, such as teacher–pupil ratios or size of school. Yet others, such as teacher expectations and teacher–pupil relationships, which are difficult to assess, may be more important. The same kind of problem relates to the range of background factors that might be used as control measures.

It is the indeterminacy of relevant factors that leads some researchers to eschew the collection of quantitative data and adopt instead an interactive approach. This involves informal interviewing and the analysis of transcripts, enabling the investigator to try to uncover the particular construction teachers and pupils bring to the situation. An example of this approach with teachers is the study of classroom deviance by Hargreaves, Hester and Mellor (1975); examples with pupils can be found in the collection of papers edited by Woods (1980). Because such studies are extremely time-consuming, they are usually limited to a few schools, or even one. The major school effectiveness studies have thus relied primarily on quantitative data. Here the problem in assessing behaviour has been whether to use teacher ratings or pupil self-reports or observations by trained investigators. Since there are pros and cons for each procedure, it is prudent to use all three as in the London secondary school study (Rutter *et al.*, 1979).

Another problem is the difficulty in disentangling school effects from the influences of other factors. It is therefore important to control for background factors as far as this is practicable. One approach is to compare schools whose pupils are taken from a socially homogeneous catchment area (e.g. Reynolds, 1976). However, backgrounds that are similar in social class may be different in other important respects, such as parental attitudes towards schooling. Another approach is to adjust the results statistically to take account of the different nature of the intakes under examination (e.g. Rutter *et al.*, 1979; ILEA, 1986a). The problem here lies in choosing the appropriate intake variables.

Then again there is the problem of representativeness. Because resources are restricted, only a small number of schools can be studied. The difficulty is choosing a sample that can be regarded as typical of schools as a whole. In this respect, the data base of the London secondary school study (Rutter *et al.*, 1979), which was limited to twelve schools in one borough, can be contrasted with the more recent London junior school project (ILEA, 1986a), which involved fifty schools selected on a random basis from the whole London area.

Finally, there is the problem of interpreting the results, since the same data can be used to support quite different theories. For instance, Hargreaves (1981) has pointed out how the finding of Reynolds (1976), that schools which adopt a rigid attitude to rules have greater deviant behaviour, could be interpreted in terms of pupils being 'typed' through the infringement of alien rules (labelling theory) or in terms of the stress generated in pupils who experience a regular assault on their autonomy (strain theory) – and other interpretations are also possible.

None of these problems can be eliminated. But an appreciation of some of the difficulties researchers encounter should help us to evaluate their work intelligently.

FINDINGS FROM SCHOOL EFFECTIVENESS STUDIES

An increasing interest is now being taken in the question 'Do schools matter?' Most of the studies have related to academic achievement (see reviews by Reynolds, 1982, 1985; Purkey and Smith, 1983; Rutter, 1983). This chapter will concentrate on those investigations in which social behaviour has been included in the terms of reference.

One of the earliest British studies to point to the impact of the school on children's behaviour was by Burt and Howard (1952). From evidence relating to almost 400 children between six and fourteen years of age, these writers concluded that the most important influences on maladjusted behaviour were not poverty, physical conditions or pathological effects. Instead, Burt and Howard believed that 'the evidence gathered ... leaves little doubt that in many cases the main, if not the sole, cause of maladjustment arises out of current conditions at the child's school' (p. 129).

The school characteristics that seemed to be related to emotional problems in pupils were the personal relations between the child, his teacher and his peers, while transfer from infant to junior school, or from primary to secondary, could also be a factor, especially if accompanied by a change in teaching method. Moreover, in follow-up studies of earlier cases, Burt and Howard found that 'in quite a high proportion, remedies directed solely to an alteration of the school conditions have been followed by a complete and apparently permanent disappearance of every overt sign of maladjustment' (p. 130).

In a later investigation concerned with social relationships among fourth-year pupils and their teachers in a northern secondary school, Hargreaves (1967) suggested that the school itself actively helped to produce disaffection and delinquency by progressively dividing pupils into two subcultural groups. On the one hand were the 'A' streamers, who came to identify themselves with the formal objectives of the school, and whose good behaviour was reinforced by consistent staff approval; on the other hand were the 'D' streamers, pupils of low ability who in the first two years showed little difference from 'A' streamers in value orientation, but who, by the fourth year, demonstrated marked feelings of rejection by the school. It was Hargreaves's contention that these deepening attitudes of hostility amongst pupils in the lowest stream were a function of the grouping system, an emphasis on arid learning, and inflexible attitudes amongst the staff.

At about the same time, in another report on deviant behaviour, Power *et al.* (1967) demonstrated that the official annual delinquency rates for boys in the secondary schools of Tower Hamlets, east London, varied from 0.7 per cent in one school to 19 per cent in another. Power and his colleagues went on to suggest that, given the homogeneous nature of the area, these variations could be attributed to the schools rather than to neighbourhood factors. Unfortunately, the controversial nature of this conclusion made the schools defensive and unwilling to allow further investigation that would have allowed Power to confirm or refute his hypothesis. Subsequent criticism of Power's methodology (e.g. Baldwin, 1972) tended to discredit this particular piece of research.

The first major British study into school effectiveness was that of David Reynolds (1976). This involved an investigation into nine secondary modern schools which accounted for the bottom two-thirds of the ability range in a former mining community in South Wales. Delinquency rates were found to vary from 3.8 per cent to 10.5 per cent, and the attendance rates from 77.2 per cent to 89.1 per cent. The more successful schools appeared to be those with 'a high proportion of pupils in authority positions ... low levels of institutional control, low rates of physical punishment, small overall size, more favourable teacher–pupil ratios and more tolerant attitudes to the enforcing of certain rules regarding "dress, manners and morals"' (Reynolds, 1982, p. 228). Reynolds also found that it was the schools that consciously fostered good personal relationships with pupils and their

Accounting for Children's Behaviour 35

parents that experienced the lowest incidence of problem behaviour. These schools were less likely to perceive pupils as 'socially deprived', involved them in the running of the school and included their parents in decision-making processes. Although Reynolds claimed that pupils in schools with the better behaviour records were not materially different in their social backgrounds or personality from those in schools with the less acceptable behaviour, a major criticism of this study is the failure to control for a range of background variables.

In the late 1970s, another major study was undertaken by Michael Rutter and his colleagues (1979), this time in an inner-London borough. The progress of children in twelve secondary schools was compared with regard to a range of factors, such as attendance, examination results, behaviour inside school and delinquency outside it. Although the results were complex, the authors were left in no doubt about their conclusion that schools with the best intakes were not necessarily those with the best outcomes, and that schools with similar intakes could have different outcomes:

> Secondary schools in inner London differed markedly in the behaviour and attainments shown by their pupils ... Although schools differed in the proportion of behaviourally difficult or low achieving children they admitted, these differences did *not* wholly account for the variations between schools in their pupils' later behaviour and attainment.
> (pp. 177–8)

As far as school behaviour is concerned, a broad range of conduct was assessed before entry by teacher ratings, and then re-assessed at various age levels in the secondary school through a behavioural measure based upon observation and pupils' self-reports. From their own observations, the researchers noted the incidence of pupils wearing school uniform, the amount of broken chairs and windows, the amount of wall graffiti, the prevalence of violence in the playground and fights between lessons, how often pupils were late for lessons, the needs to borrow pens and pencils, and whether coats were worn in class. During lessons they also noted the degree to which pupils were 'on task' and 'off task', as well as the amount of chat, mild disruption (e.g. rhythmic tapping on desks, humming, combing hair, chewing gum) and more serious disruption (e.g. loud singing, swearing, throwing pencils). Pupils were asked questions concerning the frequency with which they cut lessons, absconded after registration, played truant, did not wear uniform and drew or wrote on the school building.

The results showed that differences in behavioural outcomes were associated with particular kinds of teacher actions in the classroom as well as certain sorts of general school factors. Specifically, better behaviour occurred in classes where teachers arrived on time, started lessons without fuss or delay while materials were sorted out, gave few unofficial punishments, planned lessons so that there was less need for disciplinary interventions, made ample use of praise, attended to the whole class rather than just part of it, and kept pupils engaged in productive activities. General school conditions that were linked with the better behaviour ratings included pleasant working conditions, the approachableness of staff, the extent to which children were given posts of responsibility, the onus put upon children to care for their own resources, low rates of corporal punishment, senior staff providing a clear sense of direction and a staff consensus about values and aims.

The Rutter et al. (1979) report emphasized that individual factors on their own were of less importance than their combined influence. For instance, a teacher in one school could successfully leave children alone to work, whereas in another school the same action invited disruption. The difference in response seemed related to the general school ethos, the success of any particular action depending on the general influence of all the school factors.

Various criticisms have been made of the methodology used by Rutter et al. and their interpretation of the data (see Acton, 1980; Goldstein, 1980; Tizard, 1980; University of Exeter, 1980). The authors claimed that the study was 'not designed to test any one particular theory about schooling, nor was our analysis based on pre-conceived ideas about which particular aspect of school processes *should* be important' (p. 107, authors' italics). This is difficult to accept. Any selection of measures used to assess behavioural and academic outcomes reflects some ideological stance. It may be, as Rutter and his colleagues suggested, that the behaviour inventory 'encompassed the expectations *shared* by all the twelve schools' (p. 48, authors' italics), but these common assumptions do not make the research value free. Running through the report is a clear notion of what constitutes a 'good pupil'. Furthermore, the notion is one that is based upon measurable behaviours, some of which seem comparatively trivial (e.g. wearing coats in the classroom). Aspects of behaviour that would be difficult to measure (e.g. the pupils' perceptions of school authority, or the extent to which the pupils shared the values implicit in the curriculum) were ignored. As the researchers themselves point out, it is possible that aspects of behaviour that were not measured are more strongly related to family and neighbourhood factors.

However, within the framework of the research, the report does demonstrate the differential effects of schools on some aspects of pupil behaviour, and the fact that these effects remain reasonably stable over at least four or five years. The results also suggested that the school makes an impact on the children's behaviour outside its premises, though not so dramatically as in the classroom. Particularly important here was the balance of intake. Delinquency rates were higher in schools in which there was a disproportionate number of less able pupils. Heal (1978) has shown that primary schools too can make an impact on children's behaviour outside school. However, in a recent longitudinal study of 400 boys from age eight to twenty-five, West (1982) concluded that differences between school delinquency rates disappeared when a wide range of intake factors were taken into account.

Another indicator of variations in the ability of schools to contain unacceptable pupil behaviour comes from a study by Galloway et al. (1982) concerning exclusion and suspension rates from secondary schools in Sheffield. Amongst the schools, huge differences were found in the numbers of pupils suspended, or excluded for at least three weeks. More than half these pupils had attended only five of the thirty-nine schools. Moreover, no obvious relationship was found between these rates and aspects of the catchment areas such as parental occupation, quality of housing, or size of family. Specifically, schools which had the most socially disadvantaged pupils were not those who excluded or suspended the most. Galloway and his colleagues concluded that 'a pupil's chances of being excluded or suspended are influenced at least as much, and probably more, by which school he happens to attend, as by any stress in his family or any constitutional factors in the pupil himself' (1982, p. 33).

Since background and personal variables did not help to explain why some schools were 'high excluders' and others 'low excluders', it seemed that the schools themselves were responsible for this differential treatment of their pupils. Interviews with the heads and senior staff confirmed this to be so. It was not just that schools with the lower exclusion rates tended to contain disruptive behaviour internally: they also experienced serious problems from fewer pupils. The Hargreaves Report (ILEA, 1984) on London secondary schools also revealed how some institutions contributed disproportionately to suspension rates between 1979/80 and 1981/2, and that the discrepancy could not be attributed to intake factors.

The London Junior School Project (ILEA, 1986a) is the most recent of the school effectiveness studies, and the largest primary school survey to be undertaken in the United Kingdom. Almost two thousand children in fifty randomly selected London schools were followed in a longitudinal study from the age of seven until transfer to secondary school. To assess the impact of school factors on learning and behaviour, account was taken of each pupil's social, ethnic, language and family background, as well as cognitive attainment and behaviour at entry to the junior school.

Using a measure called 'The Child at School' (Kysel et al., 1983), specially developed for the junior age range, three aspects of behaviour problems – those related to learning (concentration, motivation and perseverance), aggression and anxiety – were recorded by class teachers with respect to each child during the autumn and summer terms of Years 1 to 3. This broad definition of behaviour should be borne in mind when interpreting the results. Assessments made over this period were summed, thus smoothing out aberrations due to the different criteria by which different teachers judge behaviour to be 'acceptable' or 'difficult'. The findings showed that, even when background factors and initial attainment were taken into account, differences between children's behaviour in the junior years could still be partly explained in terms of the school attended. Furthermore, there were marked differences between schools in their effects on children's behaviour, some schools having strong positive effects and some negative effects.

The quality of children's behaviour in junior schools was found to be related to the head's managerial style, to teacher actions in the classroom and to class size. Behaviour tended to be better in schools where the head saw parents at regular fixed times. This strategy presumably created the opportunity for children's behaviour problems to be discussed with their parents, and for parents to tell the school of any factors which could have a bearing on their child's behaviour. The school and parents could thus work as partners in their attempts to resolve the difficulty. Behaviour was also better in schools where the head rewarded pupils with stars or certificates. As we shall see in Chapter 7, the use of tangible rewards in schools is a controversial issue; as in the ILEA study, it is not necessarily associated with better cognitive outcomes, but it may help to foster a positive school atmosphere which encourages good conduct. Better behaviour was found, too, in schools where the staff as a whole were involved in decision-making. This suggests that feelings of involvement among teachers in the making of school policy help to produce a positive school ethos which is conducive to good behaviour. At the same time, worse behaviour tended to be found where the head had been in office for longer than eleven years. Such heads seemed less likely to involve staff in decision-making or meeting parents, and so may have been less successful in promoting a climate of trust and co-operativeness.

At classroom level, better behaviour was associated with the amount of time which teachers spent in giving feedback on work, in asking questions about work and in promoting a work-centred environment in which not too many different kinds of activity were going on at once. Children clearly respond positively to classroom situations in which they are given plenty to do, when they are given help in overcoming learning problems, when the teacher provides them with challenging experiences and when the activities of other pupils in the room are not distracting. Also important was a firm but fair classroom management style which encouraged self-control. Teachers who were constantly criticizing children elicited less good behaviour. Perhaps these teachers needed to reprimand more because they did not take sufficient steps to prevent disruption developing in the first place; pupils would also feel frustrated and less inclined to be co-operative with teachers who are constantly reprimanding. Finally, in contrast to the findings of Rutter *et al.* (1979) in London secondary schools, class size was found to be important: where numbers were large, behaviour was worse, possibly because teachers had less opportunity to deal with individual problems and felt the need to reprimand more.

In short, from our review of a number of studies, it seems that schools play a significant role in children's behavioural patterns and development. We can conclude that the responsibility for problem behaviour in schools cannot be placed simply at the door of the permissive society, home background or factors in the child. The school factors which appear to be particularly important are control and management styles which convey competence whilst diminishing the need for reprimand and punishment, purposeful teaching in which pupils are given regular and positive feedback, firm leadership from the head and senior teachers whose decisions take good account of staffroom feeling, and an ethos in which teachers, parents and pupils feel significant in the school community.

LEARNING DIFFICULTIES AND CURRICULUM OPPORTUNITIES

A fair amount of evidence points to an association between antisocial behaviour and learning difficulties, such as poor reading attainment (Rutter, Tizard and Whitmore, 1970; Berger, Yule and Rutter, 1975; McGee, Silva and Williams, 1984; ILEA, 1986a). Whether there is a causal relationship and, if so, which is the cause and which the effect is not easy to say. Stott (1981) has argued that adverse family situations, such as overcrowding and stress, help to produce both conduct and learning problems. At the same time, from his analysis of assessment records of over one thousand five-year-olds in Ontario, Stott considered that poor attainment in reading and arithmetic was a consequence of maladjustment rather than the other way round. This conclusion has been challenged by

Youngman (1982), however, who has criticized Stott's methodology, and maintains that the cause–effect issue remains unresolved. From their findings in the London junior school survey, the researchers concluded that attainment and behaviour are linked in a complex way, each influencing the other: 'Poor reading tends to encourage poor behaviour, and poor behaviour leads to poor reading attainment' (ILEA, 1986a, Part A, p. 24). It certainly makes intuitive sense to believe that the situation is a vicious circle, bad behaviour being both a cause and an effect of poor attainment.

A major influence on pupil disaffection in secondary schools is the 'message' generated by the nature of the curriculum and the manner of its implementation. In Raven's (1977) study of attitudes in secondary schools, half the pupils considered subjects to be 'boring' or 'useless', bearing little relevance to their interests or career expectations. As long as status is seen in terms of academic achievement, the pupil who cannot succeed in these terms has nothing to lose by being disruptive. In contrast, those whose goal is to succeed academically, and whose career depends on this, will have a vested interest in behaving co-operatively. Not only do these pupils appreciate that 'mucking around' prevents learning, they also realize that paying attention willl be taken by the teachers as a sign that they are worthy of their goal and are committed to school values. In short, as the criteria for success in school change, or become more flexible, so it is likely that patterns of behaviour will change also.

David Hargreaves (1982) argues that secondary pupils, particularly those in urban working-class neighbourhoods, experience a destruction of their feelings of personal worth. This is because schools tend to emphasize success in terms of subjects that involve cognitive-developmental skills and individual achievement, whilst also downgrading the expressive arts and community-orientated studies in which more pupils could experience a feeling of fulfilment. In consequence, some pupils create a school counter-culture that represents an attempt to remove and negate the indignities suffered as a result of these hidden messages:

> My argument is that our present secondary system, largely through the hidden curriculum, exerts on many pupils, particularly, but by no means exclusively from the working-class, a destruction of their dignity which is so massive and pervasive that few subsequently recover from it. To have dignity means to have a sense of being worthy, of possessing creative, inventive and critical capacities, of having the power to achieve personal and social change. When dignity is damaged, one's deepest experience is of being inferior, unable, and powerless. My argument is that our secondary schools inflict such damage, in varying degrees, on many of

their pupils. It is not intended by the teachers, the vast majority of whom seek and strive hard to give their pupils dignity as I have defined it.

(Hargreaves, 1982, p. 17)

Hargreaves goes on to argue that comprehensive schools have an important part to play in bringing back a sense of belonging and corporate solidarity, and that this might be achieved through a reorientation of the curriculum towards community-centred programmes and other activities that give pupils a sense of their own significance and competence.

The tendency for the curriculum and assessment procedures to create disaffection with school life by confronting pupils with their own failure has also been brought out in a study by Cathy Bird and her colleagues (1981), who interviewed over one hundred pupils in six outer London comprehensive schools. However, these researchers found that misbehaviour did not necessarily imply disaffection from the school itself, but could equally spring from the more pressing demands of the peer group. Further, pupils created alternative identities outside school that were incompatible with school expectations. For instance, many were involved in part-time employment, or helping out in the home, in which they experienced new authority relationships and levels of personal responsibility not recognized by the school. For fifteen- and sixteen-year-olds, these alternative roles seemed incompatible with the subservient pupil roles still expected at school.

ADJUSTMENT TO SCHOOL

In the previous chapter, one of the points brought out in our review of influences outside the school is that some boys and girls are particularly susceptible to stress, which in turn can trigger off disruptive behaviour. One of the ways, then, in which schools and class teachers could help themselves and the children is to minimize situations in which stress is unnecessarily created. This is not easy, for the nature of institutionalized education is bound to promote anxiety to some extent. In the case of young children, for instance, as Irene Caspari (1976) has suggested, transition from home to school is bound to be stressful because children are being separated from their mothers, often for the first time, and may be jealous of younger siblings left at home. They have to accommodate themselves to new sorts of demands, such as timekeeping, lining up, being silent and concentrating on learning tasks. They also have to secure the acceptance of their peers and to cope with being rejected or physically challenged by them.

Of course, it is good for children to experience a limited amount of anxiety in order to learn how to cope with the demands of living. But beyond a certain level, anxiety inhibits the capacity to learn and adjust. In one study, for instance, Moore (1966) found that, while most 6- to 11-year-olds adapted to school over the years, almost one in five remained generally unreconciled up to the end of junior school. Moreover, many of the problems could have been alleviated by the school since they were attributable to faulty school organization and the inappropriate attitude of some teachers. Moore's conclusion was that children could be helped to cope with social pressures more effectively, not by 'smoothing away all difficulties, nor adding to them gratuitously' but rather by 'fortifying the child in the belief that he can overcome his difficulties and find solutions to the problems he meets' (p. 70). Specifically, he recommended limiting forms of competition that reduce the child's sense of personal worth, and a style of pupil management that combines firmness with respect for the child's individuality.

Evidence concerning the relationship between frustration, aggression and school organization comes from a study by Johnson and Krovetz (1976). Marked differences were found in the playground aggression of 6–9-year-olds in two racially mixed working-class schools in California. The school, which was 'pluralistic', providing several distinct types of learning environment to meet the different intellectual and psychological needs of the pupils, had less physical aggression and verbal abuse in breaktimes than the 'traditional' school, which did not make such a provision. The researchers were properly cautious about generalizing this result and pointed to other contributing factors. None the less, they considered that pupils at the 'pluralistic' school experienced less frustration because the teaching arrangements varied according to the children's individual predicaments, and so helped to prevent the development of feelings of failure.

The transition from primary to secondary school can be anxiety-provoking for some children who react unfavourably to the larger, more impersonal environment of secondary education, and experience for the first time a range of teachers with differing standards, teaching styles and expectations (see Galton and Wilcocks, 1983; Measor and Woods, 1984). Transition from primary to secondary school is likely to be a less stressful experience if the staff in each institution regard themselves as equal partners in a co-operative enterprise. This has implications for school organization, curriculum continuity and teaching arrangements.

As regards organization, the Thomas Report on London primary schools (ILEA, 1985a) has suggested that clusters of primary and secondary schools might be formed in localities to help ease problems of transfer from one level of schooling to the next. Primary schoolchildren would then be introduced into their secondary schools in a gradual way, possibly transferring towards the end of the summer term of their last year. As far as curriculum continuity is concerned, there is a clear need for frequent discussion between teachers of the two age phases not only about syllabuses but teaching styles. In a national study concerning transfer from middle to secondary schools, Stillman and Maychall (1984) found that almost all the teachers surveyed thought that there should be frequent discussion on curriculum links, yet only 13 per cent worked in such schemes. As regards teaching arrangements, some secondary schools have found that behaviour is better when first-year pupils are not immediately exposed to the full range of specialist teachers or re-grouped for different subjects, but are taught in their form group by a limited number of teachers. This arrangement provides stability and exposure to consistent kinds of demands and expectations; it also provides the means whereby teachers can get to know individuals easily.

THE INTERACTION OF HOME AND SCHOOL INFLUENCES

Because school factors appear to be important in the creation and amelioration of problem behaviour, it does not follow that family circumstances should be ignored. On the contrary, the impact of experiences in the home cannot be underestimated. In one urban comprehensive school, Lawrence, Steed and Young (1977) found that about two in every five children were suffering from stresses such as father's unemployment, chronic illness in the family, death of a parent after a prolonged illness, being in care or thrown out of home. It would be remarkable if children's home circumstances and their relationships with parents did not carry over into the school situation and affect their classroom behaviour. Reynolds (1985, p. 193), whilst emphasizing the role of the school in promoting good behaviour, has commented that 'the assertion of the *independence* of the school may prove damaging if it prevents us from seeing the interaction between pupils from specific home backgrounds and certain specified features of their schools'.

Behaviour in school is certainly influenced when the co-operation of parents is enlisted, as studies at both secondary (Reynolds, 1982) and junior (ILEA, 1986a) levels have shown. Persuading parents to operate a system of sanctions based on the child's behavioural record at school is also effective, judging from a scheme operating in Norfolk (Melton and Long, 1986) that is described in Chapter 10. None the less, parental co-operation alone will not be sufficient because the school, in providing the context for children's behaviour in their role as pupils, also exerts an impact for better or for worse. Further, of all the factors that impinge upon pupils' emotional development and behaviour, those related to the school are probably the most amenable to change. Later chapters in this book will therefore examine the significance of particular practices for school behaviour, discipline and control.

FURTHER READING

Hargreaves, D. (1982) *The Challenge for the Comprehensive School*, Routledge & Kegan Paul, London.
(A stimulating argument on the adverse effects of the hidden curriculum on pupils' feelings of personal worth. The diagnosis is intuitively compelling; the recommendations are more controversial.)
Inner London Education Authority (1986a) *The Junior School Project*, ILEA London; and Rutter, M. *et al.* (1979) *Fifteen Thousand Hours*, Open Books, London.
(Accounts of the London research mentioned in this chapter.)
Reynolds, D. (1976) The delinquent school, in M. Hammersley and P. Woods (eds.) *The Process of Schooling*, Routledge & Kegan Paul/Open University Press, London.
(Describes the South Wales research mentioned in this chapter.)
Reynolds, D. (ed.) (1985) *Studying School Effectiveness*, Falmer Press, Barcombe, East Sussex.
(A collection of papers, given at the first conference organized by the School Differences Research Group. Looks at problems that face researchers who investigate the impact of the school on children's achievement and behaviour.)

4
THE PLACE OF DISCIPLINE IN SCHOOL

Discipline is a general notion concerned with the learning and observance of rules. All societies depend for their existence on conformity to rules. As Alexander (1973) has pointed out, 'A society without rules is inconceivable, and rules without some attitude of disapproval towards breaking them are inconceivable. ... Anyone who seeks to change a society rather than to abolish society altogether must be aiming at something with some rules, however exiguous' (p. 149).

Yet discipline is a contentious issue, especially in schools. For some it is associated with repressive regimes and brutal punishment, as in 'disciplining' and 'being a disciplinarian'. Here the argument turns on the extent to which it is held that children are being manipulated, treated as means rather than ends. For others, discipline is associated with ideals and principled behaviour, as in 'disciple' and 'disciplined thinking'. Here the argument is about the kind of rules that are felt to be right in a civilized society and an educational institution.

In this chapter the nature of this controversy will be explored by considering four reasons why discipline is considered to be an important issue in schools. These reasons are not mutually incompatible, but they do represent conceptually distinct notions of discipline. Briefly, they are concerned with beliefs that discipline is necessary for the social and economic needs of the community, for the psychological needs of the individual, for successful classroom management, and for educative learning.

(1) 'SOCIETY DEPENDS UPON A DISCIPLINED COMMUNITY'

First of all, discipline in school is often seen to perform an important function in ensuring that children conform to the mores of their society, internalizing the behavioural values of the dominant culture and acting accordingly. Without discipline, society would cease to be an orderly community, and would suffer in terms of industrial efficiency and world competition.

The notion that society depends upon a disciplined community has strong historical roots. In Sparta, because of its exclusive military ideals, schooling involved 'the complete submergence of individuality in a system where the state possesses the child body and soul' (Castle, 1961, p. 24); discipline was therefore construed in terms of 'obedience to immediate superiors in a hierarchy of persons themselves obedient to a static community tradition' (ibid., p. 25). In the English elementary schools during the last century, fear that the ambitions of the new industrial working class posed a threat to social stability, plus a belief in the natural moral inferiority of children, produced elaborate formulations of the concept of discipline in terms of obedience training. Joseph Landon, the vice-principal of Saltley Training College, was particularly adroit at this exercise:

> By disciplinary influence in the narrow school sense is meant the combined agencies which the teacher brings to bear upon the child in order to make him amenable to law and order, and to arouse such energy as he possesses in a way to induce him voluntarily to put forth his efforts in the direction we wish; to train him to steady application and prompt and willing obedience.
>
> (Landon, 1895, p. 188)

The vice-principal's conception of a good teacher was unsurprisingly 'an enthusiast but no visionary ... checking insubordination before the thought of it has taken form ... and controlling the very motives of action like the hand of fate' (ibid., pp. 186–7).

In this century, the French sociologist Emile Durkheim (1961), while rejecting the coercive view of discipline to achieve societal ends, argued that the moral objectives of schools can be determined by identifying the corporate interests of society. These he saw as a collection of societal 'facts' – rules, habits, customs, laws – which, through schooling, could become internalized by all members of society. To this end Durkheim believed that it was in the interests of public morality for teachers to cultivate in their pupils what he called 'the spirit of discipline'. By this he did not mean inducing uniformity of behaviour or controlling children to make them work, but 'regularizing' the child's conduct, moderating his egocentric desires and encouraging him to respect authority. Although Durkheim's central interest was the provision of an education appropriate to times of social change, he saw such change as rooted in existing culture, the transmission of which guaranteed the survival of society. Teachers therefore had a high responsibility: 'Just as the priest is the interpreter of God [the teacher] is the interpreter of the great moral ideas of his time and country' (p. 155). At the same time, Durkheim assiduously warned teachers not to allow their authority to become personalized or repressive, for he considered it essential that the child viewed the regulations of the school as a reflection of the regulations of society, not as the expression of the teacher's will.

Essentially, Durkheim's thesis was that schooling should focus on the good of the individual by emphasizing the interests of the group. In being subjected to the discipline of the school, the child learns the importance of accepting general rules and developing self-discipline. However, in times of ethical pluralism, as is the case today in most Western societies, the basis on which a consensual moral code could be determined is less clear. One way in which schools could deal with this problem is to impose their own code of behaviour. This is the position the National Association of Schoolmasters/Union of Women Teachers (NAS/UWT) adopted in a policy document, significantly entitled *The Retreat from Authority*, which appeared in the late 1970s. In a section headed 'The Permissiveness of Society', the authors regret that those who once stood as the undisputed representatives of authority no longer do so: 'This had had a disastrous effect on the established standing of the priest, the schoolteacher, the parent and the policeman. ... It is an important function of teachers to counter the blindness of a generation which has sought to rid itself of conventions necessary for social stability' (p. 4). A similar view was expressed in the 1985 Disraeli lecture by the chairman of the Conservative Party, Norman Tebbit, who maintained that the increase in violence and crime in our society was a direct consequence of permissive attitudes that scorned traditional standards in all aspects of life from behaviour in the classroom and the family to art and grammar.

However, pupils today will not easily accept an imposed code of behaviour. On the basis of observations in a group of secondary schools in South Wales, Reynolds and Sullivan (1979) have argued that teachers who adopt an 'incorporative' approach to discipline, i.e. involving the pupils in the authority structures and being prepared to be flexible about rules based on conventions rather than moral principles (e.g. those concerning dress or eating chewing gum in class), will paradoxically elicit more conventional behaviour from working-class adolescents than teachers who adopt a coercive approach. The National Union of Teachers (NUT) seems more sensitive to this state of affairs than the NAS/UWT: 'Teachers can no longer expect "respect" from society simply because they are teachers. The esteem of parents and pupils must now be earned and this change presents new challenge and makes new demands on teachers. It directly reflects the relationship between teacher and pupil' (NUT, 1976, para. 1.3).

During the 1970s, various writers tried to demonstrate how the interests of ruling groups are served by subjecting children to particular kinds of disciplinary regime at school. Shipman (1971), for instance, argued that the revised 'moral courses' laid down by the Japanese government from the 1950s created conditions for rapid industrialization. Although no longer tied to the rigid Confucian principle that the people must not be informed, and avoiding the prewar emphasis on indoctrination, the new courses included such items as respect for service, good manners, impartiality, the observance of rules, the difference between rights and duties, the appreciation of labour – all of which, according to Shipman, illustrates the faith of the Japanese in the power of an education system. However, these attempts to impose an inflexible behavioural code have recently met with much resistance, judging from press reports of a surge in pupil violence and vandalism, and the system also seems to be contributing to the alarming incidence of bullying and child suicides (Boseley, 1986).

Life in American high schools provides another illustration of the means by which a school's disciplinary regime has been said to serve the interests of the dominant order. In an influential book called *Schooling in Capitalist America*, Bowles and Gintis (1976) argued that the system of sanctions used in American schools plays a crucial part in reproducing the American capitalist way of life. Writing from a Marxist perspective, they asserted: 'Since its inception in the United States, the public school system has been seen as a method of disciplining children in the interests of producing a properly subordinate population' (p. 37). Although the accent was no longer on unconcealed disciplinarianism, it was still on subordination: 'Teachers are likely to reward those who conform to and strengthen the social order of the school with high grades and approval, and punish violators with lower grades and other forms of disapproval, independent of their respective academic and cognitive accomplishments' (p. 39). To support this contention, the authors cited various research studies which, it was maintained, demonstrate how the reward system in American schools operates to inhibit those manifestations of personal capacity which pose a threat to hierarchical authority. All this was seen by Bowles and Gintis to reflect the force of business interests in America and the ideology of efficient management.

However, in more recent Marxist writings, emphasis has been given to the way in which many pupils, particularly those from working-class backgrounds, bring to school their own values and resist attempts by the dominant culture to impose theirs. Willis (1977) and Corrigan (1979) emphasize the general opposition to school authority by working-class adolescents and the force of counter-school culture. Apple (1982), who, in an earlier publication, had held a deterministic view about the relationship between schooling and business forces, now argues that this theory does not do justice to the complexity of school life, in which large numbers of inner-city pupils 'creatively adapt their environments', 'simply reject the overt and hidden curricula of the school' and resist as far as possible 'the covert teaching of punctuality, neatness, compliance and other more economically rooted values' (p. 96). These 'resistance' theories 'restore a degree of agency and innovation' to groups outside the dominant culture (Giroux, 1981, p. 260). However, the new school of writers also point out that resistance to expected norms is only partially successful since the working class, in spite of its show of resistance, accommodates to the system.

A third example relates to the USSR. Bronfenbrenner (1971) has vividly illustrated the ways in which the Soviet school system is used to bring about a submergence of individual interests when these conflict with those of the 'collective'. Russian children are trained to behave by means of community influences, parents and teachers being given detailed guidance concerning the behaviour expected of children in the home, school and community. The Academy of Pedagogical Sciences decrees precisely the conduct of children required at each age. The detail is impressive. At seven years, children must be told not only to arrive in school on time, but to 'wipe their feet upon entering, greet the teacher and all technical staff by name, give a general greeting to classmates and a personal greeting by name to their seatmates' (quoted on p. 28), while the twelve-year-old is expected, among other things, to 'participate in getting fuel for heating the school (chopping wood), cleaning up and repairing school property and equipment, removing snow ... assist young children in developing habits of good conduct towards parents and elders' (quoted on p. 34). Sanctions are not punitive, but are based on rewards, praise and competition in which the appeal is always to the group. It is not the individual but the row in the classroom and the class in the school that receive rewards – though the trend is towards greater individuality. These codes and the means of their enforcement must be seen in the context of Soviet collective upbringing where the classroom is a unit of the Communist youth organization, in which all activity is in keeping with Soviet ideology.

In a modern industrialized society, there is bound to be a tension between those who, on the one hand, believe that schools should emphasize the growth of personal autonomy, and make ample provision for individual freedom and choice, and those, on the other hand, who believe that the job of schools is essentially to prepare children for the 'real world', in which competition and respect for authority are all-important. Bertrand Russell (1932), who founded an independent 'progressive' school at Beacon Hill in Hampshire, believed that traditional school discipline 'has led to the teaching of respect for competition as opposed to cooperation, especially in international affairs' (p. 163). In regular primary schools that are avowedly 'child-centred', the principles and the practice of discipline do not always match, as Sharp and Green (1975) revealed in their observational study of three infant classrooms. It is the pupils who conform to a disciplinary regime that values being 'busy' and 'getting on, on your own' who can be the most favoured, even though theoretically all pupils are supposed to be considered of equal worth.

(2) 'CHILDREN NEED DISCIPLINE FOR THEIR OWN GOOD'

So far we have considered some of the problems involved in 'disciplining' children to take their role in society. A second reason why discipline is considered an important issue in school focuses on personal rather than on societal needs. Children are held to 'need discipline' for the sake of their happiness and feelings of emotional security. Here discipline is seen in terms of a consistent application of external constraints so that children develop stable personalities and do not become maladjusted.

Durkheim, whose views on the social role of discipline were reviewed in the last section, also recognized that happiness is dependent upon self-restraint, and that this has to be learned through the experience of external constraint. The discipline of schools, he thought, saved man from 'anomie', where each is ruled by individual insatiable desires; because these cannot all be satisfied, the result is perpetual unhappiness. Even A. S. Neill, who detested harsh authority, observed how 'the child of spirit can rebel against the hard boss, but the soft boss merely makes the child impotently soft and unsure of his real feelings' (Neill, 1960, p. 52).

More recently, the American psychologist Ausubel and his colleagues (1978) have emphasized the role of discipline in providing children with emotional security: 'Without the guidance provided by unambiguous external controls they tend to feel bewildered and apprehensive. Too great a burden is placed on their own limited capacity for self-control' (p. 511). Rutter (1975) points out how 'extremely lax discipline by mothers and rigidly overrestrictive discipline by fathers is particularly common in families of delinquent boys' (p. 146). Evidence also suggests that inconsistency and lack of supervision in parental discipline is associated with aggressive behaviour (Riley and Shaw, 1985), and that a deliberate emphasis on unpunitive but firm guidance is necessary for the development of a positive self-concept (Coopersmith, 1967).

These are important considerations. At the same time, an over-emphasis on the role of discipline in this context sometimes leads parents and teachers to overlook the fact that children's personal adjustment also depends upon a regime of warmth and affection, as we saw in Chapter 2. In other words, it is important to get the balance right. Certainly discipline is important for the development of an adjusted personality, but it is the quality of that discipline that is crucial. As Ausubel *et al.* (1978) emphasize, discipline must be 'as rational, nonarbitrary, and bilateral as possible ... Above all it implies a dignity of the individual ... Hence it repudiates harsh, abusive, and vindictive forms of punishment and the use of sarcasm, ridicule, and intimidation' (p. 511). The way in which style of punishment can positively and negatively affect children's feelings of emotional security is examined in Chapter 8.

In the development of a positive self-image, the perceptions teachers and parents have of children are as important as firm guidance. This was established in studies during the early 1970s by Lacey (1970), working in a grammar school, and by Nash (1973), who investigated classroom interaction in primary school and the first year of secondary school. Nash concluded that 'children who have the bad luck to be unfavourably perceived by their teachers have a tough time in the classroom'. A review of more recent studies concerning teachers' perceptions of pupils is provided in the next chapter.

(3) 'YOU CAN'T TEACH WITHOUT GOOD DISCIPLINE'

The reason most teachers are likely to give for believing discipline is important in school is that certain rules must be enforced in the classroom in order that instruction and learning can get off the ground. 'Discipline' in this sense is used in the sense of social control.

The use of the word 'discipline' coterminously with 'control' is prevalent in educational literature. The *International Dictionary of Education* (Page and Thomas, 1977) defined 'discipline' as a term 'Used to describe teacher's classroom control or general restraint of pupil behaviour' (p. 106). The entry for 'control' takes us no further: 'Used synonymously with *discipline* in the sense of having control in the classroom' (p. 85)! In educational psychology texts, 'discipline' and 'control' are similarly often conflated. Thus Ausubel *et al.* (1978, p. 510) insist that 'By discipline is meant the imposition of external standards and controls on individual conduct', while self-discipline is simply the internalization of external standards.

The control concept of discipline rests on the assumption that the curriculum cannot of itself generate sufficient interest to command a class's undivided attention, and that therefore 'discipline problems' are bound to arise. Control measures are therefore needed to produce orderly conditions that enable teaching to go on. This is a facilitative view of discipline, and was clearly favoured by the authors of the Pack Report (Scottish Education Department, 1977) on truancy and indiscipline in Scottish schools: 'Discipline can perhaps best be described as the maintenance of an orderly system that creates the conditions in which learning may take place, and that allows the aims and objectives of the school to be achieved' (para. 3.1). Teachers also consider an 'orderly system' to be important because they see it as a sign of their professional competence. In a recent ethnographic study of a comprehensive school, Denscombe (1985) found that teachers were sensitive to noise in the classroom, not only because it interfered with instruction and learning but because 'noisy classrooms might be interpreted by colleagues (and some pupils come to that) as a sign of poor classroom control and as the outcome of inadequate standards of teaching' (p. 161). At the same time, as Hargreaves (1978) has pointed out, other teachers are often hesitant to help each other to develop more competent class control because to do so would be to impute incompetence to their colleagues.

Conditions that allow a class to function harmoniously as a group, and are conducive to learning, will not occur on their own accord, even when teachers are blessed with a natural flair for getting on with children of all kinds. Control techniques must therefore be employed. At the same time, there is always the danger, as Silberman (1973) has vividly illustrated, of control in schools becoming an end in its own right rather than a means to learning, so that the real business of teaching is forgotten and a 'schooling for docility' prevails. For it is easy to slip into a situation where there is a preoccupation with efficiency, where orders are given in the interests of smooth administration rather than related to the task of educating. Stenhouse (1975) gives examples of how the means of discipline can determine the ends rather than vice versa. A history teacher, for instance, sets a test involving one-word or short answers, and, during regular lesson periods, fires questions at children he knows are ignorant of the answers (perhaps ignoring those he knows will have something interesting to say). Why does he do this? Not, suggests Stenhouse, because he believes that these kinds of exercise could be defended in terms of what history or educative learning is really about. The reason is that teaching in this way makes it easier to dominate and control the class. Thus education is sacrificed in the interests of classroom control.

Of course it need not be like this. Some methods of keeping order go beyond minimal managerial requirements, and, far from inhibiting educative learning, are likely to promote it (Docking, 1985). We describe some forms of class management style that meet this condition in Chapter 6.

(4) 'DISCIPLINE IS EDUCATIVE'

A fourth reason for regarding discipline as an important issue in school is that submission to rules is central to the development of a 'disciplined mind'. The reason for submitting to these rules, however, is crucial. It is that the learner willingly regards them as right.

Consider the following episode in which Otty (1972, p. 83) describes a day during his first year of teaching in a secondary school:

Mr. Daniels, the senior master, was standing just outside the door as the class whooped and cheered their way home after yesterday's lesson.

'Could I have a word with you, Mr. Otty?'

'Certainly.'

We step into his room which, I notice with a chill, is directly across the corridor from my Monday 2B lesson.

'I'm sorry to have to mention this, but there seems to be rather a lot of noise coming from your second-year class. Would you like any help? I mean if I can give them a rocket or something. ...'

Now, Mr. Daniels is a nice man. A good man, I insist. He does use mild corporal punishment (the gym shoe) but with a cheerful conviction of its value and effectiveness. He is not a mean bully. Most important the children really like and trust him, even the ones he hits. He is an experienced and successful teacher.

From the front of my head I hear a distant, calm, reasonable voice. It tells Mr. Daniels things I like to think, and it has no connection with the deep centred panic in my mind.

'That's very kind, Mr. Daniels, but I would rather carry on on my own.'

'Oh well, that's fine, as long as you feel you have a grip on them when you need it.'

'No, I have no "grip on them", but then I don't want to have.' His eyebrows shoot up spreading wrinkles towards his bald crown.

'You see I don't want them to work for me because of *my* control. They must learn their own control, the value of cooperation and the intrinsic value of what they are studying. ...'

Brave words, brave words. But he takes them – and he appears to be convinced.

This passage brings out well the dilemma facing the young teacher with ideals. Otty does not want to emulate the methods of the senior master, even though he recognizes him as a successful teacher who is well liked by the pupils, because 'having a grip' on a class would involve relinquishing a concept of education that involves helping children to 'learn their own control' and to develop an intrinsic interest in their work. It was, of course, naive of Otty to assume that 'an intrinsic value in what they are studying' could be achieved without imposition of external constraints; but at least this young teacher appreciated that any consideration of the problem of discipline in school should take account of the function of schooling in relation to educational values.

The emergence of an official recognition of discipline in the educative sense can be seen in changes made in the Board of Education's *Suggestions for the Consideration of Teachers*, which was issued regularly between 1905 and 1948. In the first edition, discipline was construed in terms of our first perspective, a 'training for society'. In a section entitled 'The formation of character', teachers were urged to use the biographies of heroes and heroines in order to 'furnish the most impressive examples of obedience, loyalty, courage, strenuous effort, serviceableness, indeed all the qualities which make for good citizenship' (p. 9). At the same time, the teacher was to set a personal example of kindness, patience, punctuality, good manners, a 'determination to be obeyed' and 'a cheerful obedience to duty'. From the late 1920s, the equivalent section was given added status by being headed 'Character training the teacher's chief responsibility'. Discipline was now seen partly in terms of control – 'a means for enabling the ordinary classroom work to be carried on' – but also 'as an end, a habit to be developed, a constituent of character', the hallmark of a socially mature person.

In 1937, when the Board's handbook received its final revision, there was a further shift of position. There was no talk of obedience training. The crucial test of a school's discipline now was 'whether it represents a real sense, on the part of the children, of the rightness of the behaviour that is expected of them' (p. 24). It was further noted that 'one of the greatest changes in elementary education in the last half century lies in the gradual recognition on the part of teachers that the superiority of the adult over the child is a matter of length and width of experience and not of moral quality' (pp. 27-8). This view, that children could and ought to be able to reason about behavioural matters and be helped to see the point of rules rather than follow them through fear or force of habit, can thus be contrasted with that taken in earlier editions of the handbook which emphasized the importance of 'cheerful obedience'. It also represented a markedly different perspective from that taken a hundred years earlier by Thomas Arnold. Commenting on the moral status of the child and the adult, the famous public school headmaster maintained that 'there exists a real inferiority in the relation, and it is an error, a corruption of nature, not to acknowledge it' (quoted in Gibson, 1978, p. 65).

In his book on the values of a comprehensive school, Daunt (1975) comments on the connection between discipline and children seeing right reasons for action. Rigid school practices, he argues, such as always standing up when a teacher comes into the room, focus on 'upward' rather than mutual respect, and demonstrate more concern about the pupil's respect for those in authority than about pupils' respect for each other. While this cynicism about ritual in schools may not be generally shared, Daunt is surely right to insist that the kinds of rules imposed and the manner of their enforcement can help to educate children in the way they come to conceptualize authority. On the basis of interviews with pupils in some northern, urban schools, Paul Corrigan (1979) has dramatically related how some less able working-class adolescents have little but contempt for school authority because 'there is no perception of the teacher-pupil interaction as being a joint "coming together" of minds. Rather, there is a great distance between Them and Us; despite this, They push Us around' (p. 54).

In the educative view of discipline, a 'disciplined' pupil is one who recognizes that the kind of behaviour he is morally obliged to follow is that based on principles he himself accepts as right. It marks the difference between, on the one hand, someone who has been subjected to 'character training' and follows rules from force of habit and, on the other, someone who has been educated to 'have character' and deal with new situations and temptations in an intelligent way.

This point about educative discipline involving principled behaviour can be extended from interpersonal conduct to behaviour in relation to curriculum activities. A rigorous analysis of the concept of discipline on these lines has been made by P. S. Wilson (1971). He argues that, in so far as a teacher should help children to develop a liking for activities that are valued for their own sake, engagement in these activities must be carried out in a disciplined way if the interest is not only to be sustained but deepened. However, the compulsion of this kind of discipline does not arise because of the teacher's imposed control (even when this involves humane and attractive strategies) but emanates from values intrinsic to the activity itself. It follows that relationships between teacher and pupil based on discipline in the educative sense are of quite a different kind from those based upon external controls, since, as Wilson puts it, '*both* parties to the relationship (the teacher as well as the class) submit to the educative order of the task in hand' (p. 79, emphasis added). 'Discipline' therefore involves helping children to understand the rules of procedure implicit in curriculum activities and the implications these have for behaviour.

We might illustrate this point as follows. Suppose a class of children are engaged in a science project. If they are to 'do' science as scientists do, and to develop a 'scientific interest' in things, then they have to appreciate that certain sorts of behaviour are required of them: they must, say, observe accurately, collect data systematically, record it carefully, analyse it according to certain scientific conventions, and so on. In other words, there are certain rules intrinsic to the pursuit of science that make certain behavioural demands on the participants. Only by obeying these rules can an interest in science be developed. The same applies to any activity that is taken seriously, and is, of course, most obvious in games, where the rules are explicit.

A similar sort of point has been made by Paul Nash (1966), who distinguishes between making lessons interesting as a means and as an end. Teachers who see interest essentially as a means to some end will try to capture children's interest through various devices and by force of personality. However, this concept of 'interest' in school learning assumes that young people 'can be aroused from a pervading lethargy only by dramatic tricks or colourful gimmicks' (p. 131). What matters is not so much that lessons are 'made interesting' but that children are helped to 'see what there is of interest' in what they are doing. However successful interest-arousing techniques may be in attracting pupils' attention initially, it is only by allowing pupils a vision of the interest intrinsic in an activity that they will see a reason for engaging in the activity more than momentarily.

We have seen in this chapter that discipline is a multifaceted concept. It may refer to 'training for society'; to a consistent application of external constraints in order to promote a stable personality; to something teachers do before they teach in order to bring about a proper attitude to work; or to the adoption of certain kinds of behaviour that the pupil himself understands to be morally right or necessary for deepening interest in a particular activity. Each of these notions of discipline has a place in schools. However, it does not follow that teachers who concentrate successfully on one aspect of discipline will be successful in any other. In particular, it must be appreciated that a controlled child, even a *self*-controlled child, is not the same as a disciplined child in the educative sense. It may be that class control is a necessary condition for the development of 'educative discipline', but it is not a sufficient one since the achievement of the first does not guarantee the second.

FURTHER READING

Corrigan, P. (1979) *Schooling the Smash Street Kids*, Macmillan, London.
(A study of the resistance offered by working-class adolescents to traditional school discipline.)
Denscombe, M. (1985) *Classroom Control: a Sociological Perspective*, Allen & Unwin, London.
(An ethnographic study of three comprehensive schools, looking at the way teachers regard control in school and how this is affected by organizational factors.)
Smith, R. (1985) *Freedom and Discipline*, Allen & Unwin, London.
(A very readable exploration of the philosophical issues involved in discipline and related notions, such as freedom and responsibility.)

5
TEACHER–PUPIL RELATIONSHIPS: PERCEPTIONS AND EXPECTATIONS

Few entrants to the teaching profession these days are insensitive to the need to establish with pupils a working style that is at once considerate, relaxed and purposeful. Yet relationships that were intended to be firm but friendly can all too easily end up in a cycle of conflict and confrontation. One reason why teacher–pupil relationships can break down is that insufficient attention is paid to the perceptions and expectations teachers and pupils have of each other and themselves. Some teachers may put constructions on pupils' behaviour that, on reflection and examination, do not do justice to the pupils' intentions. They may also not be sufficiently sensitive to the way in which their own actions are being perceived by the pupils, and they may fail to live up to the pupils' expectations of what a good teacher should be like. These ideas will be explored in this chapter. But first we shall consider what it means to establish 'good relationships' in the classroom.

THE MEANING OF RELATIONSHIPS IN SCHOOL

It is not easy to say just what it is that characterizes 'good teacher–pupil relationships'. The Plowden Committee on primary education (CACE, 1967, paras. 738–9) saw it as a matter of teachers gaining 'affection and respect', of not imposing 'arbitrary authoritarianism' but a climate in which 'each child is valued for himself' and where children 'know where they stand and what to expect'. The Newsom Committee on secondary education (CACE, 1963, para. 197) saw it as the 'need to make some gesture of recognizing the more adult status of the older pupils, even those who are not troublesome or not very bright, and who do not seem responsive' (para. 197). That these ideals are still wanting in some schools has been shown in several recent studies that will be reviewed in later sections.

R. S. Peters (1966) has made the important distinction between 'liking pupils' and 'respecting them as persons'. He recognizes that teachers are bound to find some pupils easier to get on with than others; but respect for persons

> is the feeling awakened when another is regarded as a distinctive centre of consciousness, with peculiar feelings and purposes. ... It is connected with the awareness one has that each man takes pride in his achievements, however idiosyncratic they may be. To respect a person is to realize all this and to care.
>
> (pp. 58-9)

But, as Peters goes on to argue, teachers are confronted with *developing* centres of consciousness. This means that they should both encourage children to defend their points of view (so that children come to know what they really think and feel) and also demonstrate a commitment to the principles they care about (for otherwise there is no teaching).

In a school, 'good relationships' are not established simply by 'being nice', but rather by treating the pupils as significant, enabling them to cope with their frustrations in a socially acceptable way, and making them feel that their point of view matters. Harold Entwistle (1970) has noticed how teachers who know that they lack histrionic gifts to compel attention sometimes feel that they are more likely to be successful with pupils – particularly those in deprived inner-city areas – if they adopt a 'love' relationship with the children. The motive is to offer the child something he would otherwise lack in his association with adults. Entwistle acknowledges that such 'love', in the idiom of the New Testament, denotes 'a relationship which is disinterested, long-suffering, patient, modest, kindly, seemly, enduring, hopeful, incapable of rebuff or revenge' (p. 70), and that this may be the way to effective disciplinary relationships. But he argues that, in an educational context, such love must not be seen as an end in itself because there is more to an educative relationship than personal rapport: 'The teacher gives not himself, but the skills, knowledge and attitudes – the discipline – which he mediates' (p. 71). To 'have a way' with children is important in the classroom, but it is not a substitute for education. Indeed, as Entwistle notes, it is the discipline of the teacher's material that is the child's ultimate safeguard against authoritarian teaching.

TEACHERS' JUDGEMENTS OF PUPILS

The significance of terminology in describing pupil deviance

In a previous publication (Docking, 1982), the present author argued that perceptions of behaviour are reflected in the terminology in which deviant behaviour is described:

> To characterize a child as 'disruptive', for instance, is not to offer an objectively neutral description, for the term tends to carry implications of disposition and possibly of intent – i.e. the child is seen as a disruptive agent or influence. The term 'disturbed', on the other hand, suggests that the child is not being held responsible for his abnormal, handicapping behaviour. Yet the presented behaviours of a 'disruptive' child and a child who is 'disturbed' could well be identical.
>
> (p. 240)

The practical importance of terminology is that the word employed tends not only to reflect but also to promote particular constructions of the situation. Further, it may influence the kind of response we make to the child whose behaviour we find unacceptable. As Leach (1977) has pointed out, terms such as 'emotionally disturbed', 'maladjusted', 'culturally deprived' and 'slow learning' 'can develop into negative typifications that merely serve to maintain or even to enhance the very behaviours which are subsumed by them' (p. 195). Coulby (1984) has noted out how the word 'disruptive' applies more appropriately to behaviour than to people, since children are not disruptive all the time but only at certain times, in certain places and with certain people. He goes on to argue that, by attaching the label 'disruptive' to pupils and then providing special units to which they can be referred, we may have helped to create a new institutional category of child as a feature of mainstream schooling.

In general it is probably best to use words that do not evaluate the problem in terms of the responsibility of the child or as evidence of a 'deficit', but that simply describe the outward manifestations of the behaviour. For this reason, some writers recommend the term 'disaffected pupils' rather than 'disruptive pupils' (e.g. Bird *et al.*, 1981; Lloyd-Smith, 1984b). Certainly it may make all the difference to a child whether he is said to be 'a disruptive pupil' or one whose behaviour is disrupting, for, as Tattum (1985, p. 12) has observed, 'concentration on the social pathology of the individual permits us to ignore deficiencies in the system'. It may be that a change in the school situation and the teacher's behaviour will help the child to behave more acceptably. Tattum also observes that confrontation may arise in cases where the pupil lacks the social skills to 'please teacher'. Thus social education rather than referral for 'treatment' might be the more appropriate response on the part of the school.

We have seen how, in attributing dispositions to children, or in locating causal influences, teachers may make inferences that go beyond the information actually available to them. Jones and Nisbett (1971) have argued that the kinds of attribution people make depends on what aspects of the situation are salient for them. For a teacher, we could say that it is the behaviour that is personally threatening that is more likely to be attributed to the pupils' disposition or intentions than to the situational circumstances in which it occurred. It is because such behaviour engulfs the perceptual field of the teacher that he or she may see a child's behaviour as an instance of a quality possessed by him rather than as precipitated by the circumstances of the classroom. Teachers may thus sometimes misattribute intentions to children and so build up distorted views about them, thus jeopardizing the chances of establishing an equitable social relationship.

Teachers' perceptions of pupil behaviour

There is probably a tendency in us all to behave not as 'unique individuals perceiving other unique individuals' but to see others through our 'perceptual set' (Brophy *et al.*, 1981). A good deal of evidence suggests that teachers possess a picture of the 'ideal' pupil, and that they interact more often and more favourably with pupils who conform to this image. According to Brophy and his colleagues, teachers seem to get on best with pupils who are helpful, neat, happy, physically attractive, socially mature and unlikely to be daydreaming. These are also the qualities teachers of pre-school children prefer, according to a recent study carried out by Driscoll and Reynolds (1984). Denscombe (1980) has shown how teachers react unfavourably towards 'noisy' pupils since their behaviour might be interpreted by other teachers as evidence of professional incompetence. Teachers' images of the ideal pupil can also lead to gender bias. In one comprehensive school, Lynn Davies (1984) found that teachers preferred to teach boys because, compared with girls, they were seen as 'more forthcoming', 'full of ideas', 'livelier' and less inclined to 'bear grudges'. Girls, on the other hand, were seen as more likely to have 'tantrums' and to be 'surly', 'catty' and 'vindictive', even though they were perceived as also less aggressive and more conformist.

Colin Lacey's (1970) sociological study on classroom interaction in an exclusive boys' northern grammar school showed how teacher's attitudes can be based less on the quality of pupils' actual behaviour than on matters to do with physical appearance, health, and whether the pupils' interests matched those of the staff. Thus, in observing the class of an English master who also taught music, one boy called Cready, a diligent member of the school choir, could make mistakes and receive no reprimand. In contrast, Priestly, a nervous fat boy who suffered from catarrh and asthma, not only attracted ridicule from his classmates but was reprimanded by the teacher for his errors. Lacey comments how the behaviour of pupils such as Priestly was not within their own control but was a function of the system:

> anything he tried to do to improve his position only made it worse. His attempts to answer questions provoked laughter and ridicule. His attempts to minimize the distress it caused – a nervous smile round the room, a shrug of the shoulders, pretending that he had either caused the disturbance on purpose or did not care – served only to worsen his position with the teacher.
>
> (p. 55)

Even when teachers champion the importance of giving equal consideration to all pupils, they do not necessarily practise what they preach. This is probably because pressures of the school situation make it difficult for them to live up to their ideals. In an investigation which focused on the primary school, Sharp and Green (1975) looked at the way in which teachers who hold a 'progressive', child-centred ideology differentiated between 'normal' and 'problem' pupils. From a series of observations, it emerged that the teachers had an image of the 'ideal' pupil that was centred in a 'bedrock of busyness'. This was inferred from statements to pupils in which teachers would express approval for those who were 'getting on' and producing 'interesting work'. The authors concluded that 'while the teachers display a moral concern that every child matters, in practice there is a subtle process of sponsorship developing where opportunity is being offered to some and closed off to others. Social stratification is emerging' (p. 218). In another study, Kedar-Voivodas and Tannenbaum (1979) found that teachers who had previously maintained that they regarded acting out and withdrawn behaviour as equally serious and deserving of a constructive response, reacted more negatively to children displaying acting out behaviours when it came to the actual classroom situation.

Relationships between teachers and pupils can also be affected by the system of grouping. In a classic study, Hargreaves (1967) concluded that boys in the 'D' stream of a secondary school were treated in a less flexible way than those in the 'A' stream, and this in turn seemed to promote the development of an anti-school 'delinquescent subculture' amongst the

'D'-streamers. More recently, Ball (1981) has suggested that the move from streaming to banding in many comprehensive schools has created its own pupil-stereotyping problems. From his study of 'Beechside' school, he observed that the middle-band pupil was expected to be 'not interested in school work' and 'difficult to control', whereas lower-band pupils were seen as less belligerent because they were judged to be emotionally unstable and immature. Ball noticed how a move from banding to mixed ability grouping in this school reduced the incidence of bad behaviour since the disaffected pupils were no longer clustered together. Indeed, the movement towards mixed ability grouping in secondary schools may have been motivated more by beliefs that this arrangement would reduce behaviour problems than by beliefs that it would improve academic achievement.

Although much evidence suggests that teacher-pupil interaction is influenced by the teachers' images of the 'good pupil', studies have also shown that some teachers are less biased in this respect and are more successful in developing positive perceptions of all pupils and in furthering productive relationships with them. Following a study of a group of secondary modern schools in a working-class district of South Wales, Reynolds and Sullivan (1979) explained teachers' perceptions of pupils and their parents in terms of two strategies. Schools in which the staff employed an 'incorporative strategy' tried to involve pupils and their parents in the organization of the school. In the classroom, pupils were encouraged to participate without explicit invitation from the teacher and to work in groups; outside lesson times, prefects and monitors, chosen from the whole ability range, carried out supervisory duties – a strategy that appeared to inhibit the growth of anti-school subcultures because the senior pupils were themselves involved in the control of the school. In general, pupil-teacher relationships of the schools in this category were developed by relying on only a minimal use of overt control and physical punishment, pupil 'deviance' evoking a therapeutic rather than a coercive response. In contrast, schools that adopted a 'coercive' strategy made no attempt to involve pupils or parents in the authority structures. Rigid and punitive means of control were adopted because the staff believed that an integrative approach would be abused.

Reynolds and Sullivan (1979) argue that schools in which teachers use an 'incorporative strategy' are more successful in promoting academic success and better behaviour. The 'coercive' schools are less successful because they underestimate the pupils' ability and assume the need for character training and institutional control to make good the deficiencies of their upbringing. These schools appear to 'externalize their failure by identifying their pupils as of less potential and as "under-socialized" (p. 52). Moreover, such perceptions are passed on to new teachers and pupils, so perpetuating the syndrome.

In a similar way, Hargreaves et al. (1975) distinguish between 'deviance-provocative' teachers, who believe that deviant pupils avoid work at all costs, no matter what is done to improve the learning conditions, and 'deviant- insulative' teachers, who believe that deviant pupils really do want to work and that they will do so if school conditions are improved. Teachers in the first category control deviance through regular punishment and confrontation; in contrast, teachers in the second category avoid confrontation and derogation, take an interest in deviant pupils' personal problems and encourage signs of improvement.

Of course, teachers do not in reality divide neatly into those who are 'coercive' or 'incorporative', or who are 'deviant-provocative' or 'deviant-insulative'. These categories represent extremes of a continuum. Further, where the strategy is not pervasive throughout the school, those teachers who use it may not succeed because pupils perceive them as 'soft'. Behaviour is likely to be better in schools where the staff as a whole operate on the expectation that the pupils will want to work, and who try to provide a teaching–learning environment in which energy is directed towards helping pupils to develop as persons rather than towards obtaining conformity for its own sake.

Teachers' images of pupils from different ethnic groups

The tendency of some teachers to engage in racial stereotyping has been documented in a succession of studies (see reviews by Taylor, 1983; Taylor and Hegarty, 1985). In this respect, children of Afro-Caribbean origin seem to come off the worst, and they suffer psychologically and educationally as a result.

In one study, involving interviews with seventeen London heads and teachers, Giles (1977) found that, compared with white pupils, black pupils were perceived as more quick-tempered, more excitable in a group, more open to voicing their own opinions, more prone to give strong emotional expressions of love and hate, and less achievement-orientated. In contrast, Asian children are usually favourably perceived, often more so than whites. Short (1983), for instance, found that girls of Asian origin, compared with their white counterparts, were seen by a sample of sixty-five London primary school teachers as quieter, less talkative, less resentful of punishment and more self-controlled; Asian boys were seen as less attention-seeking, less aggressive and less rude.

The Swann Report (1985) on children from ethnic minority groups confirmed earlier findings that teachers tended to have a more favourable view of pupils who belonged to certain ethnic groups. Chinese were considered the most desirable group to have in school, and Afro-Caribbeans the least. The Swann Committee considered that ethnic stereotyping was partly an historical legacy from imperial days when some nations and peoples were seen as 'inferior', partly a consequence of associating lighter skin colour with greater academic ability and partly a result of images perpetuated by the media.

Whatever the reasons, there is no doubt that many black pupils believe that some white teachers are prejudiced against them, and some recent evidence has demonstrated the validity of these beliefs with examples of personal insensitivity and structural injustice. In a recent study that involved conversations with black pupils and their white teachers at two Midlands comprehensive schools, Wright (1985a) found that the teachers would frequently make sarcastic jokes at the black pupils' expense. One told the researcher, in front of the class, that he had once, 'in good fun, nothing malicious', threatened to send a black girl 'back to the chocolate factory'. The teacher expressed amazement that the girl had gone home and related the incident to her parents, who had then decided to take the matter to the Commission for Racial Equality. Wright found that teachers were sometimes quite open about their stereotypic images and prejudice, but seemed unable to alter their attitude. A Year Head said, 'I find it very difficult to accept the immigrant people and children that I come into contact with. I cannot change my feelings because it is part of my upbringing – I feel that the English culture is being swamped' (p. 13).

In another report related to the same two schools, Wright (1985b) gives clear instances of black pupils being victims of structural injustice. For instance, at one of the schools, although the reading scores of Afro-Caribbean pupils at entry were the same as, or even better than, those of whites and Asians, nearly one-fifth were assigned to remedial groups, compared with 7.7 per cent of Asians and no white children at all. At the other school, the Afro-Caribbean children were allocated to the lower band even though they had the best mean performance scores of all groups. In view of these policies, it is not surprising that only one Afro-Caribbean child in each school finished up with five or more O-levels, compared with 24.5 per cent of white children at one school and 18.5 per cent at the other school. Wright argues that the staff appeared to disregard the ability of Afro-Caribbean children when assigning pupils to groups, and operated instead on the basis of perceived behaviour.

Another effect of teachers' ethnic stereotyping relates to the image children have of themselves. Green (1985) has demonstrated that children's levels of self-concept in a multi-ethnic classroom is related to factors in the school situation in a complicated way. His study involved 75 white teachers and their 1,814 pupils of European, Afro-Caribbean and Asian origins in three middle and three junior schools. He showed that the mental image children have of themselves is associated with the teachers' beliefs and attitudes concerning schooling and race. These include (1) 'tender-minded' v. 'tough-minded' attitudes, (2) beliefs in conservation or change in education, and (3) levels of ethnocentrism – i.e. the tendency to consider inferior the features of ethnic groups other than your own.

For instance, 'tender-minded' teachers reacted more positively than 'tough-minded' colleagues towards children of Asian or Afro-Caribbean origins. This appeared to have consequences for the pupils' self-concept, although there were gender differences. In classes taught by 'tough-minded' teachers, self-concept levels were significantly lower among girls of Asian and boys of Afro-Caribbean origins. As regards teachers' views about change or conservation in education, white boys received the most positive responses and the least authoritarian comment among 'conservative' teachers, and these pupils had also developed the more positive self-concepts. Among the 'radical' teachers, self-concepts were positive not only among European pupils but also among girls of Afro-Caribbean origin. With respect to levels of ethnocentricity, teachers who were ethnically 'highly intolerant' gave more opportunity for white pupils than for blacks to initiate ideas and opinions. Overall, it was children of Afro-Caribbean origin who were the most adversely affected by the teachers' ethnocentricity.

Local education authorities have a special responsibility to eradicate ethnic typing by teachers, not only because of the psychological harm and injustice produced, but because it helps to perpetuate racism in our society. The influence of adult models is clearly important in counteracting racist tendencies, which are prevalent among our children from a very early age (see review by Milner, 1984). Some education authorities (e.g. ILEA, 1983) are making strenuous efforts to counter both personal and institutional racism in schools; but, as the research reviewed earlier in this section demonstrates, negative images of pupils from different ethnic backgrounds are still material factors in the development of pupil–teacher relationships in some schools. What must be constantly kept in mind is that part of a child's identity is his ethnicity, and to recognize and to value that is to respect the child's individuality and personhood.

Labelling pupils

According to labelling theory, a person who thinks that others believe he can never do right, may himself come to believe that he can never do right, and give up trying. The individual takes on the identity of the label and thus transforms the conception he has of himself. In school, pupils who are labelled will therefore tend to adapt their behaviour to fit the label. Labelling can be positive and produce desirable effects, but it is the negative aspects that have received most attention in the literature.

Labelling theory was developed in the writings of Howard Becker (1963), who called his book *Outsiders* because he argued that deviance arises when some people are labelled as such. It is then difficult to behave in a manner that is inconsistent with the label since one's status depends upon living up to the others' expectations. Public labelling thus becomes a self-fulfilling prophecy, the labelled person taking on the characteristics attributed to him by others. In this way, according to Becker, deviance is socially constructed since it is a response to a label, the existence of which depends upon the way in which the person's behaviour is interpreted.

Flew (1976) has warned against the dangers of assuming that all differences in human behaviour can be explained in terms of the expectations of others: 'Such expectations themselves may be, and often are, grounded in knowledge of antecedent talents and temperaments. Nor are we all, even within the limits of our various talents, the creatures of other people's expectations' (p. 20). However, while the act of labelling may not in general be the source of deviant behaviour, it exacerbates the risk of deviance and makes the task of reform more difficult. For some people, conforming to a negative label enables them to be distinctive, for being bad is being somebody (Emler, 1983).

Hargreaves (1976) has argued that the degree to which a child will accept the label teachers and others give him is likely to depend upon four factors: the frequency of the labelling, the extent to which the child sees the adult who labels as significant to him, the degree to which the label is supported by other adults and friends and the amount of publicity surrounding the label. Identifying a child as 'maladjusted', as 'disturbed', or as 'coming from a broken home' may lead to the child being labelled as a 'problem'. If the teacher then takes on rigid attitudes towards the child, the child's behaviour may become more and more a reflection of the label. The expectations of adults who provide the label thus effectively prevent the child from acting otherwise.

Egglestone (1979) has distinguished between overt and covert labelling in schools. *Overt labelling* includes not only the direct labelling of children in the classroom but also the use of derogatory terms such as 'thick' or 'hopeless', which communicate messages of expected behaviour. *Covert labelling* occurs through the 'hidden curriculum', children picking up messages about their perceived worth through the kind of learning opportunities they are given and the way teachers evaluate their comments. Children can easily sense the teacher's disapproval of their personal interests and achievements when these are ignored or not taken up as significant. Egglestone's argument is that, as a result of mechanisms such as these, some pupils are denied status whilst high status is attributed to others. And when pupils feel that they are denied status, they may seek to attain it through strategies that challenge the teacher's authority and lead to confrontation. In this way, deviancy is socially constructed and can be avoided only through a realistic understanding of the power structure in schools.

The significance of negative labelling of pupils, in its ability to act as a self-fulfilling prophecy, has been the subject of several studies, in particular one by Hargreaves, Hester and Mellor (1975). Teachers of first-year pupils at one coeducational urban school were asked to comment on individual pupils and on the events that had occurred during lessons the researchers had observed. From these discussions, it seemed that the teachers had developed elaborate typifications of pupils, and that this had come about during the course of three overlapping stages. In the 'speculative stage', teachers began to type the pupils in their new classes on the basis of information already possessed from sources such as primary school records, the experience of teaching older brothers and sisters, a medical problem that had been disseminated amongst the staff, or gossip in the staffroom. Before long, a few pupils would begin to stand out from the rest and become categorized as deviant in terms of their appearance, behaviour, ability and attitude to work, likeability and relations with other children.

The slender evidence on which deviance could be based is illustrated in the following interview extract:

T. Lewis. A little blond lad. I suspect that Ted could be bothersome later on. I detect an air of sort of anti-establishment about him. That's just purely a feeling because at the moment he's very co-operative. He does as he's told; does more than he's told; does all that he can to help you, really. I just detect that in the end he might turn out anti-establishment. It's just one of those things.
I. What I'd really like to know is what you are basing that on.
T. It's experience of seeing other lads of a similar nature. It might be his relations – you see you can't always pin it down to any particular incident

because you've never had a row with him. He's never been sort of bolshie with you. It could be in his relations with other children if he's more aggressive possibly. He won't be aggressive with the teacher at this stage because he's only a first year, but if he's showing some aggression to other children, then this might transfer to teachers later on in the school. That might well be it. And often you feel this rather than seeing anything. It might well be that. You've seen lads like this growing up. It might sometimes be the look of the child. I think that Ted has this look of slightly drawn cheeks; rather a hardened look and a slightly hardish look in the eye. These things give me the impression that he might be bothersome this type of lad. (p. 172)

In later weeks, teachers attempted to verify their initial hypotheses, finding out whether each pupil really was the sort of person he was originally thought to be, and revising their pictures accordingly. This was the stage of 'elaboration'. Finally, in the stage of 'stabilization', the teacher felt confident in predicting an individual's behaviour. Actions of the deviant pupil that did not fit a label such as 'conformist', 'helpful', 'troublemaker', 'truant', would tend to be disregarded, so that any efforts by the pupil to change the picture were frustrated. Detyping occurred only rarely, in which case the process reverted to the earlier stages.

According to Hargreaves, Hester and Mellor (1975), the outcome of such negative labelling is that the teacher adopts an attitude towards the pupil that is different from that adopted towards 'normal' pupils. He is 'guarded, suspicious, wary, cautious, apprehensive, and even fearful' (p. 240). When the pupil who has been typed as deviant is disruptive, the teacher avoids intervening for as long as possible to avoid confrontation; then, because the pupil finds that his attempts to annoy the teacher have failed, he commits further deviance. Thus 'paradoxically the avoidance-or-provocation reaction can itself constitute a provocative act from the pupil's point of view: the teacher's reaction has effectively exacerbated the deviant conduct it was intended to control' (p. 248). The prophecy is fulfilled!

More recently, Bird (1980) has challenged the idea that labelling is a phenomenon of secondary schooling. From interviews conducted over an eighteen-month period with a group of 'difficult' fifth-year girls in a large comprehensive school, she became convinced that the likelihood of one particular label being repeatedly applied to a pupil was small. This was because a pupil would be taught by up to fifteen teachers, each of whom may see between 150 and 300 pupils each week. Further, teachers' labels in relation to any one pupil are constantly changing as individuals move in and out of favour. Again, because they are exposed to a range of teachers, pupils are also exposed to different interpretations of deviance and thresholds of tolerance. As a result, few pupils see behavioural labelling as a matter of concern: 'While pupils may accept that they are seen as problems by certain teachers in certain lessons, they do not internalize deviant labels and do not embark on deviant careers as a consequence of that labelling' (pp. 102-3).

However, in another recent study, Beynon (1985) has confirmed the operation of pupil labelling in the first year of secondary schooling. From observations of teachers' initial encounters with pupils in a comprehensive school, Beynon found that, within the first few weeks, teachers were confident about which children were 'difficult' and would treat them differently as a result. Like Hargreaves, Hestor and Mellor (1975), Beynon found that teachers put much faith in the 'sibling phenomenon', by which pupils were assumed to be behaviourally and academically similar to older brothers and sisters, and that they would often base their assessment on incidental factors and hearsay rather than on hard evidence.

Hargreaves, Hestor and Mellor (1975) suggest various practical implications that arise from their study on labelling. These may be summarized as follows:

(1) Obviously rules are needed, and, to be effective, must be enforced; but since deviance arises only if a rule is broken, abolish any rule not serving an important purpose.
(2) Make the rules clear to reduce the possibility of deviance occurring because the pupil is confused about what is expected of him.
(3) Label the *act*, not the person. The pupil is thus given an opportunity to dissociate his behaviour from his 'real' self. Because he can regard what he has done as not typical of him, he can retain the self-image of an essentially well-behaved person: 'It is when a person believes that he really is deviant that the commission of further congruent acts is facilitated' (Hargreaves, 1975, p. 259). King (1978) noted in his study of infant classrooms that teachers who avoided labelling children as naughty (e.g. 'You naughty boy') but instead pointed out the behaviour that was naughty, were more successful in keeping order. King suggests that to draw attention to undesirable behaviour poses a norm for all children, whereas to concentrate on the naughtiness of a child gives that behaviour an individual personal property.
(4) Avoid public labelling in large classes or school assembly. This is likely to have a particularly damaging psychological effect, partly because it is humiliating and partly because the more who hear the label the more will use it.
(5) Adopt a sceptical attitude to staffroom discussion that denigrates

particular pupils. Try to discount the negative evaluations of other teachers or your own knowledge of brothers and sisters since misbehaviour may be promoted through children perceiving they are expected to misbehave.

(6) Avoid frequent derogatory comments, particularly those which imply stable dispositions (e.g. 'You're a persistent troublemaker').
(7) Encourage any sign of improvement. Try to believe that the child who misbehaves 'isn't really like that'.

In short, the adverse effects of labelling probably arise when the child's mind is dominated by the persistent derogatory comments made by adults in authority, who hold fixed expectations while doing little constructive to help. This suggests that teachers can reduce the chances of a pupil becoming unco-operative if they are sensitive to the dangers of typing pupils, if they make efforts to see them in as positive a light as possible, and if they remember that home and neighbourhood experiences, important as they are, offer only a partial explanation of a child's behaviour in school.

PUPILS' JUDGEMENTS OF TEACHERS

Pupils' expectations of 'good' teaching

We now turn to the ways in which classroom relationships can be affected by what pupils expect of a 'good' teacher. The argument here is that positive working relationships will be difficult to develop if teachers do not in general live up to the pupils' criteria of professional behaviour.

Table 5.1 summarizes the findings of twelve recent studies concerned with children's perceptions of 'the good teacher'. McPhail and his colleagues (1972), whose work related to adults in general and not only teachers, based their analysis on the written accounts of 800 adolescents. The Wragg and Wood study (1984b) also involved written responses to open-ended questions, but also included ratings. Dawson (1984) used a questionnaire, while Carnell (1983) and Gannaway (1976) used both interviews and questionnaires. Nash (1976a) elicited the personal constructs held by children by use of a structured interview technique which enabled him to build a 'repertory grid'.

The remaining studies cited in Table 5.1 relied exclusively on analyses of statements made during the course of informal interviews which were conducted in the style of a conversation. Conclusions from such 'open' approaches are bound to be influenced by the researchers' presence and interpretations of what the pupils say. The intention of such studies,

Table 5.1 Children's perceptions of a 'good' teacher

Age-range	Study	The good teacher is one who
10–11 years, 'open-plan' type class	Davies, 1979	helps you to learn, explains makes the day a pleasant one with a few jokes organizes the class so that the pupils feel work is being done gives guidance about what is 'good' work is just, and punishes for bad behaviour but not too severely allows pupils freedom to express themselves negatively or positively does not get upset, disturbed, or angry as a result of misbehaviour
12–13 years	Nash, 1976a	keeps order, is firm but not overbearing teaches you explains, is clear is interesting is fair, doesn't have favourites, punishes justly is friendly
12–16 years, comprehensive	Wragg and Wood, 1984b	would help explain things clearly would call you by your first name would help the slower ones catch up in a nice way would help you to learn a lot in every lesson would be a good listener
12–16 years, off-site support unit	Tattum, 1984	never pushes you around but helps you treats you with respect applies rules consistently is tolerant of jokes and horseplay
13 years, disturbed pupils in six special schools and units	Carnell, 1983	has good teaching skills is patient has a sense of humour has good control can build up friendships can be sympathetic
13–18 years, all types of school	McPhail et al., 1972	(Incidents of being well treated by adults in general, including teachers) encourages you to make choices and reach your own decisions

Table 5.1 Continued

Age-range	Study	The good teacher is one who
13–18 years, all types of school	McPhail et al., 1972 (cont.)	helps with a problem or difficulty without being invited to do so is quietly efficient in teaching, in handling an awkward situation, in organizing work, etc. listens, tries to understand, is tactful, does not impose formality for the sake of preserving distance is predictably considerate provides standards and offers a good example, stands up for what he believes and doesn't sit on the fence has a sense of humour, a sense of proportion, doesn't take himself too seriously, accepts people with their weaknesses
14–15 years, low-ability girls' secondary	Furlong, 1976, 1977	convinces pupils they are to 'learn a lot' (*not* necessarily of practical relevance, but not 'boring' or a 'waste of time') is strict *provided that* they enable you to learn
14–15 years, non-selective school	Woods, 1976a, 1979	is helpful and explains is friendly, kind, and understanding provides variety allows freedom (is democratic) is cheerful, humorous
Secondary girls' private academic high school, Scotland	Delamont, 1976	'makes you learn very, very hard', 'makes things clear', can get her subject across doesn't wear outlandish clothes is young (because not embittered) is married (if a woman, because she will be happier and more placid) is efficient, can keep order has a degree from a respectable university
Secondary comprehensive	Gannaway, 1976	can keep order without getting upset or being aggressive; is 'like us, but if she wanted to be firm she could be' 'has a laugh with you', is not overstrict teaches in an interesting way 'you can really sort of talk to', is not too aloof but approachable

Table 5.1 Continued

Age-range	Study	The good teacher is one who
Secondary comprehensive	Gannaway, 1976 (cont.)	is young (because more acceptable) understands pupils, i.e. puts something of interest in the lesson, shows that the activities have a rationale (e.g. not note-taking just to fill in time, but whether the activity makes sense now); doesn't demand work for work's sake takes you out of school and on trips
Secondary comprehensive (council estate on outskirts of town)	Marsh, Rosser and Harré, 1978	treats you as a person, knows your name helps you to learn and feel confident takes your ideas seriously, isn't arrogant doesn't pick on you is 'pretty strict' but will 'let you feel a bit free'
Secondary 'disturbed' boys in three residential and three day schools	Dawson, 1984	goes out of his way to help you lets you talk about your personal problems does something about your complaints encourages you to talk about your feelings

however, is to elicit the hidden, unwritten rules by which pupils give meaning to their school experiences.

A number of interesting points emerge from summaries in the table. First, there is remarkable agreement between pupils of all ages and ability levels. With few exceptions, the girls at a formal academic high school admire essentially the same characteristics in teachers as juniors in an open-plan classroom; and adolescents in special and mainstream schools look for the same basic qualities in their teachers. Two issues crop up again and again. One concerns the pupils' insistence that a good teacher is one who can keep order in a firm but relaxed and non-punitive way. Even the disturbed adolescents in the Carnell (1983) study, whilst also putting 'understanding' among those qualities they most admire in teachers, gave 'good teaching skills' first place among fifteen attributes listed in a questionnaire.

The other teacher quality that almost all pupils admire relates to the teacher's ability to make the pupils feel they are learning something worthwhile and efficiently. As Brian Davies (1979) noted in his study of 10- to 11-year-olds, 'A good teacher helps you to learn or makes it possible for you to learn and also makes the day a pleasant one with a few jokes' (p. 52). 'Mucking about' occurs in lessons that are 'boring' or 'a waste of time'. This does not mean, however, that the curriculum has to serve a clear instrumental purpose. Furlong (1976) noted how history lessons could be as successful as those in typing; and Gannaway (1976) found that the English teacher was the most liked and respected, especially if, as one boy put it, 'you could really sort of talk to her' but not if 'it was all English compositions, English speaking and things like that' (pp. 57–8). Helpfulness, readiness to explain, clarity of presentation, quiet efficiency and resolving difficulties without fuss – these are the qualities that characterize 'good teaching' for all children.

Secondly, children dislike both the 'soft' teacher who cannot keep order (and even more the one who gets angry or upset) and the 'hard' teacher who is overbearing and indiscriminate when reprimanding and punishing. They like firmness, even strictness, but it must be seen to be just. As Nash (1976b) observed, it is the poorly behaved children as well as the well behaved who like firm control. None the less, pupils like order to be kept in such a way that they feel some freedom to express themselves. They therefore welcome a fairly relaxed classroom and the opportunity to express their ideas to teachers who treat them seriously.

They also like teachers who are prepared to have a joke. From a list of thirty expressions, Gannaway (1976) found that fourth-year pupils ranked first the item 'has a sense of humour'. In a discussion of the place of laughter with a group of secondary pupils, Woods (1976b) concluded that humour was significant 'as a life-saving response to the exigencies of the institution – boredom, ritual, routine, regulations, oppressive authority' (p. 185). Woods feels that teachers could help themselves by harnessing some of the pupils' 'ingenuity, creativity, brilliance and *joie de vivre* as a contribution to, rather than as an antidote to, schooling' (p. 186). Similarly, Stebbins (1980) notes how humour can function as a comic relief, offering refreshing momentary respite from the efforts of lengthy group concentration. Indeed, Walker and Goodson (1977) have shown how the language of classroom humour can help to build up a special kind of cultural identity. Joking relationships have a meaning shared only by the participants, and it is this that gives them special significance in the establishment of personal relationships.

Thirdly, pupils like teachers who behave considerately towards them. They do not mind punishment if it is perceived as just, but they resent teachers who pick on pupils, who are disrespectful, or who 'push you around'. In the Wragg and Wood (1984b) study, pupils expressed a clear preference for teachers who called pupils by their first name, who helped slow learners in a nice way, and who were good listeners; in contrast, they demonstrated a distaste for teachers who hit pupils, who were bossy, or who were too busy to talk to pupils. The disturbed pupils in the Dawson (1984) study, which concerned views about staff support and strictness, clearly valued a teacher's willingness to spend time talking informally and to take personal feelings and problems seriously. In an investigation by Thompson (1975), involving 2,400 secondary pupils, teachers were rated more favourably than adults in general with respect to their professional role, such as being interesting or wise, but less favourably with respect to personal qualities such as kindness, fairness and warmth. Tattum (1982) found that pupils whose behaviour was regularly disruptive were critical of teachers who publicly abused them and who lacked understanding and compassion. Tattum asks whether the views of the few who are openly critical of school are the sounding board of larger numbers of pupils who are discontended and frustrated but do not openly express their feelings.

Finally, it is important to note how older children want to be treated in an adult-like way whilst they also depend on adults for security and guidance. They like to feel free yet also controlled; and they like adults who come clean with their own views about controversial issues, but not those who pontificate and moralize.

Pupils' perceptions of fairness

Another series of studies has shown how seemingly malicious behaviour is sometimes viewed by the pupils, particularly those from working-class backgrounds, as an attempt to restore self-dignity. The hidden rule at work here involves what Rosser and Harré (1976) see as a principle of reciprocity, according to which the pupils try to restore themselves as human beings in situations where they feel they are not being treated as persons.

One of the earlier studies related to this issue is that of Werthman (1963), who investigated the educational achievement and classroom experiences among a group of working-class black delinquents in an American high school over a two-year period. Why, he asked, did these adolescents (of whom more than two-thirds had spent some time in jail) cause disruption with only some teachers and not others? Werthman concluded that it was a mistake to view disruptive classroom behaviour as a product of culture conflict between working-class boys and middle-class teachers. Rather, the problems suggested something more specific about the teachers. For these boys, authority was not considered acceptable unless it was exercised on suitable grounds in a suitable way, and the burden of proof lay with the teacher. Four criteria seemed to govern the acceptance of authority:

(1) In cases of inattentiveness in class – talking, reading comics, turning round, chewing gum, etc. – the teacher must have good reason to reprimand you; the right could not be taken for granted.
(2) In cases involving race, dress, hair-style, and mental capacities, the teacher was *never* within her rights to make pronouncements.
(3) Authority was unlikely to be accepted if it was exercised by the use of imperatives, which were seen as insulting.
(4) The award of formal grades must be manifestly fair. For instance, it was unacceptable for a teacher to give a low grade for bad behaviour or a high grade as an inducement to behave better. Moreover, teachers should be able to give an account to justify the award of a particular grade; the boys would feel insulted if the teacher thought it demeaning or unnecessary to explain a grade.

When teachers failed to comply with these unwritten rules, the boys felt justified in resorting to dissenting behaviour, such as arriving late for a lesson, not saying 'Sir' when addressing the teacher, 'looking cool' by bearing a slight smile or wearing a hat indoors. The significance of these postures lay in their symbolic rejection of authority. Although provocative, teachers found it difficult to find anything specific to attack. Yet the other side of the picture was equally important. When the boys perceived that the ground rules were being observed, that the teacher was really interested in teaching them and treated them with respect, then they would arrive at class on time, raise their hands before speaking and generally act in a conforming way.

Several subsequent studies in Britain have produced similar results to those of Werthman. Furlong (1977) found that less able Afro-Caribbean girls resented those teachers whom they perceived as treating them unfairly: in these circumstances they would feel no guilt in reasserting themselves, even shouting and swearing. 'Unfair trouble' might include being told off when others were also misbehaving, being shouted at or being ridiculed. Yet strictness, which was perceived as in the interests of effective learning, was not only tolerated but valued. More recently, Davies (1984), working in a girls' Midlands comprehensive school, found that the greatest hostility was aroused when pupils were presented with contradictions in teachers, who, while demanding polite behaviour, would demonstrate bad manners themselves. As in Furlong's study, behaviour that was seemingly insolent could have a rational basis in terms of the preservation of self-esteem: 'bad manners could be returned only by equally bad manners, if status and principles of reciprocity were to be preserved' (Davies, 1984, p. 29). Similar views were expressed to Tattum (1984) by the pupils in an off-site behavioural unit, e.g. 'some talk to you like you're blinking dogs. And that's what makes me go mad then, see' (p. 98).

In a study of working-class boys in their final year at a tough Midlands school, Willis (1977) argued that 'the most basic, obvious and explicit dimension of counter-school culture is entrenched, generalized and personal opposition to "authority"' (p. 11). He saw the boys' rejection of school as a blanket rejection of teachers' authority and what the school stood for, the opposition of hard masculinity representing an attempt to achieve status in a context that is perceived to rob the boys of their dignity. Willis found that, in their attempt to promote a distinct alternative culture, 'the lads' searched out incidents to create trouble and to have a 'laff'. They rejected and felt superior to the conformist pupils, whom they appropriately dubbed 'the ear'oles'. Willis sees working-class counter-school culture as symbolic of a recognition that schools are less inclined to liberate working-class pupils and more inclined to maintain a social system of 'us' and 'them'.

In another account of working-class counter-school culture, Corrigan (1979) has reported conversations with Sunderland 'smash street kids' that reveal the resentment felt about the amount of power teachers could wield. However, Corrigan's conclusion was that for these adolescents there was no concept of legitimate teacher authority. The boys maintained that the distance between them and their teachers precluded any meaningful relationship. For them the role of the teacher was *'inextricably* linked with the idea that someone pushes you around' (p. 55, author's italics).

The recent study by Wright (1985a), mentioned in an earlier section, reveals a succession of disturbing perceptions by black pupils of demeaning behaviour on the part of some teachers towards them. The following comment by a black pupil is one of several cited: 'It's like once the man [referrring to the teacher] come in the class, and ask me in front of the class, 'Why me coffee coloured?' He say, 'How come Wallace dark, and Kennedy black and Kevin a bit browner? How come that you a half-breed?' (p. 12). As a reaction to the frustration such treatment aroused, black pupils felt justified in displaying disruptive behaviour in the interests of reciprocity. Wright quotes one as saying of teachers, 'You then treat them without any respect because they don't give you any, so really it's just a two-way thing' (p. 15).

In a series of intensive observations and interviews among fourth-year pupils in a Lancashire comprehensive school, Sharp (1981) identified three categories of dissenting behaviour which arose because pupils found school 'boring'. The first was attention-seeking, representing an 'individual message' of an underlying emotional need. One girl, for instance, would arrive late and without an apology, close the window noisily, sit at right-angles to her desk gossiping with other girls. The second category represented a 'pedagogic message', and was related to teachers' approachability and their skill in explaining things, whether they shout too much, were humourless, and generally treated pupils with learning difficulties in an inconsiderate way. Finally, some dissent was seen as carrying a 'social message', conferring on the dissenting pupil an informal social status by the expression of disdain for other pupils who needed to pay attention. This might be authentic in some cases, or it could be a rationalization of feeling of academic failure. Like other investigators whose work we have reviewed, Sharp concluded that 'disruptive behaviour cannot be dismissed as mindless hooliganism, immaturity, poor upbringing, or some similar vilification'; rather 'typical dissenting behaviour is a meaningful response by pupils to their experiences of schooling' (p. 150).

It is easy to dismiss statements from pupils as defensive reactions rather than as objective appraisals of their experiences. Is there not a tendency in us all to blame others for our lack of success? None the less, the weight of evidence that emerges from the various studies, some very recent, does seem to suggest that it is dissatisfaction about the quality of some teacher–pupil relationships, and not simply mindless devilment, that gives rise to some dissenting behaviour in schools. This is certainly not to deny the existence of serious, malicious behaviour. Nor is it to suggest that teachers as a whole are racist or insensitive to the needs of working-class pupils. But it is to say that productive relationships in schools do depend upon treating pupils with respect, being sensitive to their feelings and avoiding public, derogatory comments. As we saw in the last section, pupils respect teachers who are firm and who punish justly; but they also want to be treated as persons, individuals whose feelings matter and who are inherently responsible agents.

FURTHER READING

Furlong, V. J. (1985) *The Deviant Pupil: Sociological Perspectives*, Open University Press, Milton Keynes.
(Critical reviews of sociological studies concerned with school behaviour.)
Hargreaves, D. H., Hester, S. K. and Mellor, F. J. (1975) *Deviance in Classrooms*, Routledge & Kegan Paul, London.
(An ethnographic study of pupil labelling.)
Schostak, J. F. (1983) *Maladjusted Schooling: Deviance, Social Control and Individuality in Secondary Schooling*, Falmer Press, London.
(An analysis of pressures in school that inhibit individuality.)

Wright, C. (1985) The influence of school processes on the educational opportunities of children of West Indian origin, *Multicultural Teaching*, Vol. 4, No. 1.
(An ethnographic study prepared for a project directed by John Egglestone, of 14- to 18-year-olds from minority ethnic groups. The full report is available from Multicultural Studies in Higher Education, University of Warwick, Coventry.)

6
THE MANAGEMENT OF PUPIL BEHAVIOUR

It is clear to even the most casual observer of classroom interaction that some teachers seem to be more successful than others in establishing good relationships with pupils and in achieving class control without recourse to constant reprimand. Why should this be? Some teachers, no doubt by virtue of their personality and temperament, seem to get on naturally with all types of children and young people. Pupils respond to them positively simply because they want to do so. However, there seems to be more to it than this. One obvious point is that teaching must be interesting. But interest, though a necessary condition for successful teaching, is not a sufficient one.

From a range of studies that owe much to the work of Kounin (1970), it seems that the teacher who is most successful in establishing conditions that are conducive to co-operative behaviour and positive relationships with pupils is one who employs skills and tactics that forestall possible disruption and prevent the occurrence of incidents that attract reprimand and punishment. Essentially this involves regarding the class not only as a collection of pupils requiring individual attention, but also as a group with collective needs. The argument of this chapter, then, is that teachers who see themselves functioning as *group* leaders will be more effective as managers of group behaviour. Not only this, they will also be more successful in helping children to learn effectively.

THE SIGNIFICANCE OF THE CLASS AS A GROUP

A group has psychological needs that go beyond the individual requirements of its members. For a group to function harmoniously and productively, it needs integration, security and status. The teacher has therefore to influence both the growth of the individual and the growth of the group.

The complications inherent in this dual responsibility have been brought out in a series of illustrative examples by Redl (1966). A boy in an infant school acts the clown to gain group prestige. The teacher could perceive this as nothing more than a phase in the child's development and turn a blind eye – but this would be to ignore the group situation, in which the clowning behaviour is disturbing. Yet if the teacher punishes the boy for the benefit of the group, she may worsen the child's adjustment problem (and, ultimately, the group situation). Redl therefore suggests that if the teacher enlists the co-operation of other pupils to help the boy understand the limits to which he can go, this should check the clowning behaviour for the sake of the group without making the boy's problem of adjustment more difficult. In a contrasting illustration, Redl gives the example of a girl who sits at the back of the class daydreaming. This behaviour is innocuous from the group point of view, but is a sign that the child needs help at an individual level.

The significance of the teacher as a group leader in urban classrooms has been brought out by Joan Roberts (1971), who distinguishes between two broad dimensions of leadership:

(1) *Consideration and integrative behaviour:* this involves encouraging group members to work together towards common goals in harmonious ways that give satisfaction to each person.
(2) *Initiating, directive, task-oriented behaviour:* this involves specifying means to achieve goals, and co-ordinating activities.

Many teachers see themselves primarily in terms of the second of these dimensions, i.e. as task specialists, initiating and directing subject-matter. However, if the class is not held together as a whole, this role will be ineffective, and the teacher may be forced to adopt the role of a disciplinarian in order to restore group cohesiveness. According to Joan Roberts, the teacher's mistake may be to assume that she is the only leader in the classroom. She is likely to be more successful if she encourages the pupils to be involved in performing some of the leadership functions, and does not try to fulfil all these alone. This can be done by encouraging children to give feedback, to express feelings, to voice opinions, to evaluate the ideas of others, to contribute information, to make suggestions for possible ways of action and to test the feasibility of group suggestions.

In short, the role of the teacher as group leader will include being a receptive audience to group ideas. Teaching is thus at once teacher- and pupil-centred. As Roberts emphasizes, it is *interacting with* rather than *reacting to* pupils. It is not simply asking questions of fact and reinforcing the right answers, but focusing on concepts and ideas that take up the children's suggestions.

Another reason why classes sometimes fail to be cohesive is that the children do not value being members of their class. Teachers sometimes tell an unco-operative class that their reputation in the school is bad ('You're the worst class I've ever taught'). But what child wants to feel that he belongs to a group of low prestige? The effect of such remarks, far from reversing an unco-operative group spirit, can be to drive the children further into their informal groupings associated with an anti-school culture. From Johnson and Bany's (1970) experimental work, it seems that teachers who were successful in developing group cohesion were those who made favourable group appraisals whenever this was appropriate, who avoided group criticism, and who relayed to the class the favourable comments of other teachers, the head or visitors. Teachers successful as group leaders were also those who encouraged activities that involved joint planning and the implementation of ideas together.

The professional skills involved here should not be underestimated. Getting children to solve a problem is not just getting them to vote on it. Indeed, voting can divide groups and promote factions, as any committee member will testify. The teacher has to help pupils to formulate the question in a way that is conducive to a solution, to help pupils to discern where factual data is required and where hypotheses need to be tested, to point out areas in which agreement has been reached, to summarize points of disagreement, to clarify points of view, and so forth. Moreover, the success of such activities depends on the teacher's belief that the class is really capable of working out solutions to their own social problems. Further, should the class's decision turn out to be a mistake, the teacher must refrain from attributing blame to the group, since this could appear threatening and elicit a defensive attitude.

Another aspect of the teacher's function as a group leader relates to informal groupings in the classroom. Hargreaves (1975) has suggested that teachers should endeavour to identify the leaders of these 'cliques' because they are central in the communicative structure of the class, regulating the norms of behaviour and the criteria by which group prestige is achieved. If the teacher unthinkingly gives public praise or a position of responsibility to a pupil who is at odds with his peers, she thereby ascribes high formal status to a pupil of low informal status. In this way, relations between pupils may unwittingly be severed still further. Thus a teacher who recognizes the leaders as perceived by the pupils themselves will be a more effective manager of inter-pupil relations.

At the same time, the teacher has a responsibility to integrate the pupil of low informal status into the group. The tactics teachers employ can be instrumental in this respect, as Manning and Slukin (1984) have illustrated from their observations of nursery school children. Teachers who deal with aggressive children only by reprimanding them seem only to increase the problem behaviour, since the child who is told to stop antagonizing other children in one way will find another socially unacceptable means of achieving his purpose. However, teachers who carefully help aggressive children to meet their needs in friendly ways, such as by being given tasks to help other children, and by being invited to share their interests with other children, will gain the social status for which they are striving without resorting to hostility. The skill involved here is one that enables aggressive children to feel differently about situations: such a strategy is more likely to enlist co-operation that attempts to contain the situation by diverting such children into quieter pursuits.

THE SIGNIFICANCE OF VERBAL AND NON-VERBAL COMMUNICATION

Most teachers are aware of the effects a judicious use of words can have on classroom control, and that they can use this knowledge to establish a position of dominance. Hammersley (1976) has explored ways in which some teachers try to mobilize the attention of young adolescent pupils in traditional-type urban schools through a display of vocal superiority, sarcasm, or a comparison of one pupil's behaviour with another's. A careful choice of words, often with a hint of sarcasm, can elicit attention: 'Are we ready to start now? Have we come down from the clouds of insanity down to the ground? Do we know when our tongues are wagging, eh Bannister?' (p. 106); or 'Manners maketh man, that's why you must be a boy then, you haven't any' (p. 110). Questions are sometimes designed to test attention rather than understanding, and they are sometimes made too difficult in order to display superior knowledge and therefore power. Such devices, Hammersley argues, seem aimed to bring about a 'proper' attitude to lessons. The implication conveyed by the teachers' remarks is that unacceptable behaviour is childish.

However, as we saw in Chapter 5, verbal devices that comment unfavourably upon pupils' characters may be resented by them and therefore be counter-productive. On the other hand, much depends on the manner and circumstances in which they are used. Such remarks can sometimes be both acceptable and managerially effective if delivered with a twinkle in the eye and not as part of the teacher's routine behaviour. Indeed, the use of humour of a kind that respects the pupils as persons is particularly potent in a classroom, as we noted in our review of pupils' expectations of good teaching in the previous chapter.

The teacher's style of reprimand is another type of action that can either consolidate or estrange group relations. Research on the 'ripple effect' is of relevance here. Kounin (1970) noticed from his classroom observations that, if a teacher fairly reprimanded a child whose peer status was high and succeeded in checking the misbehaviour, the effect on the rest of the class was usually strong and positive; but if the teacher reprimanded unfairly, the ripple effect could be negative and the teacher's action counter-productive.

In a series of case studies, Amidon and Hunter (1966) have illustrated how pupils can easily feel rejected by the way a teacher reprimands. For instance, commands such as 'Susan, stop daydreaming and get on with your work!' may be perceived as rejections although they were intended simply as directions. When pupils give answers that are silly and the class laughs, teachers sometimes react with a sarcastic comment, such as 'You know very well how that word is pronounced, but, as usual, you have to be funny.' An important skill teachers can learn is responding to problem behaviour positively rather than negatively. Thus, in the first of the above examples, the teacher might have said, 'Susan, how can I help you?', while in the second she might have supplied the correct pronunciation rather than make a personal issue out of the incident.

While teachers are generally aware of the significance of their verbal behaviour, they are probably less sensitive to the impact of their body language. For instance, by shifting the head or changing posture, the teacher can help to convey her verbal message. Non-verbal communication will also have an impact on classroom relationships. The manner in which a teacher exchanges glances or catches the eye of individual children can affect the way in which the pupils come to regard her. The teacher who avoids looking at individuals directly, perhaps by gazing into the space above the class, may give an impression of disinterestedness in the pupils as individuals; by avoiding their gaze by looking down, she conveys submissiveness.

Non-verbal language is also significant in defining the status-image the teacher conveys to the class. Style of dress is of significance in this respect, and so is posture. Standing erectly at the front of the room will set up a more formal relationship than sitting in a relaxed position next to a pupil to be on the same eye-level. Thus, through non-verbal communication, teachers give cues about the kind of persons they are and the kind of control message they wish to convey. Neill (1986) has recently demonstrated how adolescents perceive teachers who present different non-verbal behaviours. For instance, a teacher who looks sad and leans back against the blackboard is seen as boring and unhelpful; and one who stands with hands on hips, leaning slightly in a calm posture, is seen as mildly threatening. Pupils too, of course, convey their feelings and expectations through body language. Boredom and frustration are somehow more acceptable if communicated to the authority figures non-verbally, and it is therefore important for teachers to be sensitive to such cues before the pupils express themselves more directly!

FIRST ENCOUNTERS WITH A CLASS

A question that faces all teachers, and is especially important for those new to the profession, is 'How shall I face my new class? Should I be dominant, showing them who's boss in no uncertain way? Or should I develop friendly relations from the start?' Clearly, the teacher who is new to a class must be assertive and confident. In his analysis of statements made by pupils about teachers' initial classroom encounters, Ball (1980) comments how it is the teachers who either take no action at all or those who show signs of confusion who are particularly vulnerable to the pupils' testing. This is consistent with the view of Wragg and Wood (1984a), who have observed the contrasting behaviour of experienced and student teachers in secondary schools. As might be expected, the former are much more likely to give the impression that they are firmly in charge, not only in what they say but also in their eye movements and gestures; and they temper their commands by a judicious use of humour.

In this section, we shall consider two models of initial classroom encounters. At first sight, these may seem to reflect very different standpoints, but, as we shall see later, a synthesis may be possible.

The 'integration' model

Elizabeth Richardson (1967) sympathetically related how the teacher faced with a new and hostile class will tend to fall back on her authority and deal briskly with timetables and other administrative announcements, doing all the talking and displaying organizational efficiency in an attempt to preserve anonymity. Whilst this reaction may give immediate reassurance to the teacher, the non-verbal message, Richardson argued, is one of benevolent autocracy in which pupils' feelings are of no account. Rather than adopt an impersonal approach in which all the communication is formal and between the teacher and the pupils, Richardson suggested that the teacher should start off by encouraging a general discussion in which pupils' thoughts and feelings are shared. This would demonstrate the teacher's belief that the pupils' opinions matter to her, and that the class does not consist of anonymous members, but persons. Specifically, Richardson suggested that an opening session with first-year pupils might invite exchanges about their primary schools and their anticipations about the new school; second-year pupils might be invited to comment on the best and worst aspects of the previous year, while fourth-year pupils might be encouraged to discuss the implications of choosing some subjects and dropping others. Such tactics 'set a pattern for future exchanges by freeing the pupils to talk about the matters which are important for them in the present' (Richardson, 1967, p. 26).

Listening to the real concerns of pupils is undoubtedly an important part of the development of classroom relationships. As we saw earlier in this chapter, for a group to function harmoniously and purposefully, its members need help in communicating with each other. The integration model therefore meets an important criterion for the development of group relationships.

In some secondary schools, however, teachers may fear they would lose their grip if they encouraged discussion of this kind when first meeting a class. The integration model is therefore more usually evident in classes of younger children. Hamilton (1984) has described the first days of school for a class of twenty-two five-year-olds. With this age-group, the teacher must both provide a welcoming environment and initiate children into the conventions of schooling, its rules and standards of expectation. In this study, the teacher had spent three days preparing an attractive classroom and allowing easy access to materials. Because she knew that she would be unable to attend to all the newcomers at once, the children were admitted in subgroups over the day, and provided with activities that needed little supervision and enabled the teacher to spend some time with each child individually. Certain rules, such as those about tidiness, were carefully explained, and children who could not read their name were taught how to recognize the place to put their belongings. Later in the day, the teacher talked to the children as a group, inviting the children to say something about themselves, thus learning to take their turn in discussion. In short, the teacher demonstrated that her concern for children as individuals in school involved helping them gently to become integrated members of the group.

The 'dominance' model

Hargreaves (1975) has argued that when children meet a teacher for the first time, they will both expect to be controlled and try to 'define the situation' in a way that suits their purposes. According to Hargreaves, the teacher's first priority on meeting a new class should therefore be to take the initiative in defining the situation, and not allow the class to do this for her:

> This is a lesson learned the hard way by countless generations of student teachers who, believing that their pupils ought to be treated with respect as mature persons, try to create a definition of the situation that is congruent with their beliefs. Almost always the result is disastrous. The pupils do not respond in the expected way [because] the pupils' perspective or definition of the situation is not congruent with that of the teacher, whereas the student teacher assumes that is is.
>
> (Hargreaves, 1975, p. 205)

This approach takes account of the fact that pupils are inclined to 'suss' the new teacher through a series of challenges. As Beynon (1985) has recently illustrated, older children are liable to try out strategies such as subversive laughter, asking stupid questions, answering back, a lounging posture, desultory obedience, combing hair and generally 'mucking about'. Beynon sees sussing as 'a plotting and mapping of teacher management skills and degrees of tolerance' (p. 132). It serves the interest of both parties since teachers and pupils reveal and prove themselves. The teacher's ability to forestall challenges and to deal with any that arise with competence will reveal to pupils the teacher's management skills, rules and toleration limits, consistency of treatment and temperament.

The 'dominance' approach thus makes a good deal of sense. However, it is important for the new teacher to beware of four dangers. The first is to confuse 'dominance' with 'being domineering' or adopting a strategy of domination. As Denscombe (1985, p. 143) has put it, 'domination relies on and exaggerates institutionalized disparities in power'. Hargreaves (1975) is well aware of this possibility when he says, 'By "tough" I do *not* mean to suggest a ruthless and punitive autocracy [but] firmness, clarity and consistency. ... In being "tough" the teacher can, and should, be humorous and reasonable' (p. 211). This is a far cry from the teacher described by Waller (1932) who, in setting out to 'define the situation', 'did everything to be disagreeable ... contested almost everything of consequence that happened during those first four weeks ... I bawled them out mercilessly, sarcastically, and impersonally' (p. 298). It is thus the *manner* in which the teacher insists and asserts that is crucial if dominance is not to degenerate into domination.

A second danger is to ignore the kinds of relationship to which the children have become accustomed with their previous teacher. Davies (1979) observed a new junior school teacher who was failing in an informally structured school because he did not listen to the children when they attempted to engage in the open negotiations they had learned from their previous teacher. It may therefore be more important for a teacher to continue the style of her predecessor (assuming this was successful), than to adopt a dominant role automatically. As Nash (1976b, p. 94) has commented: 'A new class is not a clean slate passively waiting for the teacher to inscribe his will on it. It is an ongoing social system with very definite expectations about appropriate teacher behaviour. If these are not confirmed the pupils will protest.'

Thirdly, it is vital that the teacher's dominance is seen as a means to an end and not an end in itself. The achievement of dominance can be rewarding for a teacher who might therefore be tempted to rely upon that kind of management style. Again, Hargreaves (1975) recognizes this point when he recommends that teachers gradually redefine the situation after the initial definition has been established. The authority of the teacher can then become more personal, and power can be based on the pupil's respect and admiration.

Finally, in her concern to achieve dominance, the teacher must not allow control to dominate the curriculum. Interest is not a sufficient condition for keeping order in the classroom, but it is a necessary condition for education to take place and for any worthwhile relationships to develop. Control techniques must therefore be regarded as subservient to the larger educational aims. As we shall see in the next section, it is probably best to develop management skills in which the pupils are controlled through the style of teaching, rather than to regard the two processes as separate.

The two models compared

So is the 'dominance' model reactionary compared with the 'integration' model? Is the achievement of dominance inconsistent with encouraging exchanges of information and ideas? The 'dominance' model certainly puts the teacher in the focal position, whereas the 'integration' model allows the teacher to adopt a more facilitatory role and an immediate open relationship. Yet in certain respects the two models are not at odds. As we have emphasized, 'achieving dominance' should not be taken to mean 'being domineering'; nor should welcoming contributions from the pupils be taken to mean a negation of the teacher's right to be assertive. In the 'integration' model, the teacher is still defining the situation: she remains a figure of authority, ensuring that the conversation is well regulated and at an appropriate level. Which model should be adopted will depend partly on personal preference and confidence, partly on a knowledge of how classes in the school generally behave, and also on the kind of relationships the pupils have enjoyed with previous teachers.

CLASSROOM MANAGEMENT SKILLS

The discussion in the previous section might confirm the widely held view that successful classroom management depends on personal maturity, imagination and insight, which a teacher has either 'got' or not. Various writers have described a range of strategies teachers who evidently lack these qualities use to 'survive' (Woods, 1979) and 'cope' in order to protect their self-image and control stress (A. Hargreaves, 1978; Pollard, 1982, 1984). However, whilst some teachers seem to have a natural flair for managing children without fuss, it is a mistake to believe that classroom management skills cannot be identified and learned.

The term 'classroom management skills' is used to refer to those strategies that have been shown to be effective in preventing the occurrence of misbehaviour. They are therefore concerned with providing conducive conditions for learning through foresight, planning and management, rather than allowing problems to arise and then coping and surviving.

Kounin (1970) has defined classroom management as successful if it (a) maintains a low rate of deviant behaviour and (b) produces a high rate of work involvement. By analysing video-taped recordings of almost fifty teachers of elementary school classes containing 5- to 11-year-olds (including some classes of emotionally disturbed children), Kounin was able to assess the way different types of teacher behaviour elicited different types of responses from the pupils. The results of the research left him in no doubt that the technique of dealing with misbehaviour as it arose was not significant in modifying it. What appeared to matter was not the frequency or nature of the teachers' 'desist' techniques but the general style of classroom management by which the occurrence of misbehaviour was made less likely.

The dimensions of classroom management Kounin found to be significant in determining pupils' co-operative behaviour and work involvement were each given a label, and can be summarized as follows:

(1) *Withitness:* The teacher's communication to the class by her actual behaviour that she knows what each child is doing: she has 'eyes at the back of her head', and can handle more than one issue at a time.

Handling the right child on time is important too: teachers who become preoccupied with one issue allow misbehaviour to spread, and then, not knowing exactly what is going on, often reprimand the wrong child!

(2) *Overlapping:* Attending to two matters simultaneously, e.g. by dealing with misbehaviour without interrupting work with a reading group, or by continuing to 'teach' whilst also dealing with a child who wants to show the teacher some work. For instance, the teacher might say 'Keep on reading, Mary' while she walks over to two boys making paper aeroplanes, looking back at the child who is reading.

(3) *Helping the lesson to flow smoothly.* This depends upon *avoiding* the following:

   (a) *Thrusts:* A sudden 'bursting in' with an order or question when the children are busy, without being sensitive to the group's readiness to receive the teacher's message, e.g. by pausing and looking around.

   (b) *Over-emphasis:* Deflection from the main stream of activity, e.g. making a fuss about paper on the floor or about slouching on the desk when the children are endeavouring to concentrate on their work.

   (c) *Dangles:* Starting an activity and leaving it hanging in mid-air by going on to another activity, e.g. asking a girl to read and then asking why someone is absent.

   (d) *Flip-flops:* Going back to an activity that has just been terminated, e.g. saying 'Put away your spelling books and take out your arithmetic books' and then asking some further questions about spelling.

   (e) *Overdwelling:* Engaging in a stream of talk beyond that necessary for the children's understanding or knowing what to do. This can take the form of nagging unduly about behaviour, or talking on and on about sitting up straight or how to hold a pencil when the children are trying to master an arithmetic problem, or dragging out the time needed in the distribution of art materials, or overelaborating on a point the pupils have already understood.

   (f) *Fragmentation:* Unnecessarily asking each child in turn to do something, so keeping other children waiting.

(4) *Maintaining the focus of the group:* This can be done through the use of:

   (a) *alerting cues* to keep the attention of those children who were not immediately contributing to the lesson, e.g. pausing to look around before asking a child to read, ensuring that discussion is not confined to a few children, presenting new and unexpected materials in order to arouse interest;

(b) *accountability cues* to ensure that the children know that the teacher knows what they are doing, e.g. by asking children to hold up their work, by circulating and checking, by asking pupils to demonstrate their skills and knowledge.

(5) *Variety:* E.g. of subject matter, in type of response required, in materials to use, in group configuration, in the allocation of responsibilities, in the use of teaching aids.

To summarize, the hallmarks of successful classroom management, according to Kounin (1970), are: smoothness in maintaining an activity and in transition from one activity to the next; skill in handling misbehaviour whilst not interrupting the flow of learning; maintaining the momentum of the lesson, partly by ensuring all children know what to do, and partly by avoiding making an issue out of matters that could wait; keeping children accountable for their performance; and planning lessons to ensure variety in content, type of work and mode of presentation. Teachers are thus more or less successful in keeping order not because some are more skilled than others in dealing with trouble when it arises, but because some are more skilled than others in reducing the number of occasions when trouble could occur.

Kounin's findings are of practical importance because they point to specific matters. General slogans such as 'creating rapport', 'making it interesting' and 'being warm and understanding' are desirable attributes but will not by themselves secure successful classroom management. Further, the research corrects a common idea that children's behaviour can be appropriately affected by the manner of reprimand or punishment alone. Finally, Kounin (1970) emphasizes the significance of dealing with a class *as a group* and building up a *class ethos*. Such a strategy does not diminish the significance of individual teacher–pupil relationships; on the contrary, attending to the class as a group will provide an atmosphere in which it is easier for individual attention to be given.

Follow-up studies have confirmed and extended Kounin's findings. When Brophy and Evertson (1976) studied the managerial behaviour of some teachers who were responsible for classes of 7- to 9-year-olds of mixed ethnic origin, they found that the qualities of management that had been identified by Kounin (1970) were related not only to better behaviour but also to more effective learning. Presumably, if teachers are relatively free from control problems they will have more time to teach and the general atmosphere will be more conducive to learning. But there could be another explanation too. In a review of literature concerning classroom management skills, Anderson, Evertson and Emmer (1980) noted that teachers who employed the kind of tactics that Kounin identified helped to create a general atmosphere of purposiveness and seriousness about learning, and this would be picked up by the pupils. It is also worth noting how Anderson, Evertson and Emmer did not see the more effective managers as authoritarian taskmasters: rather, they saw them as teachers whose classroom atmosphere is congenial and pleasant while the focus was unmistakably on learning.

The Brophy and Evertson (1976) study identified three other key factors that are associated with successful classroom management. The first is provision for a high level of pupil involvement. This is consistent with the approach advocated by Roberts (1971) discussed at the beginning of this chapter. The second factor is the provision of effective facilities for assisting pupils with learning problems. Examples are setting aside special times for helping, systematically checking work and identifying difficulties, writing instructions on the board so that pupils who are unclear about what to do can check without interrupting the teacher. Thirdly, instructions in a classroom need to be clear and flexible, so that children know what is expected of them yet can work at their own developmental level. For instance, some children (particularly in a mixed ability class) will be more capable than others in choosing appropriate work tasks, in working independently or in contributing to a group project.

British studies in classroom management have come to conclusions similar to those of the American studies. Wragg (1978) describes a teacher he observed to be particularly skilful and unfussy in the way she handled her informally structured junior school class. Of particular significance were the subtle methods by which she transmitted her vigilance to the whole class. Apart from a watchful eye that could split attention between an individual or group and the rest of the class (thus enabling her to practice what Kounin (1970) called 'overlapping') she would periodically and publicly review the class's progress (thus providing what Kounin called 'accountability cues'). For instance, she might say, 'Now, you two are still painting; Ian, you're preparing assembly; Neil, I think it's time you left that, isn't it?' She thus alerted everyone to the fact that she knew what was going on, but did this without being unduly bossy. This teacher also encouraged individuals to have faith in their own judgement. This would help them to become more self-assured and also reduce the occasions for having to ask others for help.

As part of the Teacher Education Project (TEP) funded by the

Department of Education and Science, Partington and Hinchliffe (1979) recorded 'critical events' during lessons taught by fifty-six postgraduate students during English and science lessons in secondary school teaching practice. These bear a close resemblance to Kounin's findings. The successful teacher–manager emerged as one who

(1) *Established good personal relationships*, e.g. they learned pupils' names; they divided the lesson time to provide opportunity to get to know pupils while they were working or outside lesson time and so could respond to their interests; they used humour without putting pupils down.
(2) *Prepared lessons thoroughly* so that they were confident about the content material, had thought about appropriate organization of activities in the light of the time available, and had anticipated possible problems that might occur and how these would be dealt with (e.g. if chairs had to be moved the instruction would forestall possible disruption: 'Now, very quietly, move your chairs to one corner. Quietly.').
(3) *Organized the pupils appropriately*, e.g. arrived at the room in time to admit them in an orderly way, began lessons briskly, predetermined the way pupils would be organized for group-work.
(4) *Developed specific teaching skills*, such as explaining, questioning, commenting on pupils' work, reading correctly the pupils' non-verbal cues of boredom, lack of understanding – and responding appropriately.

In the main TEP study (Wragg and Dooley, 1984), over two hundred lessons in secondary schools were observed. Serious misbehaviour, such as aggression towards other children, was rare; but much was irritating (noisy talking was the most common problem). The results showed that the more pupils were involved the less there were behaviour problems, while control got out of hand most easily during transitions from one activity to another. The same conclusion was reached by the London Junior School Project team (ILEA, 1986a): 'Children talked more when there was less work for them to do and also when they did not appear actively to be interested in the task in hand' (Part B, p. 114).

A workbook (Wragg, 1981) based on the Teacher Education Project has been published to help students develop managerial skills during teaching practice. As a result of another DES-funded project undertaken by six educational psychologists, a pack of materials aimed at prevention rather than cure, together with a video for use in training courses for teachers, has been produced (Lake, 1985).

SEATING ARRANGEMENTS

The science of behavioural ecology in the field of education is concerned with the effects of environmental factors on children's learning and behaviour. In a review of research in this area, Glynn (1982) has cited studies that demonstrate how the introduction of parents and other familiar adults into pre-school play situations can lead to an improvement in the children's behaviour. This would seem to be a consequence of ample opportunity being provided for the children to perform tasks that receive praise as reinforcement. Other studies have shown how children eat more, engage in more conversation and behave better at meal-times if adults join them at the table.

Seating arrangements constitute another ecological aspect of classroom management that has received some recent attention in the research literature. In secondary schools, it is customary for pupils to sit in rows, whereas infants usually sit around tables. With children between seven and twelve years, the practice varies not only between schools but sometimes within schools too, some teachers preferring one arrangement and some the other.

Some recent evidence has thrown light on the effects of different seating arrangements. In one American experiment, Axelrod, Hall and Tams (1979) observed classes of 7-8 and 12- to 13-year-olds in which the pupils sometimes carried out individual tasks while seated in groups of four or five around tables, and at other times did so in rows. With the younger children, on-task behaviour was 82 per cent when they sat in rows compared with 62 per cent when they faced each other around tables. With the older class, verbal disruption was at least 50 per cent during tables compared with 30 per cent during rows. It thus seemed that a row formation reduced the incidence of disruptive and off-task behaviour because the pupils, by not being placed in face-to-face relationship, were less easily distracted by each other. One might also surmise that the teachers would find it easier to monitor pupils in rows.

A similar study in Britain was carried out by Wheldall et al. (1981) with two classes of 10- to 11-year-old boys and girls who were accustomed to sitting round tables. In the experiment, the pupils worked for two weeks in their familiar table arrangement, then two weeks in rows, and then returned to tables for two weeks. As in the previous study, on-task behaviour was higher (about 15 per cent) in the row arrangement, especially with children whose initial on-task behaviour when working in tables was low. In another British study, this time involving children classified as educationally subnormal (moderate), Ng (1982) concluded that seating in rows led not only to improved behaviour and more time spent on work, but also yielded a four-fold increase in the rate of approving remarks made by the teacher. These findings were seen to be interconnected: because the pupils were not distracted by facing each other, their behaviour was less disruptive, which in turn increased the on-task behaviour, which in turn elicited greater amounts of praise and less disapproval from the teacher, which in turn helped to perpetuate the good behaviour.

Since the lessons observed in the above studies were concerned only with conventional individual work, it would be wrong to conclude from the results that sitting pupils in rows is always the best arrangement. Other ways of grouping seats might be preferable for other types of activity. Support for this possibility comes from a study by Rosenfield, Lambert and Black (1985). In this experiment, three classrooms of 10- to 11-year-olds were observed during discussion lessons, the pupils being seated sometimes in rows, sometimes around tables and sometimes in a circle. The results showed that pupil involvement in discussion was highest in the circle arrangement and weakest in rows. Indeed, the researchers are brave enough to comment that 'teachers need not fear an unruly class when pupils are seated in a circle' (p. 106).

It thus seems that different seat arrangements facilitate better behaviour for different kinds of tasks. When the goal is pupil participation in discussion, circles appear to produce the best behaviour and work, whereas for individual non-group work rows seem the most appropriate. Clearly, tables might be expected to be better for small group work. It might thus be prudent, if circumstances allow it, for teachers to re-arrange the classroom furniture according to the nature of the task in order to provide optimal conditions for learning and good behaviour. It costs no money (and needs no special training!). However, further research is needed to see if the quality of work, as well as the rate of on-task behaviour, is improved under certain seating arrangements since other studies indicate that increases in on-task behaviour do not necessarily result in better academic output (Glynn, 1982).

A WHOLE-SCHOOL POLICY FOR THE MANAGEMENT OF BEHAVIOUR

Studies in school effectiveness have pointed to the fact that good behaviour is more likely to be achieved if the staff as a whole work in relation to a common policy. For instance, Rutter *et al.* (1979), referring to school process measures that correlated with pupil behaviour and other outcomes, state, 'It was striking, however, that their *combined* effect was much more powerful than that of any individual factor considered on its own. For this and other reasons, we have suggested that some kind of overall school "ethos" might be involved' (p. 182, authors' italics). Similarly, the authors of the London Junior School Project comment: 'It is essential to realize that the school and the classroom are in many ways interlocked. What the teacher can or cannot do depends, to a certain extent, on what is happening in the school as a whole' (ILEA, 1986a, p. 38). The management of pupils' behaviour is thus not only the concern of the individual classroom teacher. Success in the creation of a non-disruptive school climate is more likely if a concerted effort is made by the staff as a group to ensure that children experience similar sorts of treatment with different teachers. But apart from this, some aspects of management can only be realized at school level.

This point is illustrated in the research carried out by Lawrence, Steed and Young (1984a) in two multiracial urban comprehensive schools. Unlike most of the research on classroom management skills, these investigations relied upon teachers' self-reports through interviews plus the completion of special forms whenever disruptive incidents occurred. A report was then prepared and discussed with the staff, not to impart criticism but to encourage discussion and reach agreement on possible ways of reducing disruption.

One general source of misbehaviour this research technique threw up concerned movement around the school. In large secondary schools, changing classes can involve a good deal of travel for both pupils and teachers, allowing opportunity for disruption to arise in the corridors. Teachers often have to calm down a boisterous class when they eventually manage to arrive themselves. Thus careful timetable planning and room allocation could be instrumental in reducing the development of disruptive behaviour.

A similar piece of action research was carried out in a Nottingham comprehensive school by Gillham (1984). The staff agreed to a whole-school policy that involved:

(1) timetabling to minimize the number of occasions that might provide an opportunity for disruption, e.g. by alternating academically demanding periods with lessons involving more practical pursuits;
(2) provision for helping children with learning difficulties, e.g. by remedial staff helping subject specialists to ensure that demands were made at suitable levels for all children in mixed ability classes;
(3) lesson planning that took account of classroom management strategies on the lines discussed earlier in this chapter; and
(4) giving first-year form tutors sufficient teaching time with their own classes to initiate pupils into the school's expectations.

There is certainly a case for some individual variation in classroom management style, since different teachers, by virtue of their different personalities and skills, find different, but equally effective, ways of dealing with children in a group. However, it is an important point for these variations to be such that pupils can recognize a common framework of understanding.

Every school should have a 'whole-school' behaviour policy that is founded on agreed principles and the ongoing monitoring of behaviour by all staff. Pupils are more likely to behave well when they are treated in a reasonably consistent way by teachers who share a common set of expectations. Sharing information about disruptive incidents can act as a morale booster to teachers who might otherwise believe they are alone in having difficulties; and the accumulated knowledge of strategies that work should be of benefit to all.

FURTHER READING

Recent research studies

Beynon, J. (1985) *Initial Encounters in the Secondary School*, Falmer Press, London.

Manning, M. and Slukin, A. M. (1984) The function of aggression in the pre-school and primary school years, in N. Frude and H. Gault (eds.) *Disruptive Behaviour in Schools*, Wiley, Chichester.

Wragg, E. C. (ed.) (1984) *Classroom Teaching Skills*, Croom Helm, London.
  (A collection of papers covering classroom management, students' experiences on teaching practice and teaching skills.)

Practical advice

Laslett, K. and Smith, C. (1984) *Effective Classroom Management*, Croom Helm, London.

Robertson, J. (1981) *Effective Classroom Control*, Hodder & Stoughton, London.

Saunders, M. (1979) *Classroom Control and Behaviour Problems*, McGraw-Hill, London.

7
PRAISE AND REWARDS

Teachers are often advised to be liberal in their use of praise and rewards. Thus Laslett and Smith (1984, p. 51) state: 'The frequent use of praise is the quickest and most effective route to promoting a positive atmosphere in the classroom.' On rewards, the Association of Educational Psychologists (1983) is equally unequivocal: 'Rewards of all kinds should be encouraged and given out as often as possible, thereby placing the whole emphasis of the school on achievement, effort, and positive aspects of life in general.'

In practice, however, teachers do not appear to heed this advice. Brophy (1981) has cited studies that show that, although teachers are more likely to praise good answers and good work than to criticize bad answers or bad work, they are more likely to criticize conduct that is socially unacceptable than to praise that which is desirable. Indeed, Brophy found that the frequency of teacher praise for good behaviour varied from as little as once in two hours to only once in ten hours, and was negligible with older children. Rutter *et al.* (1979), in a sample of twelve London secondary schools, found an average of only three or four positive comments per lesson for pupils' work. Third-year pupils reported twice as many reprimands as instances of praise and three times as many punishments as rewards. Similar findings emerged in a survey of Sheffield secondary schools (Galloway *et al.*, 1982).

In the recent London Junior School Project (ILEA, 1986a), it was found that teachers spent only one per cent of their time praising pupils for work, while praise for good behaviour was even less frequent. A further finding was that teachers were observed to reward for work more often than they punished, whereas for behaviour the reverse was the case.

At secondary level, the low incidence of classroom praise and rewards, especially for behaviour, may reflect the difficulty which teachers experience in commenting favourably upon children whose behaviour is normally threatening, and with whom, as Brophy (1981) points out, they may therefore wish to avoid any form of interaction. At primary level, however, teachers seem to praise good behaviour more often in the case of pupils who are generally naughty than in the case of those who are usually well-behaved – though it is still a fairly rare event (ILEA, 1986a). The question to be asked, therefore, is whether teachers should make the effort to use praise and rewards more frequently. The argument to be presented in this chapter is that such devices certainly can be used to good effect, but that they should not be used indiscriminately if they are to help pupils educationally.

It is important to appreciate that two kinds of criteria can be used in evaluating the use of praise and rewards. One is *managerial*: Does praising or rewarding help the teacher to control pupils so that their overt behaviour changes for the better? The other criterion is *educational*: Does the use of praise or rewards make a direct contribution to the task of helping pupils to think more maturely about their behaviour and how it is affecting others, to be successful in their learning and to develop an intrinsic interest in curriculum activities? The distinction between these criteria is important since, as was argued in Chapter 4, a controlled classroom, while important, is not necessarily one in which effective learning is taking place. In a recent study of primary classrooms, Bennett *et al.* (1984) noticed how children can be working cheerfully and industriously even if they are also working unproductively, at inappropriate levels, and are totally confused!

REWARDS AND INTRINSIC INTEREST

One reason for believing that rewards are problematic educationally is that their use may have adverse effects on the intrinsic interest children take in an activity. In a classic study by Lepper, Green and Nisbett (1973), nursery school children were promised a reward for drawing, an activity they had previously chosen in preference to others available. Some of the children were promised a certificate with a gold seal and a ribbon, others were given the reward but not told about it until they had finished their drawings, whilst a control group was neither promised nor given a reward. After a week or so, the children were observed in their normal classroom situation where drawing materials were available along with other objects to play with. It was found that those who had expected a reward in the experimental situation now demonstrated *less* interest in drawing, whereas the other children showed an undiminished or increased interest in the activity. Furthermore, the quality of drawings produced by the children who expected a reward was judged to be inferior to those of the other children in both the experimental and classroom settings.

This experiment lent support to the hypothesis concerning an 'over-justification effect', which predicts that the offer of a tangible reward for undertaking an activity that has previously been enjoyed for its own sake will diminish intrinsic interest in that activity. This detrimental effect of rewards on subsequent intrinsic interest has since been confirmed in numerous studies involving children of all ages and adults, with respect to a variety of activities and different kinds of rewards (Lepper and Gilovich, 1981; Lepper, 1983).

What is the explanation for the over-justification effect? One possibility suggested by Lepper is that the promise of a reward causes children to shift their focus of attention from the features of the activity that make it interesting to the hope of receiving the reward. A related reason is that the knowledge of a reward adversely affects the children's feelings of personal competence in that they attribute their success to the external incentives rather than to their personal efforts and ability. Rewards thus seem to make children feel less interested in doing the activity for its own sake and also less in control of their success. Lepper also points to evidence that suggests that the desire to receive a reward can also cause children to 'play safe', so impairing creative, insightful responses and encouraging the choice of less challenging problems.

However, rewards can be educationally productive if certain conditions are met. First of all it helps if the reward is contingent on the achievement of certain standards, and not just on simple engagement in the activity (Boggiano and Ruble, 1979). A second condition is the provision of feedback to children about their success. In a recent study involving 9- to 10-year-olds (Boggiano, Ruble and Pittman, 1982), rewards by themselves were found to diminish intrinsic interest in a moderately difficult task, thus demonstrating the 'over-justification effect'. However, when the rewards were accompanied by feedback concerning the children's competence, interest in the activity was enchanced. Presumably the feedback provided the children with the means to deepen their insights into the problem. According to Deci (1975), we are most likely to become intrinsically motivated when we are enabled to accept challenge. Thus teachers can help children to enjoy learning for its own sake, and thus prevent classroom disruption, by (a) providing tasks which are moderately challenging, and also (b) providing regular feedback concerning each pupil's level of performance. Rewards may help in this task, but are no substitute for challenge and feedback.

THE EFFECTS OF PRAISE

Some experiments with children (e.g. Anderson, Monoogian and Reznick, 1976; Swann and Pittman, 1977) have demonstrated how verbal praise, as distinct from tangible rewards, can enhance rather than reduce intrinsic interest in an activity. Undoubtedly, the reason lies in its facility to provide information for the pupil. It seems, too, that cues concerning performance of a pupil can have vicarious effects on other members of a class, who pick up specific information that allows them to assess their own performance (Morine-Dershimer, 1982).

However, as with tangible rewards, an indiscriminate use of praise can be detrimental in terms of the educational interests of pupils. Why should this be so? First of all, a distinction needs to be made between specific and general praise. The problem with general praise statements, such as 'Good!' or 'Well done!' is that, although they may make the pupil feel good, they do not tell him just what behaviour is being admired. Kanouse, Gumpert and Canavan-Gumpert (1981) cite an unpublished experiment by Scheer in which fifty 10- to 11-year-olds were asked to sort fifty-four cards containing an assortment of symbols in various colours. During the exercise, some of the children were given praise that described clearly what was good about their sorting strategy (e.g. 'Great, I like the way you are sorting by shape'), others were given unembellished praise for every three cards sorted (e.g. 'Great!'), whilst a control group was given no praise at all. The results showed that the children who were given the descriptive praise were more successful than the other two groups. Indeed, whether the children were given unembellished praise or no praise at all made no difference to their performance. Yet, according to the results of a study by Anderson *et al.* (1979), teachers tend to give general rather than specific praise; and Brophy *et al.* (1976) found that teachers of 7- to 10-year-olds, whilst frequently praising children for having completed a task, rarely commented on the quality of the work when they did so.

A second kind of distinction that is important to make is between praising the pupil and showing approval of the pupil's work. Praise that is focused on the pupil as a person (e.g. 'You're a good boy!') draws attention to the personal relationship between the child and the teacher, and this can have one of two unfortunate consequences. Where a pupil already values the teacher's authority, such praise may induce feelings of personal indebtedness, the child then feeling that praise has to be earned to maintain a sense of personal worth. Where a pupil does not value the teacher's authority, praise directed at the person may produce feelings of embarrassment and be resented since it may undermine the status the pupil enjoys with his peers. On the other hand, praise that is directed to the pupil's work rather than to the pupil as a person will communicate to the child the value placed on the activity and the recognition that the performance comes up to an acceptable standard. The child is then more likely to gain satisfaction from the achievement itself rather than be dependent upon his personal relationship with the teacher.

Thirdly, as Brophy (1981) has shown in a detailed review of the literature, teachers will often use praise inappropriately. For instance, they often fail to make favourable comment *contingent* upon the desired behaviour. They will also sometimes praise pupils who give incorrect answers! This may provide encouragement to less able children, but, in so far as pupils often see through such tactics, the effect is likely to be counter-productive. Nor do teachers always appear credible when praising. The Brophy *et al.* (1976) study showed that teachers' non-verbal gestures often negated the positive intentions of praise. Again, praise-comments may be frequently neutralized by subsequent negative criticism since teachers in general find it easier to identify inappropriate than appropriate behaviour.

Finally, children may have different praise 'needs' according to their age and sex. Those in the infant school generally have an insatiable appetite for praise because of their greater dependence on adult authority. Amongst seven-year-olds, girls appear to be more anxious for adult approval but boys for peer approval (Davie, Butler and Goldstein, 1972). Burns (1978) found that 11- to 15-year-olds in general seemed to have a medium or low regard for praise; however, praise given quietly by the teacher rather than publicly in front of other pupils was quite highly valued by girls. The work of Dweck and her colleagues (1978) suggests that, although teachers do adopt different praise styles according to whether they are addressing boys or girls, this is not due to a perception of the pupils' needs, but to stereotyped views about gender roles. In this study, it appeared that, for academic achievement, boys get praised somewhat more than girls, who are more likely to receive favourable comments for matters of form, such as neatness. If these findings are typical of teachers' behaviour, it could be that this gender differentiation in teachers' use of praise contributes to the greater self-confidence that boys, in general, seem to possess in relation to academic pursuits.

BEHAVIOUR MODIFICATION

The behaviourist approach to child management

Rewards and praise play a central role in behaviour modification, which is an approach to child management based upon behavioural science. The techniques are derived from learning theory, developed and applied to the teaching situation by B. F. Skinner, who argues that inappropriate behaviour can and should be changed by systematically controlling environmental factors. By behaviour in this context is meant overt, observable behaviour. The individual's intentions and thoughts about the rightness of his behaviour are of no account.

In a book called *Beyond Freedom and Dignity* (1973), Skinner argued that the environmental factors behaviourists investigate in the science of human behaviour are 'taking over the explanatory functions previously assigned to personalities, states of mind, feelings, traits of character, purposes, and intentions. ... We have moved forward by dispossessing autonomous man' (Skinner, 1973, p. 24). This echoes an earlier comment that 'the hypothesis that man is not free is essential to the application of scientific method to the study of human behaviour' (Skinner, 1953, p. 447). It is important to recognize this standpoint when evaluating behaviour modification techniques in schools, since, in an educational context, the underlying motivation that lies behind an act is usually considered to be of importance. What matters in behavioural strategies is the shaping of the child's behaviour towards a predetermined goal, largely by a process of operant conditioning. The term 'operant' infers that the child operates on his environment, and the term 'conditioning' infers that his operant behaviours can be modified by systematically changing the environment.

In the ordinary way, a teacher might deal with misbehaviour by reasoning or reprimanding. This sort of strategy implies that children are able to reflect upon their actions in a rational kind of way, and to change their behaviour accordingly. But in behaviour modification, the notion that children deserve praise or blame, or that they can reason about their behaviour, is not considered important – at least by those of the 'hard' Skinnerian school. Instead, the child's behaviour is seen to be shaped as a consequence of his experiences. In this sense most behaviour is seen to be learned, and can be unlearned and changed through altering the environment in which the child operates. Typically, the unwanted behaviour is ignored while the desired behaviour is rewarded (positive reinforcement). Although some form of punishment might also be used in the negative reinforcement of undesired behaviour, this is frequently avoided because it effectively reinforces attention-seeking behaviour (see Chapter 7). As the child comes to act more in the desired manner, the teacher then uses rewards more sparingly, thus phasing out the behaviour modification schedule.

Behaviour modification programmes differ in their design, but the following five steps can be regarded as typical:

Step 1: The teacher pinpoints exactly the behaviour she wants, e.g. 'staying in seats' or 'speaking in turn without calling out'.

Step 2: The teacher makes a record of the incidence of these behaviours over a period of a few days, e.g. by constructing a tally sheet, and calculates the average frequency. For this to be objective, the behaviour must be defined with the utmost precision. Thus 'out of seat' might be defined as 'occasions when the child's bottom is not in contact with any part of the seat for a period longer than three seconds' (Merrett, 1985, pp. 7–8). This establishes baseline data which will be used to evaluate the intervention programme.

Step 3: The teacher systematically gives positive reinforcement (praise and/or reward) contingently and consistently upon the occurrences of the behaviour she wants, the theory being that individuals will repeat the acts they find immediately rewarding and avoid repeating acts that have aversive consequences (Thorndike's 'law of effect'). Sometimes a 'token economy' is employed, the child being given a token such as a coloured disc. This can later be exchanged for money or a tangible reward such as sweets, treats or the opportunity to engage in a favourite pastime. A further refinement is a contract system, which can be employed with the reward system; this involves an arrangement whereby the child and the teacher, and maybe the parents too, agree that certain ways of behaving will result in certain consequences. It is important to avoid giving rewards in a predictable way: like the gambler at the races, the child will find the programme compelling precisely because pay-off is unpredictable. It is also important in this experimental period to avoid the unwitting reinforcement of unwanted behaviour through thoughtless use of reprimand or punishment, which may be rewarding for attention-seeking children. If the teacher has observed that the behaviour she wants to change has tended to be prompted by certain events, it may also be possible to change the behaviour by changing the antecedent event.

Step 4: After a period, the behaviour of the children is re-evaluated by constructing another tally chart, and the results are compared with the baseline data.

Step 5: If the results of Step 4 are encouraging, the reinforcement schedule is phased out in controlled manner.

Thus the strategies are more systematized than those ordinarily practised by teachers. All teachers praise and reward from time to time, and some schools use special devices such as stars and house points. But such attempts at positive reinforcement usually lack consistency, and the potentially beneficial effects are often nullified by the proportionately greater use of negative comment and punishment. In behavioural strategies, reinforcement contingencies are carefully controlled, and the effects are monitored and evaluated against baseline data. The approach thus tries to emulate a scientific experiment.

Behaviour modification in ordinary classrooms

Behaviour modification is quite widely practised in the United States, but much less so in Britain, except in special units or special schools. However, at the Centre of Child Study in the University of Birmingham, Kevin Wheldall, Frank Merrett and others are encouraging the use of behavioural methods in general school contexts as well as in clinical and social work. They have also recently helped to found a new publishing company called Positive Products to produce behaviourist materials. To further their aim, the team at Birmingham have produced the BAT-pack (Behavioural Approach to Teaching), which was funded by the Schools Council in 1981–3, to teach behaviourist classroom techniques that will be useful to teachers in managing all children and not only those who are 'problems'. Six one-hour courses involve the use of videos of classroom lessons. As they observe a teacher's behaviour in the video sequences, course members tally the approving and disapproving responses given to children's behaviour, and then do likewise in their own classrooms. These experiences help the teachers to become more aware of the style of their interaction with children. Course members are then asked to generate ideas for positive teacher behaviours and to practise these. In this way, the focus of classroom behaviour is shifted away from the pupils and their naughtiness to the teacher and her managing skills. The Birmingham team believe that this skills-approach works best if all the staff of a school are involved and not just an individual teacher.

Merrett (1981, 1985) has produced a series of examples to describe the way in which behaviour modification has been introduced into the regular classroom situation. These cover all ages and a range of behaviours, from the improvement of eating behaviour in a nursery class, through controlling a noisy, restless class of 10- to 11-year-olds, to increasing the on-task behaviour in mathematics lessons of pupils aged 14–15 in a secondary school. Work in special schools has also been reported by Merrett (1981).

An experiment conducted by Merrett and Wheldall (1978) can be used to illustrate the kind of work being promulgated by the Birmingham centre. A young woman graduate teacher, who had just successfully completed her probationary year, was finding difficulty in gaining and maintaining class order with her unstreamed class of thirty-two 10- to 11-year-olds. Most of the children were below average in general ability and attainment. The teacher agreed to try out a special schedule, involving the use of a cassette tape that gave out a ping at irregular intervals but at an average of one per minute. To establish baseline data about the children's behaviour, the teacher would note the behaviour of the target child, as previously determined by a random method, whenever the ping sounded. At the next ping, another child's behaviour was noted, and so on. The teacher then agreed that her goal should be to reduce noise and movement in terms of three rules, which were explained to the children on a wall chart as follows: (1) We stay in our seats while working; (2) We get on quietly with our work; (3) We try not to interrupt. During the intervention programme, a house point was given to each child at the target table whenever the ping sounded from the cassette player, together with verbal praise and a warm smile. After five weeks, the programme was phased out by rewarding the pupils on half the occasions.

In evaluating this intervention programme by comparing the children's behaviour with the baseline data, it was found that the main problem now was passive inattention rather than loud talking or movement round the room. On-task behaviour increased from 44 per cent to 77 per cent and later 88 per cent. The quantity of work also increased during the experimental period (from five to thirteen words per minute) and without adversely affecting the number of spelling errors. The teacher herself felt that she had gained confidence in controlling the class. At the same time, she had found the monitoring and recording somewhat of a hindrance to her teaching, had 'felt silly' about putting up the wall chart of rules, and was reluctant, in spite of the results, to make more use of verbal reinforcements and to reduce her disapproving comments. Twelve of the thirteen children who gave comments approved of the programme, mainly because they liked earning house points. Unfortunately, we are not told the long-term effects.

This experiment illustrates a number of features that are characteristic of behaviourist strategies. First, the programme demands meticulous preparation and monitoring, as well as patience and determination. Merrett and Wheldall (1986) have recently described a reliable observation schedule they have devised to help in this process. Secondly, it requires a combination of clear specification of rules, ignoring unwanted behaviour, and rewarding and praising good behaviour. Thirdly, it can have dramatic effects in improving observable behaviour. Fourthly, it is the extrinsic factors that are motivational rather than intrinsic interest in the activity.

Is behaviour modification a good thing?

A mass of evidence has been produced to demonstrate that behavioural strategies do change children's observed behaviour. On this criterion, they can be of considerable help to teachers who are experiencing behavioural problems with children. Because behaviour is seen to be dependent on the environmental contingencies, behaviour modification avoids placing unfair blame on children, or explaining away their behaviour by throwing all the responsibility on features of the home background. Attention is therefore focused on the social environment of the classroom and the teacher actions that influence behaviour. Teachers are encouraged to look for positive responses in pupils and generally to capitalize on their good behaviour, rather than to dwell on their bad behaviour. Further, if the strategies are used in regular classroom situations, they may obviate the necessity to remove children to special classes or units.

None the less, behaviour modification is controversial in a number of respects, particularly when used in the regular classroom with ordinary children, rather than in clinical settings with children who have proved unresponsive to normal management. Some of the problems relate more to potential abuse of the technology or to technical difficulties, while others raise more fundamental questions relating to the concept of human behaviour on which behaviour modification is based, ethical considerations and educational criteria.

Technical considerations

Even the advocates of behaviourist approaches recognize the difficulties entailed in carrying out a behaviour modification programme, and the importance of training. As we saw in the example given at the end of the last section, the techniques are not easy to acquire, and most teachers find it difficult to be spontaneous and genuine in praising a child whose behaviour is displeasing and threatening. O'Leary and O'Leary (1977) accordingly suggest that a teacher should start off with a child she quite likes, and try to help herself by smiling as she praises, varying the volume and intensity of her voice and enlisting the assistance of a colleague to observe and advise. A lecture course and reading are not sufficient to become proficient in the use of behavioural techniques: special training is needed, such as that provided in the BAT-pack courses.

Harrop (1980a, b) has detailed a number of technical difficulties that arise in observing and recording children's behaviour. One point he makes is that, however carefully a behaviour is defined, subjective judgements are inescapable. Apart from problems involved in such tasks as determining 'at what level of intensity does "pupil shouting out" become "pupil muttering to himself"' (Harrop, 1980a, p. 159), the observer is forced to ignore well-motivated actions which come within the definition. For instance, there is a difference between shouting out abusive comments and shouting out comments meant to be helpful – but such distinctions would involve referring to the child's intentions.

Berger (1979) has written of the dangers of behaviour modification becoming a mindless technology in the hands of those who adopt a simplistic view of the exercise as a result of inadequate training and supervision. He points, for instance, to the dangers 'which will persist while proponents of behaviour modification try to resolve complex problems by means of a few technical tricks' (p. 419), so that if the techniques are tried and fail the approach itself may be mistakenly rejected, or the teacher may suffer yet further feelings of incompetence. Berger stresses the importance of recognizing the strategies essentially as means and not as ends in themselves, and emphasizes the care that must be given to the fading out process.

Theoretical problems

It is often said that behaviourist approaches, by concentrating on what can be seen and disregarding underlying mental states that cannot be empirically verified, can overlook the 'real' source of the problem. As we have argued in earlier chapters, features of the classroom situation are significant determinants of pupil behaviour, but other factors are also important and may be more so. As Berger (1982) points out, the source of some behaviour difficulties is poor motor co-ordination, specific learning problems or emotional turmoil because of situations in the home. It would therefore do no service to these children to act as if behaviour modification was the only legitimate approach to their behaviour problems when other influences, albeit not open to scientific measurement, seem to be at work.

A fundamental shortcoming of behavioural theory is brought out in a paper by Burwood and Brady (1984), who warn against teachers unthinkingly adopting a deterministic view of human nature. Because behaviourists emphasize the causal role played by environmental forces, the distinction is not made between voluntary and involuntary behaviour. The authors argue that 'unless one wants to be a consistent determinist ... the assumption must be that children are capable of reasoning, rational choice and self-direction, unless there is some specific circumstance that makes a child incapable of rational thought' (pp. 112–13). The point here is that the model of man behaviourists defend seems to deny people their essential humanity, i.e. their ability to choose and make decisions to change their behaviour. Looked at in this way, rewards are not external causes of behavioural change, as behaviourists maintain, but rather constitute one sort of reason a person may have for acting. However, people have other reasons for behaving as they do. In one investigation, children as young as four were found to give many sorts of reasons for their actions (Williams and Williams, 1970). While some of these, like rewards, were based on expediency or were otherwise self-related, others showed a recognition of the feelings and needs of other people. Teachers who rely on behaviour modification as a general strategy would be ignoring the ability of most children to reflect upon their behaviour and to respond to reasoning. Behaviour modification thus has a place where a child seems impervious to reason, but it is less defensible as a first resort.

Ethical considerations

An important criticism often made of behavioural strategies is that the child is being coerced and manipulated, albeit by attractive methods. To this extent he is not being regarded as a person, with distinctive centres of consciousness, feelings, and purposes. As Paul Nash (1966, p. 109) has pointed out, control that is pleasant may be just as authoritarian as control that is harsh: 'Coercive authority uses physical force: manipulative authority uses psychological persuasion. ... Manipulative authority is more gentle, more subtle, and usually more pleasant: but it is important to realize that it does not necessarily imply any greater respect for the person who is manipulated.'

Poteet (1974), himself an advocate of behaviour modification in appropriate circumstances, has acknowledged criticisms that the strategies do not take account of a pupil's self-awareness and his values, and that there is the constant danger of self-expression being stifled in the interests of management and conformity. Although believing that children who do not find life rewarding can be helped to develop a more positive self-concept through behavioural techniques, Poteet emphasizes the need for the teacher to regard reinforcement by means of tangible incentives as a means to the ultimate end of self-reinforcement.

In a recent publication, Cheesman and Watts (1985) have preferred to use the term 'positive behaviour management' rather than 'behaviour modification'. Their argument seems to reflect the idea that people are managed, machines are modified. The term 'modification' implies that change is brought about mechanistically, and seems to ignore the importance of facilitating *cognitive* changes in the pupil: 'We use the term management because this implies at least an element of cooperation between the manager and those managed. ... In our approach the term 'management' implies the active involvement of the child in bringing about behaviour change, and regular consultation and discussion with him about the way we are going' (p. 6). Cheesman and Watts therefore strongly advise teachers to negotiate behavioural management programmes with the pupils concerned: 'The pupil becomes a partner in the process, helping to decide on both the direction of change and the method used to bring it about. It is essential that behaviour change be seen as a partnership' (p. 7).

Educational considerations

In an earlier section, we referred to studies that have demonstrated how material rewards extrinsic to a task can undermine a child's wish to engage in the activity for its own sake. The danger of producing this 'over-justification effect' would seem to be a real one in classrooms where behaviour modification is used with children who already have some intrinsic interest in the work. This problem is particularly likely to occur when behavioural strategies are used with whole classes, since presumably some children are gaining some intrinsic satisfaction in curriculum activities. Behaviour modification programmes are often evaluated in terms of 'on-task' behaviour. If this means judging behaviour simply in terms of *engagement* in a task and not the quality of its performance, there is particular danger, as we saw earlier, of invoking the 'over-justification effect'. Thus, in solving a managerial problem, the teacher is at risk in creating a motivational one!

Another educational danger is the possibility of a teacher using behaviour modification as a cloak for inappropriate teaching. Whilst interesting activities are not a sufficient condition for orderly classroom behaviour, they are a necessary one for education to take place. As Brown (1982, p. 51) has pointed out, 'It would be rather unfortunate if skilful control of reinforcing contingencies obfuscated the fact that the children found the work dreary, inappropriate or unimaginative.' Ryan (1979, p. 134) puts it even more forcefully when he foresees 'the possibility that the use of this technology can encourage some teachers to remain in the profession when they might be suited for other work'. Of course, this in itself is not a criticism of behaviour modification but of its abuse. None the less, there remains the danger of teachers believing that they have achieved something educationally when their success is simply managerial. In short, behaviour modification is no substitute for a sound and imaginative curriculum and effective teacher–pupil relationships.

A further point mentioned by Ryan (1979) relates to the importance of providing opportunities for children to respond to unexpected changing circumstances. Such a capability depends on us being able to try out a variety of behaviours in childhood. However, some behaviours may not be given a chance to develop if they are stifled through arrangements that put a premium on conformity and focus on a restricted range of actions, however attractive the process may be to the children. Again, this is more a criticism of the abuse of behaviour modification, but it warns against setting up the system as a panacea for all ills.

A fundamental educational shortcoming of behavioural approaches is that they ignore the way in which the child construes his behaviour. As Dearden (1984, p. 142) has argued, 'What someone is doing and why he is doing it are unintelligible without reference to certain of his beliefs, desires, intentions, experiences, imaginings, attitudes, sentiments, or his general understanding. To see what someone is doing and why he is doing it is therefore a work of constructive interpretation.' From an educational point of view, helping children to reason about their behaviour is vital to their moral development. For instance, it is not at all clear whether it is possible to say that, as a result of behavioural strategies, a child has stopped 'stealing' or has just stopped 'taking things from other people', since whether or not a person is 'stealing' depends not only on what can be observed but how that person conceives property and ownership, and his attitude towards social rules regarding these concepts (Pring, 1981). Attitudes and conceptual understanding cannot be observed directly, but are inferred from observations.

It is thus a matter of some seriousness if teachers assess pupils' social actions only on the basis of what can be observed, without also attending to the way the pupils come to think about their behaviour in relation to others. The crucial question to ask about teachers' attempts to change behaviour in an educational context is this: Does the approach not only seem to get the child acting more acceptably but also help him to view his behaviour and those of others in a different light?

So, is behaviour modification a good thing? At the beginning of this section we mentioned a number of its strengths, in particular its propensity to encourage the teacher to look out for and acknowledge good behaviour rather than to reprimand bad behaviour. Some criticisms of behaviour modification are more concerned with its abuse or misuse than with its status as a system that has application in educational contexts. However, a number of fundamental weaknesses have also been suggested. In particular, we have questioned whether human 'behaviour' *can* be defined without reference to the person's mental functioning, since assessment of what a person is doing involves knowledge of his intentions. In this connection, we have also questioned the propriety of shaping children's overt behaviour without attending to their understanding and have noted the 'softer' and more human concept of behavioural 'management' advocated by Cheesman and Watts (1985). On the practical side, we have noted the dangers of teachers using behavioural strategies to disguise their problems in relating to pupils effectively, in developing a sound curriculum and teaching methods and in assuming that intrinsic motivation will automatically come about as a result of extrinsic motivation. It is vital, if schooling is to be about education, and not just management and instruction, that pupils are enabled to develop and deepen their interest in activities for their own sake, and, for this to happen, careful consideration needs to be given to the *teaching* arrangements. As far as classroom management is concerned, an approach that involves the kinds of preventative strategies identified by Kounin (1970) and others, outlined in Chapter 6, should be tried before resorting to behavioural techniques, with their potentially detrimental side-effects.

All that said, when other approaches have failed behaviour modification does have an important place in enabling children to adapt to social conventions and, indeed, to become happier individuals. In relation to eradicating undesirable habits such as nail-biting, aimless wandering around the room or shouting out, behaviour modification has a useful role since the pupil's intrinsic interest in such activities is of little importance. But it is a very different matter when curriculum activities and moral behaviour are involved. Behaviour modification is controversial with respect to those activities in which 'behaviour' is only superficially considered if no reference is made to the pupil's understanding and attitudes. For this reason the ability of behaviour modification to contribute to children's educational and moral growth must be questioned.

FURTHER READING

Brophy, J. (1981) Teacher praise: a functional analysis, *Review of Educational Analysis*, Vol. 51, No. 1, pp. 5–32.
(An exhaustive review of the research on praise.)
Cheeseman, P. L. and Watts, P. E. (1985) *Positive Behaviour Management: a Manual for Teachers*, Croom Helm, London.
(A very clear book that emphasizes the need for a less mechanistic approach to behavioural management.)
Lepper, M. R. (1983) Extrinsic reward and intrinsic motivation: implications for the classroom, in J. M. Levine and M. C. Wang (eds.) *Teacher and Student*

Perceptions: Implications for Learning, Erlbaum, Hillsdale, New Jersey.
(Reviews the research concerned with the 'over-justification effect'.)

Merrett, F. E. (1985) *Encouragement Works Better than Punishment*, Positive Products, Birmingham.
(Outlines twenty-six case studies that illustrate the application of behaviourist techniques in the classroom.)

Wheldall, K. and Merrett, F. E. (1984) *Positive Teaching: the Behavioural Approach*, Allen & Unwin, London.
(A detailed account of behaviour modification and its application in English classrooms.)

8
PUNISHMENT IN SCHOOL

In this chapter we will consider two main issues. The first concerns the place of punishment in *social control*. This will involve a discussion of the effects and effectiveness of punishment used to train children to behave acceptably, and will be followed by specific attention to problems surrounding the use of corporal punishment. The second issue concerns the contribution punishment might make to the *process of education*. This will involve a discussion on the possibility that punishment, if used with discrimination, can help children to feel responsible for the consequences of their actions and to reason about rules that should govern behaviour. The first issue is therefore mainly about the role of punishment in shaping children's observable behaviour, while the second is mainly about its place in children's cognitive and moral growth.

PUNISHMENT AS A MEANS OF SOCIAL CONTROL

The view of most teachers is that some punishment is necessary for deterrent purposes, and in this they are supported in law. Teachers are said to stand *in loco parentis* while children are in their care. This implies that, in the interests of an orderly community, a member of school staff would be justified in using the same amount of restraint as a reasonable parent would honestly consider necessary. Because punishment necessarily involves the infliction of pain or unpleasantness, many people would agree with the philosopher Jeremy Bentham (1748-1832) that the *only* justification of punishment is in terms of its social expediency and unique deterrent power:

'But all punishment is a mischief: all punishment is in itself evil ... It ought only to be admitted in as far as it promises to exclude some greater evil' (*Principles of Morals and Legislation*, Ch. 13, Sect. 2).

Bentham's position was a utilitarian one. This means to say that punishment is justified only in so far as it can be demonstrated to be in the interests of a law-abiding society. It would therefore be wrong to inflict punishment if it was unlikely to bring about greater social order, or if it produced problems worse than those it was designed to prevent, or if the wrongdoing could be prevented by some other means. It is essentially a means to an end and has no value in itself.

Applying this argument to the schools situation, Peters (1966) acknowledges the force of the utilitarian claim in so far as the existence of punishment in the background may be a necessary condition for the maintenance of classroom order, the upholding of rules that are morally important or are enshrined in law and the general smooth running of the school. At the same time he recognizes that punishment 'is one of the most potent devices for bringing about estrangement' (p. 273) and is 'at best a necessary nuisance' (p. 279).

However, although punishment in school may be intended to deter children from behaving unacceptably, whether it actually does so is another matter. That punishing can sometimes have an immediate impact in controlling a child is not in dispute, as common experience will testify. What is more problematic is the long-term influence on the individual and the general pervasive influence of punishment inside and outside school. Certainly the evidence suggests that there are good reasons for doubting the efficacy of punishment as a general means of social control. This is partly because, for punishment to be optimally effective, certain conditions must be satisfied. A second reason concerns the personality of the child who receives punishment. Thirdly, punishment may produce certain undesirable side-effects. Each of these issues will now be considered in turn.

Optimal conditions for the effectiveness of punishment

From their studies in clinical settings, learning theorists have maintained that punishment is more likely to be effective if it is administered consistently and at the onset of misbehaviour. Both these conditions, however, are rarely satisfied in normal school settings.

In an experiment that manipulated the consistency of punishment, Parke and Deur (1972) invited ninety 8- to 10-year-olds to put on boxing gloves and punch a large doll. The researchers demonstrated that the children who were most effectively deterred from their 'aggressive' behaviour were those who were 'punished' by being consistently subjected to the noise of a loud buzzer upon punching the doll, rather than those who either received the same treatment half the time and a reward of marbles the other half, or who were neither punished nor rewarded. The researchers went on to argue that punishment is often less effective in real-life situations because of the erratic manner in which it is characteristically employed.

There are problems, however, in drawing conclusions for everyday behaviour from studies involving highly contrived situations. For one thing, the term 'punishment', as used in laboratory-type experiments, does not have the same connotations as in real-life situations because the experiments are not concerned with *misbehaviour* as such, still less with actions that are morally *wrong*. In the above experiment, the 'aggression' was artificially induced and the children had not done anything for which they should have felt guilty. Another problem is that the form of 'punishment' in such experiments is hardly typical of normal school practice. Furthermore 'success' is measured purely in terms of the suppressive effects of an aversive stimulus and does not involve any consideration of changes in children's understanding of their behaviour.

Of course, children who are subjected to erratic and arbitrary responses, whereby an action is condoned one day but attracts punishment the next, will obviously be confused about what is acceptable and unacceptable behaviour. The oft-quoted remark that 'children need to know where they are' therefore contains a good deal of sense. However, the consistency argument often fails to make the important distinction between an erratic and a flexible use of punishment. Although punishment will not be effective if applied unpredictably or arbitrarily, it is unlikely to be effective in the long term if applied inexorably upon a particular offence being committed. This is because, as Nash (1966) has pointed out, consistent punishment without regard to the child's perception of the circumstances may serve only to suppress unwanted behaviour when its threat is present, thus encouraging a dependence upon external restraint. On the other hand, if administered discriminatively, though not erratically, punishment may successfully prompt the culprit to raise questions about his conduct and ultimately stand in self-judgement.

In relation to the findings from his South Wales project, Reynolds (1976) argued that inflexible punishment styles simply serve to alienate pupils, especially in those areas of behaviour in which adolescents believe they should have autonomy. Teachers in secondary schools who experienced the least behaviour problems with low-aspiring, working-class pupils were those who seemed to adopt an unofficial 'truce' with pupils in their stance towards regulations about eating chewing gum and smoking. In one of the schools with the least conformist behaviour, staff on break or lunchtime duty would patrol the premises *looking for* children who chewed gum or smoked. When found, the culprits were invariably reprimanded and usually hit round the head and arms before being told to put the gum in the bin or surrender the cigarettes, and they were sometimes caned as well. In contrast, teachers in the schools with the more conforming behaviour refused to make an issue out of these rules and were more discriminating in their use of punishment. In contrast to teachers in schools that did not adopt a 'truce' regime, they found that high rates of punishment were unnecessary, and that a simple telling-off or mild punishment was usually sufficient to secure conformity.

It is important, of course, not to confuse the 'truce', which Reynolds identifies with the more successful schools, with permissiveness. The findings from this study do not imply that rules should never be enforced or that punishment should not be used; rather it is that the school authority should not seem perverse and insensitive to what the pupil perceives as just and reasonable. Teachers who regard their relationships with pupils as involving a power struggle between 'us', who know what's right, and 'them', who don't, will invite hostility; and the more inexorably and severely teachers punish, the less effective will be verbal reprimand and mild forms of punishment.

Apart from the consistency factor, the timing of punishment is also held to affect success in extinguishing unacceptable behaviour. From the results of another laboratory-type experiment, in which young children were conditioned to refrain from playing with certain toys, Aronfreed (1976) argued that a child who is punished as he *begins* to act in an unwanted way will subsequently invoke the feelings associated with the punishment when he is next tempted to behave similarly, i.e. the punishment will have helped the child to develop an inhibitory conscience. But if administered after the offence, when the child may already be feeling guilty, the punishment will result in anxiety being associated with that guilt; rather than have a deterrent effect, it will increase guilt feelings and build up resentment. If this hypothesis has application to normal situations, the timing of punishment could be a significant factor in reducing the child's temptation to misbehave another time. In classrooms, of course, teachers cannot be so consistently observant as in experimental situations, and even if they were they might well think it unwise to resort to punishment before more positive measures have been tried. However, if punishment does seem in order, it may be more efficacious, circumstances permitting, to wait until the child begins to repeat the act and then punish him at that point. Another possibility, suggested by Burton (1976), is to verbally reinstate the stimulus conditions under which misbehaviour occurred and then administer punishment at the appropriate point in the recreated account.

The personality of the child

Children vary in the degree to which they appear to respond positively to punishment. Thus personality differences may be a factor that affects the success of punishment as a means of training children to behave acceptably. Eysenck (1970) has proposed that, under identical stimulating conditions, arousal levels in the cortex of the brain are higher in introverts than in extroverts. If this is true, then introverts will be more susceptible to conditioning, and therefore more likely to respond both to positive and negative stimuli. Punishment is thus more likely to 'work' with children who are extremely introverted than with those who are extremely extroverted.

The undesirable side-effects of punishment

It is probably the unintended consequences of punishment that, most of all, should warn teachers against resorting to punishment lightly. Put shortly, it appears that, however effective punishment may appear in the short term, adults who engage in a punitive style of child management may unwittingly be instrumental in producing undesirable behaviours, feelings and dispositions in children.

First of all, because punishment represents a confrontation between the culprit and the punisher, it teaches children not what they ought to do but what to refrain from doing, and in whose presence. For these reasons, Skinner (1973) has argued that punishment may simply teach children avoidance tactics and encourage them to behave acceptably only when the adult concerned is present.

Secondly, in cases where children misbehave because they feel impelled to seek attention, punishment can reinforce the very behaviour it is meant to extinguish. This is because the pupil's attention-seeking behaviour has paid off in successfully eliciting a response from the teacher, and sometimes the other pupils too: 'A student misbehaves to annoy his teacher or to be admired by his peers when he takes punishment. If the teacher's attention is reinforcing, unwanted responses which attract attention are strengthened' (Skinner, 1968, p. 190). Seeing the teacher upset can also be rewarding for some children. Teachers are therefore sometimes tempted to ignore misbehaviour rather than punish the offender. Yet pretending the behaviour has not occurred will not make it go away. For as Foss (1965, p. 8 has pointed out, 'a teacher may be fairly successful in ignoring attention-seeking behaviour, but the rest of the class will not be, and will provide reinforcement – probably irregularly, and therefore (as animal studies have shown) more potently'. It is for this reason (as we saw in the previous chapter) that behaviourists recommend strategies that involve rewarding children for their good behaviour as well as ignoring them for their bad behaviour.

A teacher's loud voice in reprimanding children can also help to maintain attention-seeking behaviour since the offender becomes the focus of attention of the whole class. Loud reprimands also disrupt the work of the class, and a constant loud nagging may create tension that leads to verbal abuse and confrontation (Rutter et al., 1979). In an experiment by O'Leary et al. (1970), based in a natural setting, teachers of children whose behaviour was disruptive were asked to use primarily soft reprimands, audible only to the offender. The frequency of misbehaviour was then found to decline. When the teachers were asked to return to their customary loud reprimands, the disruption increased. The researchers suggest that the ideal combination would be frequent praise, soft reprimands and only very occasional loud reprimands.

Thirdly, punishment can fuel disaffection with school life. This may be so not only in relation to physical punishment (considered in the next section), but also when children are 'shown up' through devices such as sarcasm or public embarrassment. From his observations, Woods (1975) concluded that when children are denigrated in front of the class, they experience an assault on their identity and feel confused. The teacher's action may have a dramatic shockwave impact, but in the end it breeds scepticism and bitterness, leading to a destruction of the self.

Fourthly, punishment in some circumstances exposes children to an inappropriate model of adult behaviour that they may copy. As Wright (1971) has pointed out, while pupils can be vicariously conditioned by seeing an offender punished, the effect will be dependent upon the degree to which the pupils regard the punishment as just or unjust. Wright goes on to warn that teachers can, without realizing it, set an inappropriate model if they 'imperceptibly slide into the habit of more or less continually setting an example of bad manners, injustice, bullying, or even mild sadism' (p. 240). According to social learning theory (Bandura, 1977), children are prompted to behave aggressively through imitating the aggressive behaviour of adults who are perceived as powerful. It is important here to remember that aggression can be unwittingly fostered not only directly, through the experience of receiving aggressive punishment, but also vicariously, through witnessing or knowing about others who are being punished. Fortunately, observational learning in punishment situations can be turned to advantage. If the teacher is seen to hold back her natural impulses to act aggressively when under stress, an appropriate model of adult behaviour is being provided for the pupils to imitate.

Finally, children who are subjected to regular punishment may be prevented from developing the virtues of kindness and sensitivity to the needs of others. To understand this, it is necessary to say something about the growth of conscience. Within the framework of psychoanalytic psychology, children in the nursery years take on aspects of the personality of those adults with whom they have close dealings, especially parents. When a child is punished or rebuked by an adult, he builds up aggression towards that adult as a result of his frustration. If he expresses this aggression outwardly, he finds he receives more punishment. The child therefore has to learn how to restrain his natural aggressive impulses. This he does by turning his aggression in upon himself, identifying with the parent and so reducing anxiety over potential punishment. According to this view, then, punishment would help the child to develop an intropunitive conscience.

However, if punishment is frequent or severe, it may influence the degree to which children develop a conscience based more on a sympathetic concern for others than on fear of detection or a wish to conform. Hoffman (1970) found that twelve-year-old children who were compassionate, who showed a concern for the consequences of their behaviour on others and who recognized extenuating circumstances, were more likely to have parents who varied their means of control, who suggested means of reparation wherever possible, who expressed affection frequently and who were less punitive. Comparable findings emerged in Light's (1979) work with four-year-olds. Pre-school children who were beginning to recognize and adjust to other people's points of view tended to be those whose mothers refrained from adopting a generally punitive style of management, preferring to treat the child on a personal level. It would seem, therefore, that the development of a strong, altruistic conscience depends on the child's perception of his parents as warm and loving. Pupils who are punished frequently at home, and who also perceive the teacher as someone who resorts easily to punishment in order to ensure implicit obedience, will have their attention focused on the personal power of adults in authority. When punished, they may then sense a feeling of rejection that in turn may impede the development of a conscience based upon compassion and concern. In short, frequent punishment may induce the child to feel self-regarding rather than other-regarding.

Practical implications

From the evidence presented in this section, it would seem that punishment is an unreliable means of social control, at least in the long term. It does not necessarily deter, and it can have a number of undesirable side-effects. However, this in itself does not mean that it should never be used. Rawls (1954) has pointed out how justifying a practice as a system of rules is one thing, and justifying a particular action falling under those rules is another. There is therefore nothing logically contradictory in being wary about punishing a particular child for a particular offence committed in particular circumstances for particular reasons whilst also justifying the institution of punishment for its potentiality to deter and control. Further, whilst children will not respect punishment administered by a hostile and rejecting adult, evidence suggests they will respect punishment used judiciously by a responsible and concerned person. In a recent investigation of comprehensive pupils' attitudes and reactions to different kinds of control strategy, O'Hagan and Edmunds (1982) showed that the teacher who never punishes, even when the class is not behaving properly, is not generally respected. On the other hand, teachers who use punishment fairly but not too severely are usually held in high regard.

Punishment probably stands a greater chance of 'working' without unfortunate side-effects if certain conditions are observed. In particular, the *focus* of punishment should be on the inherent reasonableness of the rule and not on the power of the punisher, while the *manner* of punishing should convey to the culprit that it is the behaviour that is unacceptable, not the child as a person. To prevent children becoming unduly dependent on external constraint, and to provide opportunity for them to learn what is acceptable and unacceptable behaviour, punishment should not be erratic or irrational or frequent or unnecessarily severe. Rather it should be flexible in so far as it takes account of the circumstances and the child's perception of the situation, for punishment is more likely to 'work' if the culprit perceives it to be fair. 'Showing up', or punishing for offences the pupil cannot accept as serious, should be avoided since such acts generate feelings of alienation. Reprimands are best given quietly whenever possible since nagging in a loud voice may not only reward attention-seeking behaviour but disrupt the work of the whole class and create a general atmosphere of tension. Aggressive punishment should be avoided lest the culprit learns to imitate the aggressiveness of the punisher rather than respond to the intended 'message'.

No form of punishment is without its problems, which is why many teachers prefer to rely on more positive approaches to social control, as discussed in the previous chapters on management skills, praise and rewards. Given the need for some punishment, however, it is important to choose forms that enhance rather than damage the quality of teacher-pupil relationships. Isolating the offender from the group (sometimes called 'time out') may serve to provide a cooling-off period and an opportunity to reflect upon the misbehaviour. On the other hand, the experience must not be effectively rewarding, which it can be if the offender spends the time talking to his friends in the corridor or distracting everyone by looking through the window in the classroom door! The use of withdrawal classes is potentially a positive approach and is discussed in Chapter 10. Measures that involve the loss (or winning) of house points are often employed in secondary schools. Francis (1975, p. 137) has commented that this practice is 'hallowed by tradition, highly respectable, and quite useless'! No doubt its effectiveness depends on how well the offender relates to the house group. The widely adopted institution of detention in secondary schools is of dubious deterrent value. Although it can be an occasion for seeing that work gets done, it creates problems with parents who are anxious about children coming home late and with teachers who are resentful at having to give up time in this way, especially for their less resourceful colleagues.

Less problematic, perhaps, are restrictions on freedom about where to sit or the withdrawal of special benefits. These may serve to remind pupils that privileges cannot be taken for granted but have to be earned through good behaviour. Placing on report, a system that involves the pupil carrying a card teachers sign at the end of each lesson, can be used as a basis for the monitoring of behaviour and for discussion with the child about his behaviour in different situations. Enlisting the support of parents can be very helpful, provided that the bad behaviour does not stem from a rejecting mother or father who may be inclined to 'take it out' on the child. For this reason, parents need to be discouraged from adopting a punitive approach and encouraged to regulate the child's privileges in accordance with his behaviour – a matter we will take up in Chapter 10.

Whatever form the punishment takes, the reasons for it should be explicit, and it should be presented by the teacher and perceived by the pupil as a last resort after reminders and reprimands have failed to 'get through'. The alternative behaviours that are desired and by which the pupil can redeem himself must also be made clear.

CORPORAL PUNISHMENT

The 1986 Education (No. 2) Act provides that teachers in state schools who use corporal punishment in any form will be open to civil proceedings for battery. However, in view of the fact that the House of Commons reached this decision by only one vote, that large numbers of teachers still believe in the value of corporal punishment as a last resort, and that the legislation does not apply to independent schools (except to children in the Assisted Places Scheme), it is worth rehearsing the arguments that surround this controversial issue. Further, it appears from opinion polls that the general public is hardening in favour of corporal punishment, in spite of the change in legislation. In the autumn of 1986, 69 per cent of people questioned in a Gallup survey agreed that teachers should be allowed to inflict corporal punishment, compared with 50 per cent in 1946 (*Times Educational Supplement*, 7 November, 1986).

As Gibson (1978) has illustrated in his book *The English Vice*, corporal punishment has a long tradition in British schools. The view expressed in 1846 by the Rev. F. Watkins HMI sums up the prevailing judgement at the time, that corporal punishment was needed as a necessary means of restraint: 'There are natures amongst the wretched, uncultivated, and almost brutelike occupants of some of our boys' schools to which this "last appeal of force" seems the only one to which they will attend' (quoted in Gosden, 1969). Humphries (1981) has related how girls as well as boys were regularly physically punished for acts of minor disobedience in the urban elementary schools of the prewar period and that this could frequently attract protest from the parents and even pupils themselves. Between 1900 and 1939, there is no evidence from school punishment books that the incidence of corporal punishment in elementary schools fell, in spite of official claims by the Board of Education to the contrary (Musgrave, 1977).

Newell (1972, 1979) has documented the practice of corporal punishment in the 1960s and 1970s. He disputes the claim that use was limited to a last resort and notes that maladjusted and handicapped children were not exempt. Until recently, the teachers' unions have been against the abolition of corporal punishment, and in 1968 they forced Cardiff to reverse its decision to abandon the cane in primary schools. Although London abolished the practice in primary schools in 1972, this was an isolated example at the time (Newell, 1972) and corporal punishment continued to be used in about half the secondary schools of the capital city (ILEA, 1978b). By the early 1980s corporal punishment was still being used in over eight out of ten secondary schools in non-abolitionist authorities, and in from 45 to 85 per cent of primary schools in the five authorities that still permitted its use for pupils under twelve years (Newell, 1984).

In contrast to Britain, other European countries and the communist bloc have got along without resorting to corporal punishment. Greece, Italy, Iceland and Luxembourg have never practised this method of control; and, led by Poland as early as 1783, corporal punishment was gradually abandoned throughout continental Europe, Eire finally abolishing it in 1982. Since 1969 Sweden has also outlawed its use by parents. However, corporal punishment is still practised in Australia, Canada and New Zealand. It is also prevalent in most parts of the United States, where in 1976 the Supreme Court sanctioned its use as 'an acceptable method of promoting good behaviour and instilling notions of responsibility into the mischievous heads of schoolchildren' (quoted in Dubanoski, Inaba and Gerkewic, 1983). The practice, although illegal, is also rife and sometimes brutal in Japan (Casassus, 1986).

Although, according to a poll in 1984, over half the teachers in Britain still believe in the value of corporal punishment as a last resort (*Times Educational Supplement*, 21 September 1984), an alternative view is that the practice in schools is both physically and emotionally damaging and, as such, is a form of institutionalized child abuse (Dubanoski, Inaba and Gerkewic, 1983). Newell (1984) has observed that children in school are the only sector of our society who lack adequate legal protection from violence.

There is strong circumstantial evidence that suggests that corporal punishment is associated with worse rather than better behaviour, even when pupils' social background and behaviour at entry to the school are taken into account. Clegg (1962), investigating the position in thirty schools in the West Riding of Yorkshire, found that schools using corporal punishment had higher rates of delinquency. He concluded that these schools 'positively engender rebelliousness and do little to inhibit bad behaviour'. Wiseman (1964) subjected Clegg's data to rigorous analysis and concluded that the association between caning and the worst behaviour was of 'undoubted significance'. He argued that the data 'offers no shred of opposition to the hypothesis that corporal punishment encourages bad behaviour and juvenile delinquency, but does offer evidence *against* the alleged association of caning and poor school neighbourhood' (p. 164). Similar conclusions were reached by Reynolds and Murgatroyd (1977) as a result of their survey in Wales, while Rutter *et al.* (1979), after controlling for variations in ability and social background, found that behaviour in a group of twelve London schools was worse where there were high levels of corporal punishment. Hearn (1985) reports an American study by Eron, conducted over twenty-two years, that revealed that those who had been physically punished most at school committed eight times as many crimes by the age of thirty.

The arguments presented in the previous section help to explain why corporal punishment is often counter-productive, at least in the long term. In particular, the practice exposes pupils to a model of adult behaviour that legitimizes aggression in the face of unwanted behaviour. The pupil may also displace his frustration by directing it towards animals and small children who cannot hit back (Skinner, 1973). Additionally, corporal punishment may serve the interests of its recipients by helping to confirm a reputation of 'being tough'.

One argument often heard in support of corporal punishment is that it is the only 'language' some children understand. The children in question tend to be those from working-class backgrounds who are more accustomed to physical punishment at home. It is true, according to a survey by the Newsons (1968, 1976), that physical punishment amongst mothers of four- and seven-year-olds is more prevalent in homes where the father is unskilled. However, the use of such facts to support the use of corporal punishment in schools is simply to advocate the continuation of the vicious circle in which violence begets violence. Further, corporal punishment may actually reinforce attention-seeking behaviour. Writing about the punishment of maladjusted children, Evans (1967, p. 34) remarks:

> Many deprived children are so hungry for contact with an adult who has become a meaningful person to them that they would rather be hit by that person than ignored by him ... and if corporal punishment is the rule, the more outrageous one's behaviour the more contact one will achieve.

Corporal punishment is therefore unsuitable precisely in those circumstances where its use may seem most justified. The practice may also have adverse effects on sensitive pupils who, though not receiving the punishment or even witnessing it, nevertheless feel its impact by being in an environment in which it is used. There is also evidence to suggest an association between flagellation and sado-masochistic tendencies (Maurer, 1974; Ritchie and Ritchie, 1981). Gibson (1978) and Livingstone (1975), noting that much pornographic literature thrives on allusions to school beatings, have suggested that some children may deal with their fear of the cane by fantasy, where the introduction of a sexual element can make the experience more acceptable; even for those not directly affected, a caning environment can create a climate in which flagellant fantasies are allowed to develop.

Another kind of argument, based primarily on ethical principles, is that corporal punishment is wrong because it is humiliating and degrading for both teachers and pupils. This point of view is then countered by evidence to suggest that children 'do not view punishments as being "humiliating" or "degrading" but as fair or unfair, merited or unmerited' (McCann, 1978, pp. 171-2). Again, Corrigan (1979) found boys in Sunderland to be 'indignant' and 'angry' rather than degraded by their experiences of physical punishment. However, in so far as the boys in Corrigan's interviews described teachers who hit them in such terms as 'bastard', 'twat' or 'puff', it is plain that they saw their treatment as unjustified and vindictive.

An understandable fear amongst some teachers is that the abolition of corporal punishment will lead to an increase in disruptive behaviour. For instance, one teachers' union used this argument to explain a dramatic rise in the number of suspensions from London schools in the early 1980s (*Times Educational Supplement*, 18 February 1983). However, this increase could, in part at least, have reflected the more stringent procedures for recording suspensions that London introduced in 1981. Moreover, in two British studies of schools that had abolished corporal punishment (British Psychological Society, 1980; Cumming *et al.*, 1981), no noticeable decline in school discipline was detected, and acceptable alternative sanctions had been found. Similar findings have been reported in the United States (Farley *et al.*, 1978).

In 1968, the Society of Teachers Opposed to Physical Punishment (STOPP) was founded and began a long and vigorous campaign for the abolition of beating in all schools. Its painstaking collection of evidence concerning unjust and cruel treatment in some schools has undoubtedly been instrumental in bringing about a change of public opinion. In 1978 the Educational Institute in Scotland was the first major teaching union to vote for abolition. At its conference in 1982, the NUT overwhelmingly passed a resolution to this effect, and the executive subsequently published a detailed statement (NUT, 1983, 1984). Other teaching unions subsequently opposed corporal punishment or stated that they saw its abolition as inevitable. The Association of Community Homes advocated abolition in 1985. By the mid-1980s, statements in favour of abolition had also come from almost all the relevant national associations concerned with education and child care, such as the Association of Educational Psychologists and the British Association of Social Workers. Abolition was also part of Labour, Liberal, SDP and TUC policy. None the less, by 1986, only 32 of the 125 local education authorities in the UK had abolished the practice.

Towards the end of the 1970s, the right of schools in Britain to use physical punishment was first brought to the European Court of Human Rights. Although the European Convention on Human Rights is not part of the law of the UK, it has been ratified by HM government, which has taken some steps to ensure that laws in this country meet the provisions of the Convention. The test case was *Campbell and Cosans* v. *The United Kingdom*, 1978, in which two mothers objected to the use of corporal punishment in Scottish schools (see Barrell, 1983, or *Times Educational*

Supplement, 5 March 1982, for a detailed discussion). Mrs Campbell's complaint was that the education authority refused to guarantee that her nine-year-old son would not be subjected to corporal punishment. Mrs Cosan's application concerned her fifteen-year-old son, who was suspended for refusing to accept the tawse for taking a prohibited short cut home through a cemetery. Because the mother refused to accept the local authority's offer to lift the suspension on the understanding that the boy could be liable to physical punishment for future offences, the suspension remained until the boy 'left school' on reaching statutory leaving age some months later.

Whilst not accepting the complaint that corporal punishment was inhumane and degrading within the meaning of the Convention, the European Court at Strasbourg in February 1982 did uphold the complaint that the authorities had not heeded the mothers' 'philosophical convictions'. Mrs Cosan's son was eventually awarded £3,000 'moral damages' since, through missing examinations and studies, his employment prospects had been diminished and he had since been without a job.

In response to these judgements, the Secretary of State for Scotland asked local education authorities to ban corporal punishment, and by 1986 the practice had been abandoned in 90 per cent of Scottish schools (Rosenbaum, 1986). In the same year, the DES immediately issued a circular to local education authorities and schools in England and Wales pointing out that certain cases of corporal punishment might be in breach of Article 3 of the European Convention on Human Rights, which outlaws inhumane and degrading treatment. The government also awarded an out-of-court settlement of £1,200 to the parent of a fourteen-year-old girl who had been caned in school.

In July 1983, the Conservative government issued a Consultative Document (DES, 1983), the gist of which was reflected in a bill presented to the House of Commons in January 1985. This allowed schools in England and Wales the right to administer corporal punishment, but proposed that parents should be given the right to choose whether to let their children be subjected to it. A chorus of derision greeted this compromise solution, which the National Union of Teachers had earlier described as 'ill-conceived and totally impractical' (NUT, 1983), and in July 1985 the bill was destroyed by the House of Lords. During the passage of the 1986 Education Bill, the House of Lords introduced an amendment to outlaw corporal punishment. In the Commons, the government allowed a free vote on the issue, though Labour members were given a three-line whip to vote for abolition. On 22 July 1986, MPs supporting corporal punishment were defeated, though only by one vote (231 to 230) – and they might have had their way had numbers of Conservative MPs not been held up in royal wedding traffic!

CAN PUNISHMENT BE EDUCATIVE?

So far, we have seen that punishment in schools might be justified as an instrument for controlling behaviour, though it can often be ineffective and even counter-productive. Now, if punishment is seen simply as an unpleasant means to a desirable end, and especially if it is known to have adverse side-effects, teachers need not feel *obliged* to punish. Alternative means might achieve the same ends more surely and more humanely. Punishment could then disappear from schools along with slates and learning by catechism, and schools would be all the better for it. This was the view of the Plowden Committee (Central Advisory Council for Education, 1967, s. 734) on primary schools: 'Few indeed will now consider it in any way positively "good" for children to be punished. ... Punishment will be defended simply as a means to order.' Peters (1966, p. 279) has taken a similar view: 'The truth of the matter is that punishment in a school is at best a necessary nuisance. It is necessary as a deterrent, but its positive educational value is dubious.'

However, some writers have argued that punishment can serve an educative function, helping children to develop moral feelings and constructive ways of thinking about social behaviour. If this is so, then the notion that *all* punishment could be substituted by alternative practices is misplaced, and the ideal of a school that eschews punishment regardless of the circumstances is ill-conceived.

There are three main strands to the argument that punishment can serve an educative function. One is based on the idea that punishment provides a logically necessary condition for children to acquire the concept of a social rule. A second is based upon the place of punishment in the development of moral growth. And a third is based upon the notion that punishment in certain circumstances is the appropriate moral response to wrongdoing. We shall deal with each of these in turn.

Punishment and the concept of a social rule

John Wilson (1977, 1984) sees punishment as logically bound up in the idea of rule-following. This conclusion is reached in the following way. The existence of society, or social groups such as schools, depends upon the members subscribing to rules, written or unwritten. Rules entail enforcement, which in turn entails placing some disadvantage on the rule-breaker. If people do not generally see themselves as advantaged in obeying rules and disadvantaged in breaking them, the notion of rules would be unintelligible. John Wilson illustrates this by referring to the rules of the road: we may be able to minimize accidents by, say, making it impossible for cars to go fast, but 'so long as we interact, in this and in any other situation, there is always the possibility of human beings hurting or harming each other ... and that possibility can be minimized by ensuring, via rules and punishments, that we adhere to and obey the relevant principles and norms' (J. Wilson, 1984, p. 106). Authorities such as teachers must therefore enforce social rules, and this is particularly important with children who may be too young or inexperienced to appreciate the reason for rules.

John Wilson sees this issue not as one of tough-mindedness v. tender-mindedness, but rather of rules-backed-up-by-punishment v. no-human-community. However, as Marshall (1984) has argued, even if the idea of harmonious living depends on some rules being socially sanctioned, the necessity to subscribe to rules in general does not mean that all breaches of rules must be punishable. Some may be enforceable by other means such as commands, appeals, persuasion or remonstration. None the less, it may be that rule-enforcement requires a general background of punishment and that the knowledge that rule-breakers can expect to be punished is therefore logically necessary if children are to be initiated into the idea of rule-following.

The place of punishment in moral growth

Whether or not rules logically require enforcement by punishing, all children, according to cognitive-developmental theory, seem to go through a stage in which the idea of punishment plays a significant role. Both Piaget (1932) and Kohlberg (1968) concluded from their studies of the conditions for moral growth that children in infancy are in a stage of 'heteronomous morality', when beliefs of what is right and wrong are determined by experiences of rewards and punishment and the commands of adults. Moreover, young children do not distinguish between their own and other people's point of view. They have no reason to reflect upon their judgement since the notion of deliberation between alternative courses of action is quite foreign to them. Piaget (1932) also considered that the young child needs punishment to serve as expiation for a broken rule, and that 'the sterner it is, the juster' (p. 199).

However, from the age of seven or so, according to Piaget's theory, children develop feelings of co-operation and mutual respect as they interact more with each other and become less dependent on adult authority. They gradually lose their egocentrism, and learn to take the point of view of others when this conflicts with their own. The impulsive, intuitive action of earlier years gives way to reflective, deliberate action. Punishments that are 'fair' are no longer those that hurt most (expiatory punishments) but those that relate to the offence (punishment by reciprocity). Piaget thus sees the typical junior child thinking of punishment as simple retribution where the offender must put right the damage he has caused or return what he has taken. In short, the child has come to see himself as a moral *agent*, and so morally *responsible*, deserving of blame and praise. Around eleven or twelve years, feelings of justice are refined as the child appreciates that applying the same punishment for the same offence may not be fair since circumstances must be taken into account.

What are the practical implications of Piaget's ideas on punishment? Although the young child seems to develop his moral understanding partly through his experiences of external constraint, it is also likely that the more adults use punishment to encourage an authority–subject relationship the longer children take to develop feelings of reciprocity and of justice. Kohlberg's finding that even some adults still typically think heteronomously suggests that development towards autonomous ways of thinking does not just occur naturally. Rather it is dependent upon the quality of social environment experienced by the child.

Indeed, the way in which children's beliefs about punishment are affected by their teachers' beliefs has been demonstrated in an American study by Haviland (1979), who interviewed several hundred 5- to 11-year-olds and their teachers from three different school systems. Children whose teachers held strong beliefs in punishment as a means of control were themselves more punitively orientated in their thinking, and this was so at each age-level. Haviland suggests that this association between the children's and teacher's beliefs may not be due directly to the teachers' punishing behaviour, rather it arises from the general interaction style in the classroom which reflects beliefs in unilateral respect:

> The teacher who does not ask the child about his own belief creates a social situation in which she represents and teaches the moral and common good; she is the authority who teaches her students 'rules'. Teachers who explore and question the nature of their students' beliefs may not be reinforcing the younger child's punitive beliefs as much as they are communicating indirectly the social system of reciprocal communication necessary for egalitarian and restitutive behaviour.
>
> (p. 568)

Thus punishment which is based upon the power of the adult enforces unilateral respect in young children. As early as possible, then, punishment should be based more on reciprocity and the legitimacy of authority, so that the child is gradually encouraged to see punishment as arising from his disregard of the rights and feelings of others rather than from his disobedience.

Recent work concerned with children's judgements of others in relation to cause, blame and punishment (Fincham, 1983; Docking, 1986) suggests that, provided the situation is within their experiences and is presented simply, children of 6–8 years are more able than Piaget supposed to take the point of view of others and to discriminate between accidental, malicious and altruistic action. For instance, they will tend to see blame and punishment as significantly more deserving for someone who injures another out of maliciousness than for someone who injures another whilst committing an act of kindness. If these findings are valid, there is at least a limited sense in which young children are able to deliberate about their actions. Further, as Plamenatz (1967) has suggested, to act *as if* children were genuinely blameworthy can help them to *develop* the feelings of a responsible, moral agent:

> Certainly, if children were not already to some extent in the use of their reason, we could not induce these feelings in them; but it may also be that, unless the feelings were induced in children before they had reason and experience enough to foresee the consequences to others and themselves of their behaviour, no pointing to these consequences later, when they were able to foresee them, would suffice to persuade them to behave well.
>
> (Plamenatz, 1967, pp. 175–6)

Punishment is also more likely to be effective in changing a pupil's behaviour if it is accompanied by comments that help the offender to reason about his actions. Children need practice in reasoning about their behaviour to help them acquire general rules that operate across a range of comparable situations. In this connection, Wright (1972) points out how important it is for adults to give the deviant act a label, such as 'stealing' or 'lying', and to explain why acts subsumed under the label are wrong. This 'helps to draw the child's attention to those features of the situation we want him to think about ... and it can help the child to construe his actions in a certain way, to structure them cognitively and to relate them to general rules' (p. 40). It is also likely that the label helps the child to 'instruct himself' when next confronted by a similar temptation.

Punishment as a moral response to wrongdoing

An argument that justifies punishment on moral rather than utilitarian grounds was put forward by the German philosopher Immanuel Kant (1724–1804). Kant's view was that where a culprit is blameworthy, is responsible for his actions, knows the consequences of them and has gained satisfaction from his misdeeds, then it is the responsibility of society to inflict punishment as moral retribution: 'no one undergoes punishment because he has willed to be punished, but because he has willed a punishable action' (Kant, trans. 1887, p. 201). On this argument, wrongdoing *merits* punishment.

The assumption behind this retributionist argument is that people can *choose* to behave in a prosocial or antisocial way. The American behaviourist B. F. Skinner, however, unequivocally maintains that to blame individuals on the grounds that they are autonomous and the cause of their own behaviour is misleading and unhelpful. Rather, 'It is the environment which is "responsible" for objectionable behaviour, and it is the environment, not some attribute in the individual which must be changed' (Skinner, 1973, p. 77). In contrast, Kant saw man as a purposeful being, who can plan his actions. As such, individuals should be made to feel accountable for what they do. When they do not act responsibly, it is the duty of others to inflict punishment to uphold the sanctity of the moral law. If this argument is applied to children, the assumption must be that, to some extent at least, children can be regarded as responsible for their behaviour and thus deserving of praise and blame.

It is the role of punishment in treating children as responsible moral agents that is the concern of P. S. Wilson (1971). Wilson carefully distinguishes between 'penalties', which are given simply to control children's behaviour, and 'punishment', which is given to confirm for children the existence of a moral order. 'Penalties' are for breaking school rules and regulations, whereas 'punishment' is for deliberate moral negligence. It is in this sense that Wilson sees punishment as educative:

> A rule-breaker is liable for a penalty whether or not he can see good reason for the rule, but a wrong-doer is liable for punishment *because* he can see good reason for the rules (and has nevertheless broken them). ... The *force* of what we say or do in punishing hurts, while its *meaning* educates.
>
> (pp. 117–18, author's italics)

In a conference paper replying to various criticisms of his position, P. S. Wilson (1974), whilst acknowledging that the term 'punishment' is often used in the context of simple social control, insists that his conceptual distinction between 'penalties' and 'punishment' is necessary. This is because the point of 'punishment' in Wilson's sense is not to extract obedience but to communicate the moral significance of behaviour, and these two objectives must not be confused. The argument is that pupils ought to feel the pain of a teacher's displeasure when they are guilty of moral failings. This is not coercion, Wilson insists, since it is not intended to extract obedience: rather it is treating children as moral agents who have views about appropriate behaviour and some control over their own actions. P. S. Wilson is not saying that controlling children through penalties is wrong: he recognizes the social justification in stopping undesirable acts, such as crossing a road carelessly or disturbing other children who are trying to concentrate in class. What he is pointing out is that the act of inflicting pain when the culprit is *technically* culpable of breaching a rule but unaware that such action is *wrong*, as distinct from disallowed, will not aid moral learning; whereas to make a child feel uncomfortable for *moral* culpability, i.e. when the child himself recognizes the wrongness of his action and not just that it is forbidden, is to make a contribution to the child's moral growth. Certainly we might suppose that a child who, on his own account, believes his behaviour to be wrong will perceive the punishment as more justified than if he sees his breaching of the teacher's rule as a mere technicality.

Critics of P. S. Wilson, such as Royce (1984) and Smith (1985), ask how the act of punishing can be educative if the child already knows his action to be wrong. However, this argument does not seem to take account of the gap between the child *knowing* something is wrong and *caring* sufficiently to modify his behaviour accordingly. Although, as we saw earlier in this chapter, punishment can estrange relationships and be counter-productive, it may, if handled sensitively in cases of moral failings, help the child to care about what he already intellectually accepts as right and wrong.

Practical implications

It is not easy to accept the view that punishment can educate when so much evidence suggests that it can more easily alienate. One obvious problem here concerns the form punishment takes if it is to have educative potential. Punishments in schools vary from frowns, looks of displeasure and mild 'tellings off', at one end of the continuum, to sarcasm, smacks and beatings at the other. Given the research findings reviewed in earlier sections, those who argue that punishment can contribute to a child's moral growth must clearly be excluding physical and psychological punishment that is vindictive, relentless or humiliating. The anxiety brought about by punishment of this kind will interfere with the cognitive tasks of discriminating between acceptable and unacceptable behaviour and between conceptually related acts such as stealing and borrowing. That said, three main points seem to emerge from the discussion in this section:

(1) A society depends upon rules and their enforcement. Whilst rules can often be enforced by means other than punishment, it may be that a background of punishment in some form is needed to ensure that rules in general are taken seriously and that children acquire the concept of rule-following.
(2) In infancy, children seem to depend upon external constraints to develop an understanding of rules. At the same time, a punitive style of upbringing will not only alienate and estrange relationships but impede the development of empathy and independent thinking.
(3) If children are to be regarded as developing moral agents, they should be increasingly treated as responsible for their actions and therefore liable to blame and punishment. This is easier to justify with older children, who are more able to take account of others' points of view and to deliberate about their actions. But even in the infant school children are able to reason about appropriate behaviour in a limited way. Moreover, in so far as children can increasingly discriminate between what they accept as wrong and what they perceive as disallowed or unconventional, then the occasion of punishment may have a significant moral function in prompting children to care about what they themselves regard as appropriate behaviour.

Finally, if the rightness of punishment arises from the rightness of basic moral principles, then it is vital for punishments in school to bear a clear relation to the moral seriousness of the offences. If the infringement of basic moral principles, such as truth-telling or treating others as equals or not hurting people unnecessarily, is not handled as rigorously as breaches of local regulations, such as those concerning hair-style or uniform, punishment can be miseducative in conveying to children a confused picture in which infringements of moral rules and arbitrary conventions are undifferentiated and seen as equally reprehensible.

Thus for any system of punishment in schools to be educative rather than simply a crude form of training, it must help to convey to the child what matters morally rather than what others expect. Clearly, therefore, the reasons for which punishment is given, the form which it takes and the manner in which it is delivered, together with the degree to which the pupils perceive it as just, are all-important. As long ago as 1841, Kay

Shuttleworth, the first secretary of the Committee of Council for Education and one who had high visions of the part schools could play in society, summed the point up this way:

> The punishment of all children in all schools ought ... to be addressed to the conscience of the child rather than to the public opinion of the school. ... The object of all moral education is to awaken the conscience. It is plain therefore that the mind of the child should not be so much actuated by the fear of the present punishment as by the fear of doing wrong.
>
> (Kay Shuttleworth, 1841, pp. 7-8)

FURTHER READING

Bean, P. (1981) *Punishment*, Martin Robertson, Oxford.
(This book is not about punishment in school particularly, but is a readable, general discussion about the justification of punishment and its role in the penal system. Special attention is given to the problem of punishing young offenders.)
British Psychological Society (1980) *The Report of a Working Party on Corporal Punishment in Schools*, BPS, Leicester.
(An exhaustive review of the evidence, opinions and arguments.)
Pik, R. (1981) Confrontation situations and teacher-support systems, in B. Gillham (ed.) *Problem Behaviour in the Secondary School*, Croom Helm, London.
(Discusses the kinds of occasions when punishments can lead to confrontations and suggests ways in which such situations might be avoided.)
Wilson, P. S. (1971) *Interest and Discipline in Education*, Routledge & Kegan Paul, London.
(Chapter 4 contains a discussion on the moral function of punishment; for criticisms see Royce (1984) and Smith (1985).)

9
PASTORAL CARE AND SOCIAL CONTROL

THE CONCEPT OF PASTORAL CARE

Pastoral care is concerned with the promotion of pupils' individual welfare. This could amount to 'looking after' pupils in a general, conventional way, and in this sense the concept is nothing new. Recently, however, the term 'pastoral care' has developed a more particular usage to cover a range of concerns that, it is argued, need to be institutionalized and not left to chance.

Pastoral care may include any or all of the following areas: familiarizing children with school organization, rules and practices, especially when transferring from one age-phase to another; the development of a positive self-image in children; the teaching of social skills; helping children to cope with stresses in their everyday life, including those of schooling and examinations; helping children with personal problems; linking children with support agencies outside school; interaction with the pupil's home; the review of school arrangements to provide a more conducive environment for learning; and the recommendation of special educational needs. In 1982, the National Association for Pastoral Care in Education was founded to promote training for teachers engaged in these concerns, to disseminate good practice (e.g. through the Association's journal *Pastoral Care in Education*) and to encourage research. The extent to which pastoral care is seen as a responsibility of certain 'experts', or of all teachers, or of both, varies from school to school. Only in secondary schools, however, are there likely to be special posts of pastoral responsibility.

Teachers who regard their pastoral role as one that is essentially concerned with defining values for pupils may regard some of the more welfare-oriented aspects of the 'new' pastoral care, in the phrase of Best and Decker (1985), as 'cuddle therapy'. Some teachers see the pervasiveness of pastoral care as an intrusion into the main purposes of schooling: 'Teachers are educators, not social workers,' they say. At the same time, those who are committed to pastoral care as a special focus for schools recognize, as Tattum (1982) has pointed out, that bureaucratic and human relations models of organization do not easily mix since the former encourages formality and conformity while the latter implies a reduction of social distance. Not surprisingly, therefore, many school pastoral systems become burdened with bureaucratic procedures, such as record-keeping, paper-chasing and referral of pupils to a hierarchy of senior staff.

Definitions of pastoral care are usually couched in language that focuses on the personal needs of pupils. Thus for Johnson (1985), pastoral care is partly 'to identify and respond to any problems the pupil is experiencing as an individual' (p. 100), whilst for Marland (1974) one aim is 'to assist the individual to enrich his personal life' (p. 10). Yet, according to some writers, the reality of the situation is different. For them, pastoral care systems amount to an insidious form of social control achieved by welfare means and dealing with 'problem children' rather than with 'children who have problems'. The dominant order, enshrining power structures that may themselves give rise to some of the problems, is thereby preserved. Thus Guthrie (1979) considers pastoral care to be a 'welfare gloss' given to an unjust educational and social order. Williamson (1980) argues that children who are unsuccessful in terms of conventional school performance criteria have their legitimate grievances deflected through what he wittily calls 'pastoralization'. This is a process in which 'problem pupils' are 'pastoralized' into believing that their lack of success is essentially a reflection of their own inadequacies. On this argument, therefore, the pastoral needs of many children could best be met by making radical changes in the school curriculum and teaching arrangements. Indeed, this is the implication of Hargreaves's (1982) suggestion that some schools effectively rob many pupils of their 'dignity' because success, and, by implication, personal worth, is measured in terms of performance in academic subjects and public examinations. Schostak (1983), who has forcefully argued that 'schooling is maladjusted to the needs of individuals' (p. 5), sees schools as primarily agents of social control, stifling any deviation from social norms, and so rendering the individual impotent in the control of his own destiny.

A fundamental problem in pastoral care is therefore the extent to which it is the pupil or the system that should be changed. Of course, school systems do not exist independently from the structures of society and the expectations of dominant social groups. Radical changes are therefore difficult to bring about without corresponding changes in society at large. Whatever the system, there will be some children who do not 'fit in'. Although some schools can and do make fairly profound changes in the way they operate, even the most caring schools will find limits to the changes they can make, given their bureaucratic structure and the demands from powerful groups in society. As Hargreaves (1982) acknowledged in his proposals for radical curriculum reform and the abolition of public examinations at sixteen plus, no one school or even local authority can make major changes of this kind without national agreement.

PASTORAL CARE AND SCHOOL DISCIPLINE

The gap between the stated welfare intentions and the practice of pastoral care has been brought out in some recent studies of individual schools. In a survey that investigated the role of seventy-one form tutors in some secondary schools in South Wales, Raymond (1985) found that, because administrative duties, disciplinary functions and giving out notices were perceived as the main functions in practice, tutors felt that they were prevented from fulfilling pastoral roles as they would wish. In the Rivendell School study, Best et al. (1983) found that 'for some teachers at least, pastoral care was synonymous with the maintenance of discipline and the correction of pupil infractions of the school rules and rejection of the teacher's authority' (p. 254). Even those who valued the welfare dimensions of pastoral care could often find themselves preoccupied with questions of control. Similarly, Denscombe (1985) concludes from his studies of Ashton and Beechgrove schools that, in spite of the official guidelines to the contrary and the reluctance of the heads of houses, 'the house system had become bound up with the routine maintenance of control' (p. 191). Again, Johnson et al. (1980) record how teachers in four secondary schools felt an imbalance between their controlling and caring functions, while Schostak's (1983) analysis of the experiences of Slumptown School reveals how 'the unresolved tension between care and control prevents teachers and pupils from meeting as individuals who might be able to share and grow together' (p. 133).

Pastoral systems and care become bound up with problems of classroom control for two main reasons. One is that 'misbehaviour' may be symptomatic of an emotional problem that, in the teacher's eyes, may manifest itself as a discipline problem. Pupils who are unable to cope with stress, find it difficult to develop meaningful relationships with school staff. They are therefore not only a problem to themselves but to those around them. The second reason is that some teachers, especially those in large urban secondary schools, who are themselves experiencing stress, lean on the pastoral system for support in their endeavours to secure control of the class.

If pastoral systems and school discipline are in fact often intertwined, the question which then arises is 'Should this inseparability be resisted?' Some writers are quite clear that the answer is 'No'. Galloway *et al.* (1982, p. 71) put it this way: 'good discipline is wasted educationally unless combined with pastoral care. Equally, good pastoral care is probably impossible and certainly ineffective without good discipline.' Other writers, however, see room for some separation. Best *et al.* (1983), in a discussion about the relation between the pastoral, academic and disciplinary dimensions of school life, argue that while these properly overlap in some respects, in other respects they should be regarded as conceptually distinct. On the one hand, a teacher discussing bullying with her form could be contributing to both school order and individual welfare, whilst a social studies lesson on law-breaking and the role of the police could be relevant to the problem of school order as well as to the academic curriculum. On the other hand, so the authors argue, the enforcement of social order by means of external constraints constitutes a different kind of enterprise from the strictly individual welfare aspects of pastoral care, and both these are in turn distinct from the knowledge and learning orientations of the academic curriculum.

It could be argued that, by attending to the personal needs of pupils, teachers are also providing important conditions for group cohesion and school order. Evidence from the Rutter *et al.* (1979) study on a group of London schools, however, suggested a negative relationship between good behaviour and the emphasis given to pastoral work. The researchers find this result surprising but suggest that it might be explained in two ways. One is that an over-emphasis on pastoral care might have meant that less energy was put into academic work, so that those schools lost the behavioural advantages a focus on the challenge of learning can bring. The other possibility could be related to the fact that the less successful schools generally had more behaviour problems, in which case they felt the need to concentrate more on pastoral care. On this argument, then, a high quality of pastoral care can be expected, in the long run, to ameliorate behaviour problems in the classroom and therefore obviate the need for disciplinary intervention. It can also be argued that if class control is firm, though non-punitive and fair, then the stable environment produced should help pupils who are behaviourally 'at risk'. The style in which class behaviour is managed is thus integral to successful pastoral care.

PASTORAL SYSTEMS AND 'TROUBLESHOOTING'

Secondary schools vary in the degree of formality and hierarchy attached to the pastoral system. Heads of houses or years will often have very clear disciplinary functions and will expect form tutors to keep them updated with behavioural problems. Pupils may be referred to them either personally or through such documentary devices as penalty and merit cards by which pupils' behavioural careers are monitored.

Yet such bureaucratization can be detrimental to the individual interests of pupils and teachers. As we saw in the previous section, various studies have demonstrated how senior staff with special pastoral responsibility are often only minimally involved in welfare roles because they are expected to act as 'discipline specialists' or 'troubleshooters' – even when the official school guidelines tell teachers not to abuse the referral facilities. One problem encountered with 'referral upward' systems is that a particular group of teachers, typically the less experienced, use the facility because they cannot keep class control. Yet, by not dealing with the problem themselves, these teachers do nothing to develop more favourable relationships with their pupils. Further, heads and senior staff are apt to interpret frequent referrals as a sign of professional incompetence, and relationships amongst colleagues are accordingly strained. Another problem brought about by referrals to senior staff is that small misdemeanours can easily escalate into major confrontations between pupils and senior authority (Lawrence, Steed and Young, 1984a). Thus, in some schools what might begin as, say, disobedience in a lesson might end up in suspension from school because, along the way, the culprit had repeatedly failed to turn up at detention and then to accept corporal punishment. At the same time, teachers who are sensitive to the dangers and who try, by avoiding 'referring upwards', to keep face in the eyes of their pupils and the hierarchy, may be driven to battle on, using ineffective means to gain the pupils' respect. The dilemma is a real one.

What answers can be given to these problems? First of all, it is important for senior staff to provide a forum in which teachers can discuss their class control difficulties. As Galloway *et al.* (1982, p. 159) acknowledges, 'Teachers, like pupils, need to feel there is someone to whom they can regularly turn to discuss a problem before it becomes too serious. The requirement is not that someone should solve the problem [but] to acknowledge the problem and explore possible ways of relieving it.' Lawrence, Steed and Young (1977, 1984a) have shown how senior staff themselves can experience class control problems and, if these can be shared with less experienced colleagues, the staff as a whole should benefit from mutual support and the sharing of understandings. Further, it is through discussion that the senior staff can help teachers to raise their levels of perception and skill and to offer a consistent and considered approach to problems of disruption. In short, teachers can help themselves by being less isolationist and 'autonomous' and instead be more prepared to learn from each other. This does not diminish the status of the year or house head. Rather it suggests that their role is less one of troubleshooting and more one of co-ordinating a team of teachers who meet regularly to review problems and to discuss appropriate responses. Teachers are then likely to feel more confident and skilled in dealing with 'trouble' themselves.

A second and complementary approach is to enhance the status and role of the form tutor, who is in a unique position to monitor pupils' work across all subjects and teachers. To give form tutors such a responsibility, however, involves a reappraisal of staff roles, as Galloway *et al.* (1982, p. 71) illustrated in their Sheffield study. In two schools, subject staff objected to form tutors checking to see if pupils had completed their homework. This was seen as undermining their autonomy and status, particularly when junior teachers checked up on homework set by heads of department. Yet, as Galloway *et al.* point out, the form tutor, who can know her thirty or so pupils better than a pastoral head could possibly know all the pupils in a house or year, is uniquely placed to determine the scale of the problem across subjects. If a pupil's failure to complete homework is a general problem, the co-operation of parents might be enlisted; but if the problem is confined to a particular subject or a particular teacher, the remedy might lie within the teaching arrangements of one department.

Of course, however strongly form tutors are regarded as the basic unit of pastoral care, success will depend upon the opportunity they are given to attend to the personal needs of pupils in their classes. This issue relates to the concept of the 'pastoral curriculum', to which we now turn.

THE PASTORAL CURRICULUM

The idea of a pastoral curriculum is founded on the belief that effective pastoral care requires not only guidance and counselling but a coherent *teaching* programme. The pastoral curriculum can be conceived as that dimension of the total curriculum that has the distinctive aim of meeting the needs of all pupils as regards the personal problems with which they are likely to be confronted. Marland (1980, p. 157), for instance, sees it as 'the school curriculum looked at for the moment solely from the point of view of the personal needs of the pupil resolving his individual problems, making informed decisions, and taking his place in his personal world'. On this basis, pastoral care cannot be effective if pupils lack a grasp of those facts, concepts, attitudes and skills required for personal and social development.

Whether the pastoral curriculum should therefore be considered as something separate from the academic curriculum is a controversial issue. Elliott (1982), for instance, plainly considers that it should not, believing that this would be 'a tacit admission that the latter is failing to provide pupils with a truly liberal education, an education which is both intellectually challenging and personally significant for the way they live their lives' (p. 54). On the other hand, as McLaughlin (1982) has argued, some special curricular provision may be needed in order to provide a more direct contribution to those practical considerations that constitute 'preparation for life'. While the general curriculum should surely be relevant to children's personal needs, this need not prevent a school setting aside some time each week for pastoral concerns in particular.

Many aspects of the pastoral curriculum go beyond the scope of this book, but two important points must be noted. The first is that the pastoral curriculum has application for *all* pupils, and not only those who are seen to have problems and are given individual help. As Marland (1980, p. 153) argues, 'Unless we have an agreed background curriculum, we are depending upon children having crises before we can offer any help; that way we don't know their problem until they know their problem – and often they don't know their problem until it's too late to help them with their problem.' The second point to note is that the term 'pastoral curriculum' in Marland's sense is not confined to the activities of special tutorial periods, though these are important. A coherent whole-school policy is needed so that all teachers can make a contribution to pastoral care through the general curriculum.

The pervasiveness of the pastoral curriculum can be seen in the following list of objectives offered by Bulman (1984):

(1) Pupils should understand themselves: their bodies, their emotions, their own goals and limitations.
(2) Pupils need understanding and experience of a very wide variety of relationships, how to deal with people who are more or less powerful than themselves and how to understand people from other cultures and sexes.

(3) Pupils must be taught how to get the best out of their environment: people, facilities, emotional surroundings, their rights, leisure and the school itself.
(4) Pupils need to develop their own learning skills . . . not only language-related skills, information-finding skills and examination techniques, but also how best to use their teachers and the school.
(5) Pupils must learn how to make decisions: how to evaluate and cope with their consequences.

(Bulman, 1984, pp. 107–8)

Bulman sees such a pastoral curriculum being implemented partly through regular lessons in the academic curriculum (e.g. English can contribute to the development of personal relationships), partly through special courses (e.g. health education) – though these might be interwoven across the curriculum – partly through the 'hidden' curriculum (e.g. the manner in which rules are enforced), and partly through a special tutorial programme.

The content of a tutorial programme can be illustrated by reference to the work of Button (1975, 1982/3, 1983), though other schemes have been developed by Blackburn (1975), Hamblin (1978), Baldwin and Wells (1979–83), and Wells, Baldwin and Smith (1983). In Button's programme of developmental group-work, some topics, such as friendship, are re-visited by each year group to deepen understanding and increase social competence; other topics, such as an induction programme for new entrants, or support for public examinations, are relevant only to a particular year. The work is 'developmental' in the sense that the programme is based on situations directly related to the current experiences of the pupils, who are helped to explore their own feelings and to acquire special skills in a step-by-step approach. The style of tutorial leadership is of special importance since members of a class should be encouraged both to develop self-reliance and to support each other. The techniques, for which Button provides many practical suggestions, include communication skills, role play, exercises in trusting each other, receiving visitors and group discussion.

Clearly, a programme of this kind has a bearing on social behaviour in school. Pupils who are developing the skills of listening to each other, being articulate in their verbal and non-verbal communication, being supportive within a group and caring for others should feel less impelled to take on defensive attitudes and to indulge in acting out behaviours. Indeed, some empirical support for this has been presented in a paper concerning an extension of the project into junior and middle schools (Thacker, 1985).

Teachers were reported as seeming calmer, shouting less and generally viewing children more positively. The pupils in turn were reported as seeing the teachers more as human beings and feeling able to speak without fear of ridicule, while the classes became generally more cohesive. Additionally, isolates were helped to come out of their shells and to be included in the group. Similarly, the Lancashire tutorial scheme (Baldwin and Wells, 1979-83) has been shown to bring about a warmer, more open exchange between teachers and pupils, with a positive effect on school discipline (Stagles, 1985).

Whether tutorial programmes are effective will depend partly on the degree to which teachers in the school feel committed to the basic philosophy. Some teachers will feel threatened by the open relationships generated by the activities that challenge their traditional position of dominance; others may simply not feel that they have the personal qualities to implement the ideas successfully; and a likely initial reaction is one of insecurity in the face of something new (Tall, 1985). A vital condition for the success of such schemes (apart from in-service training) is the involvement of all teachers in the planning stages in order to guard against the possibility that the ideas are seen as an imposition by senior staff upon reluctant practitioners. Support for the less willing by the more willing teachers and from the school head, plus a continual review of the programme, are other conditions that will affect success. But let there be no mistake: the implementation of a pastoral curriculum has strong implications for teacher-pupil relationships in all aspects of the school life. There is little point in providing pastoral support in tutorial periods if it is taken away during regular lessons.

COUNSELLING IN SCHOOLS

Counselling is concerned with the development of self-knowledge and understanding. It is not expressions of sympathy and cosy chats but a skilled activity concerned with personal development and requiring special training. Shertzer and Stone (1974, p. 20) define it as 'an interaction process that facilitates meaningful understanding of self and environment and results in the establishment and/or classification of goals and values for future behaviour'. Such a process is not easy for the client since it involves challenge and an unblocking of repressed feelings. Although counselling has this clear function, it involves a diversity of activities that do not lend themselves to a conventional job-description. Thus Tyler (1970, p. 5) sees the counsellor as one who 'supplies what is *missing* in the imperfect human organizations to which we belong'.

Although there are various approaches to counselling (for reviews see Hamblin, 1974; Nelson-Jones, 1982), the one most often used in schools is based on the ideas of Carl Rogers (1942, 1951). According to Rogers (1942, p. 114), the counselling relationship is 'one in which warmth of acceptance and absence of any coercion or personal pressure on the part of the counsellor permits the maximum expression of feelings, attitudes, and problems by the counselee'. The counsellor must be prepared to recognize and respond to any attitude the client expresses, however negative, hostile, ambivalent or contradictory. Rogerian counselling is thus often referred to as 'non-directive', 'non-judgemental' and 'client-centred'. As the client recognizes his suppressed feelings, releases them without fear and becomes aware of their significance in social relationships, so he changes his self-image. And as he changes his view of himself, he changes his behaviour.

The Rogerian philosophy, in which personal development is seen to be dependent upon learning to accept one's feelings as valid, is usually contrasted with Skinnerian behaviourist approaches in which the counsellor takes a directive role and works towards pre-specified goals through a programme in which success is systematically rewarded (cf. Krumboltz and Thoresen, 1969). Quicke (1978), however, has argued that the Rogerian position contains contradictions because, although avowedly non-directive, the values held by the counsellor come through in subtle ways, the child ultimately having to adopt a self-definition consistent with the counsellor's school of thought. Quicke recognizes that the essentially humanistic approach of 'client-centred' counselling could be important in counteracting the impersonal social climate that is characteristic of some large schools, but he points out the danger of a counsellor focusing on a child's interpersonal relations as though these existed independently from the prevailing culture:

> For Rogers, the changing world is something that is happening outside the individual to which the individual responds, but it is not clear what role there is for the individual in actually creating this changing world. ... Adaptation to existing circumstances rather than control of one's own destiny seems, in the final analysis, to be the message of Rogerian psychology.
>
> (Quicke, 1978, p. 199)

Quicke considers that social and historical studies have a contribution to make in helping pupils to see that their own 'identity crisis' is not inevitable but avoidable, given certain fundamental societal changes. This view suggests that it is not enough to help children to cope with existing stresses if they do not also see that they can contribute towards changing the very features of society that give rise to these stresses, and so help future generations to experience less adolescent conflict and crisis. As we noted earlier in this chapter, a pastoral care that genuinely focuses on the individual's welfare needs will look not only to ways of providing therapy and guidance, but will also look to school structures, teaching arrangements and the quality of teacher–pupil relationships since these factors may be contributing to the individual's problem.

Another matter of controversy concerns the desirability of an administrative separation of teaching and counselling. A few schools, such as Mayfield in London, have employed full-time counsellors. Such an arrangement gives status to the role and indicates the value the school places on counselling. In most schools, however, one or more regular members of staff who have undergone special training combine the roles of counselling and teaching. This might be because of inadequate public funds, but often it is a deliberate policy. Some teachers would see their disciplinary role undermined by the presence of a full-time counsellor because the counsellor's therapeutic role involves focusing upon a problem from the perspective of the pupil. Headteachers, too, occupying their traditional position of ultimate authority, may find it difficult to accommodate the views expressed by counsellors, if these conflict with their own (Robinson, 1978). Thus, whether the roles of counselling and teaching are combined or separated, they must be seen as mutually supporting, and staff who have special responsibility for counselling will need to interact with teaching staff upon whom their success will ultimately depend.

What reasons can be given for believing that specialist counselling, whether full-time or combined with teaching responsibilities, can make a positive contribution to the problem of class order? First of all, the specialist counsellor brings to the situation a dimension of pastoral care that cannot easily be expected in all teaching staff. While it is true that teaching and pastoral work are inevitably intertwined, the primary role of the teacher is not therapeutic. The counsellor, by virtue of her time, personal qualities and special skills acquired during training and experience, should be better placed than most teachers to allow a pupil to talk over personal problems and to come to terms with ambivalent or hostile feelings. It is understandable if some teachers see this in terms of a facility whereby pupils can complain about school authority. It should be possible, however, for a counsellor, without breaking confidentiality, to provide staff with feedback that could be considered in curricular and organizational planning. For this reason, a counsellor should be regarded as a senior member of the school staff in order that she can carry the authority to recommend changes. Further, many of the problems a pupil brings to a counsellor are about matters in which the school is not implicated, such as problems in making friends, family discord, not getting on with parents, boy/girl-friend trouble – in short, a range of issues in which pupils seem helpless and lack confidence to deal with the situation alone.

The counsellor should thus not deprive the regular classroom teacher of her pastoral role. Rather, by helping the pupil to develop a more positive self-image, the counsellor can provide more favourable conditions in which the teacher can exercise pastoral care and guidance. Hamblin (1978) notes how some pupils present a churlish and aggressive facade because they do not know other ways of behaving in certain situations. A counsellor should be able to help pupils to present themselves more positively and to learn something of the skill in making personal relationships. If the pupils can be helped to see themselves in a more positive light and to develop interpersonal skills, they are less likely to feel the need to seek group attention in order to achieve status.

Secondly, a counsellor works not only with individuals; she also works with groups to promote more positive interaction. Of interest here is the work of Leigh (1978), who, as a group leader with adolescents in schools, has demonstrated the significance of offering a non-threatening environment in which pupils are enabled to reflect upon their experience, to evaluate it, to learn from it and to use it. Of particular importance here is the notion that pupils should come to see the interdependence of individual and group concerns, to recognize and to reconcile group and individual needs and associated ambivalent or hostile feelings, and to involve themselves in practical projects for which the group takes responsibility.

It goes without saying that counsellors and teachers should work together as partners. Yet it is more than this. The institution of counselling or any system of pastoral care should symbolize the belief that a school has clear responsibility not simply to contain problems of social relationships but to provide conditions in which pupils can drop their defensive positions, and in which it is considered right that they should analyse their feelings openly. The danger inherent in any support system for pupils is that attention to inappropriate teaching arrangements or teacher–pupil relationships may be deflected, energy instead being directed towards adapting the child to the system whilst disregarding the potentiality of the system to respond to the child. Thus, genuine pastoral care involves a preparedness to adjust the system to the personal needs of the pupils as well as helping the pupils to adjust to the system.

FURTHER READING

Two classic texts are
Hamblin, D. H. (1978) *The Teacher and Pastoral Care*, Basil Blackwell, Oxford.
Marland, M. (1974) *Pastoral Care*, Heinemann, London.

There are numerous books on pastoral care, the chief authors being Best, Hamblin and Marland. Two very useful collections of papers are provided in
Best, R., Jarvis, C. and Ribbins, P. (eds.) (1980) *Perspectives on Pastoral Care*, Heinemann, London.
Ribbins, P. (ed.) (1985) *Schooling and Welfare*. Barcombe, Sussex: Falmer.

A recent manual with much practical advice is
Raymond, J. (1985) *Implementing Pastoral Care in Schools,* Croom Helm, London.

Additionally, there are published programmes for tutorial periods, the most well-known of which are
Baldwin, J. and Wells, H. (1979-83) *Active Tutorial Work,* Books 1-5, Basil Blackwell, Oxford.
Button, L. (1982/3) *Group Tutoring for the Form Teacher*, Books 1 and 2, Hodder and Stoughton, London.

10
BEYOND THE SCHOOL'S RESOURCES?

In this final chapter, we consider some of the ways in which schools can respond to pupils whose disruptive behaviour is a continuing problem. Although such cases are less likely to arise in schools whose staff adopt positive perceptions of all their pupils, and who develop strategies and approaches that prevent pupils becoming disenchanted with school, some pupils and teachers are still likely to require help that goes beyond the resources a school can provide alone.

WELFARE AND PSYCHOLOGICAL SERVICES

The main welfare and psychological support agencies with which teachers are likely to be involved are the Educational Welfare Service, the School Psychological Service, and (less likely) child guidance clinics or hospital psychiatric out-patient clinics.

The Educational Welfare Service

The Educational Welfare Officer (EWO) can be important in securing liaison between the school, parents and various support agencies. His role extends beyond that of the former attendance officers since he deals not only with absence and truancy but with a range of social problems. Hence, although the reason for visiting homes is partly to investigate reasons for absence (and, if necessary, summon parents to the school attendance committee or instigate court proceedings), it is also to advise parents about welfare services (e.g. free meals, allowances for uniform and school trips), to encourage them to adopt a positive attitude towards their children's behaviour and the work of the school, and to help with such personal problems as schoolgirl pregnancies. This dual responsibility of attendance–enforcement and welfare is not easy to reconcile.

The Ralphs Report (1973) saw the EWO as 'a social worker in an educational setting'. Many EWOs now have qualifications in social work, though the extent of social work duties and the degree of co-ordination and commitment by the local authority vary considerably. The study by Macmillan (1977, 1980) demonstrates that high workloads – on average each EWO has 3,400 pupils – make detailed casework difficult, and the role of the EWO is therefore mainly 'liaison, support, and preventative' rather than 'specifically remedial'. Davis (1985), after reading through several thousand reports from EWOs, concluded that some officers worked more with the pupils themselves and others worked more with parents (some never seeing the children concerned), and that the quality of support provided varied from heavy-handedness to demonstrations of great sensitivity and understanding. The reports revealed the extremely trying circumstances in which many of the referred pupils lived – cramped living conditions, having to look after sick parents and brothers and sisters, parental neglect and rejection, coping with family discord, death and divorce. With some pupils, an EWO might remain in contact throughout the whole of the secondary school.

The work of an EWO is especially delicate when parents are hostile to their children and to approaches from the social services. In such cases, recommending that parents take a firm line may thus exacerbate the problem, whilst listening to parents and avoiding criticism is more likely to lead to an atmosphere of trust. Sometimes the EWO can help by encouraging hostile parents to respond positively to their children's good behaviour rather than negatively to their bad behaviour.

Some schools now have their own school-attached welfare officer to facilitate communication between agencies and home visiting. Rose and Marshall (1975) found that problems of truancy and delinquency were less severe in schools to which a social worker was permanently attached.

The Educational Welfare Service is currently part of the local education authority but many authorities have taken initiatives to improve inter-agency collaboration. Various reports (Seebohm, 1968; Ralphs Report 1973; ADSS, 1978; Society of Education Officers, 1979) have discussed the possibility of transferring the EWS to social services. The controversial nature of this debate, which concerns professional boundaries and perceptions, centres on whether the Educational Welfare Service should focus primarily on ensuring the child's attendance at school or on relieving stress in the family. For a guide to the polemic about roles and boundaries in social services related to children, the reader is referred to Skinner, Platts and Hill (1983).

The School Psychological Service

Educational psychologists working in the School Psychological Service are appointed by the local education authority. They are trained teachers, typically with a first degree in psychology and a higher degree in educational psychology. They are directly involved in schools, giving guidance to teachers about individual pupils who might be considered for special treatment or placement such as in a special unit, tutorial class or with a home tutor. Having had several years' teaching experience themselves, in addition to special training, educational psychologists are well placed to work in harmony with teachers and parents. They also have contact with school medical officers, child care officers, health visitors, probation officers, EWOs and other sources of help. The essential task of the educational psychologist is to try to stop a situation reaching a point of no return. In this process she has the advantages not only of her teaching experience and special expertise, but also of being emotionally detached from everyday dealings with the child.

A child who is referred to an educational psychologist is first assessed, a process that may involve cognitive or personality testing and observation of the child in a group, as well as evaluating reports from teachers and parents. On this basis, recommendations can be made. These might focus on the child himself, and entail counselling or a special programme of work, or they might focus on the teacher, who might be helped to see the child in a different perspective and be given help in management strategies and special work programmes. The educational psychologist will also seek the co-operation of parents, perhaps with the aid of a social worker.

Recent surveys have demonstrated the confusion that exists in the minds of teachers about the role of educational psychologists, who themselves are divided on their objectives. Topping (1978) has shown how headteachers prefer to see educational psychologists as being concerned with individual cases rather than with the general work and policy of the school. In a recent survey involving over two hundred primary school teachers in Scotland, O'Hagan and Swanson (1983), whilst finding broad support for the work of the educational psychologist also found the expression of a need to develop a closer partnership. From these surveys it would seem that schools tend to value the work of educational psychologists provided that it does not challenge their competence or directly impinge upon matters they consider to be their professional autonomy. Although the work of the educational psychologist is appreciated when it involves teaching parents skills in the management of their children, it is often less accepted when it entails evaluating teaching methods, the curriculum or school policies. Some teachers apparently prefer to seek confirmation of their own viewpoint rather than dynamic solutions to their problems, and often expect the educational psychologist to back the school where there is a difference of opinion with parents.

Galloway (1985) considers that the 1981 Act not only challenges educational psychologists to show teachers how suitable provision can be made in ordinary schools for children with special educational needs, but also challenges teachers to perceive educational psychologists as a source of help in this respect rather than as a special school 'gatekeeper'. Current moves to involve the educational psychologist in a support team that includes support teachers and an EWO (as described on pp. 162–4) should help in this respect.

Treatment services

Children with emotional problems are sometimes given psychiatric treatment. Depending on local arrangements, this might be in a child guidance clinic by an inter-professional team (consisting perhaps of a psychiatrist, a psychiatric social worker, a non-medical psychotherapist and an educational psychologist) or in the child psychiatric out-patient clinic of a hospital. The quality of relationships between child guidance clinics and schools varies considerably (see Skinner, Platts and Hill, 1983), but from the research conducted by Johnson et al. (1980), it is clear that child guidance teams generally operate with the child as a member of his family rather than as a pupil in a school.

Johnson et al. (1980) found that, following a diagnostic interview, the most frequent form of clinical treatment involved the psychiatric social worker working with the parents. An alternative treatment is psychotherapy, the effectiveness of which has been the subject of much controversy. A psychotherapeutic approach implies that the child's behaviour arises from a 'disorder' that must be 'diagnosed' and then 'treated'. This is clearly unacceptable to those who believe that the context in which the behaviour occurs must be taken into consideration, and that a more productive approach is to provide support for parents and teachers that will enable them to improve the quality of the child's social environment. A literature review by Galloway et al. (1982) suggests that the success rate of psychotherapy with children whose behaviour is socially disruptive is not impressive, though it is more promising for children with 'neurotic' types of problem. Other kinds of recommendation include attendance at a special class or school, perhaps residential, and tuition in a tutor's home. More rarely, a child might be placed in hospital, a community home or assessment centre, or be recommended to be taken into care by the local authority, or given medication.

SUSPENSION AND EXCLUSION

Whether pupils who are persistently and seriously disruptive should be debarred from attending school as a last resort is a problem which any head may have to face. The issue became a politically sensitive one at the beginning of the 1980s when local authority suspension figures were shown to have risen dramatically. The number of suspensions from London secondary schools was 1,355 in 1981–2, which, in relation to the number of pupils enrolled, represented a rise of 80 per cent during the previous two years (*Times Educational Supplement,* 18 March 1983). The rate stayed at about this level during the next two years, although the proportion of pupils who were readmitted to their own school improved from two-thirds to about three-quarters (ILEA, 1986b).

There are no official agreed definitions of the terminology used for debarment from attending school, and usage differs widely between local education authorities. The Taylor Report (DES, 1977) on school government recommended that 'exclusion' should refer to debarment on medical grounds, 'suspension' to temporary debarments on any grounds and 'expulsion' to permanent debarment. However, the term *exclusion* is more often used to cover temporary debarment on non-medical grounds in cases where the pupil's presence in school is clearly undesirable (e.g. because of a violent personality clash with a teacher), or the pupil's presence represents a danger to the community (e.g. in a case of vandalism), or the pupil will not accept what the school considers to be reasonable discipline. Exclusion in this sense is technically not a punishment but an informal procedure which is invoked to provide a 'cooling-off' period during which the pupil and teachers can reassess the situation. Moreover, parents are enjoined to discuss the position with the school, which will lay down the conditions which must be met before the child can be reinstated.

Suspension is a power given to heads, who under a school's Articles of Government have power to debar pupils indefinitely for any reason considered adequate, provided that the case is reported to the governing body, the chief education officer and the parents. The only legal restraint is that the action should be 'reasonable'. The 1986 Education (No. 2) Act does

Beyond the School's Resources? 155

not use the term 'suspension', however, but instead distinguishes between exclusion which is 'for a fixed period', 'indefinite' or 'permanent'. *Expulsion* from school, which entails the removal of the pupil's name from the register, is rare, and often prohibited by the local education authority, who would be legally bound under the 1944 Education Act to find another school which will accept the pupil. Suspension (indefinite exclusion) is therefore used as the functional alternative to expulsion, since the pupil remains on the school register.

There are a number of major problems concerned with suspension and exclusion. First of all, any debarment creates a legal anomaly since it prevents parents fulfilling their obligations under Section 39 of the 1944 Education Act to 'secure regular attendance of registered pupils'. An exception arises when readmission is conditional only upon the parents agreeing to the school's requirement (e.g. that their child wears the school uniform or submits to a punishment).

Secondly, there are no national guidelines concerning the grounds upon which pupils can be debarred from attending school. In a study of one authority, Ling (1984) identified two kinds of reason which heads give for preventing pupils attending school. One is based on what Ling calls the 'camel's back' principle, which is used in cases entailing incidents which are small in themselves (e.g. infringements of dress regulations or cutting lessons) but have mounted up over a long period. In contrast, the 'outrage' principle is evoked for a single incident of extreme, intolerable behaviour. Figures for London for the early 1980s show that these two principles account for eight out of ten suspensions from secondary schools, the 'outrage' principle operating rather more often (ILEA, 1986b).

Thirdly, studies have shown that there are marked differences between schools in their readiness to suspend pupils. Galloway, Martin and Wilcox (1985) report that, out of thirty-three schools which were studied in Sheffield between 1974 and 1977, seven had no exclusions (defined as indefinite suspensions or exclusions of at least three weeks); moreover, the variations between schools could not be predicted on the basis of catchment area variables. On the basis of these findings, the researchers concluded that 'policy on exclusion is idiosyncratic to each school' (p. 56). Similar judgements emerge in reports by Grunsell (1979, 1980) and the ILEA (1984).

A fourth problem concerns the over-representation of black pupils. The Rampton Committee (1981) on the education of children from ethnic minority groups was unable to confirm this possibility, since relevant statistical information was lacking. However, the Commission for Racial Equality (1985) found that, between 1974 and 1980, pupils in Birmingham schools who were of Asian, Afro-Caribbean or other New Commonwealth origin were four times more likely to be suspended than white pupils, and six times more likely if under the age of fourteen. This numerical bias could not be explained in terms of the greater presence of black pupils in inner-city schools or in one-parent families. The Commission's report concluded that the behaviour of black pupils was often misinterpreted by white teachers (e.g. lowering of the eyes when confronted by authority figures is considered as a sign of respect in West Indian circles, but is often interpreted as insolence by white teachers). Although they did not wish to condone bad behaviour, the ethnic minority groups told the Commission that 'within some schools, the attitude towards black pupils and their aspirations was dismissive' (p. 48); for instance, confrontation could arise because a pupil, in order to demonstrate cultural identity, was affiliated to the Rastafari movement. Birmingham now keeps track of suspension cases and whether black pupils are disproportionately represented.

A fifth problem concerns the respective powers of headteachers, governing bodies and local authorities. The press brought this matter to national attention in September 1985, when Manchester City Council demanded the reinstatement of five boys who had been suspended for daubing racist and sexist slogans on the walls of Poundswick High School, although the head and governing body wanted the offenders permanently excluded. As a result, eighteen teachers went on strike until all the boys had left school nine months later. A major difficulty in this dispute was the absence of a clear appeals procedure against the right of a local education authority to override the head and governing body. The 1986 Education (No. 2) Act deals with the powers of heads, governors and local education authorities in a rather complicated way. Broadly, a local education authority has the duty to consult the governing body about any case of exclusion, but it may direct the reinstatement of the offending pupil; the governors, in turn, may make representations to an appeals committee, whose decision is binding on both parties. A head whose governing body and local education authority give conflicting directions for the reinstatement of a pupil must apply whatever direction leads to the earlier reinstatement.

Finally, the unsatisfactory arrangements for appeals have also been a major source of anxiety for the parents of excluded pupils. Until the 1986 Education (No. 2) Act, parents could usually appeal only to the school governors, though some authorities had set up independent bodies. Galloway et al. (1982) suggest that appeals to governors are doomed to failure because the teachers are so much more articulate than the parents, only they can provide direct evidence, and governors generally see their job as supporting the headteacher. Ling (1984) concluded from his study in one authority that appeals meetings in practice serve the purpose of censuring the pupil and parents, and argued that support agencies, parents and teachers need to be brought together so that a more genuinely 'welfare' approach can be adopted. In an information sheet on suspension published in the early 1980s, the Advisory Centre for Education (ACE) noted that parents of suspended children 'often feel isolated and confused and generally have no way of knowing whether the school has acted fairly'; the ACE further noted that local authorities frequently gave no advice on procedures, and that such advice as there was could be ignored by the schools.

The 1986 Education (No. 2) Act goes some way to establish the appeal rights of parents (or of pupils themselves if they are aged eighteen or over). Every local education authority is required to make arrangements for parents of permanently excluded pupils to make representations to an appeal committee. The decision of this committee is binding on all parties. The Act also makes it a duty of the headteacher to inform the parents of excluded pupils about their rights of appeal to the governing body and local education authority. The Inner London Education Authority has also recently established a process of conciliation between schools and parents of pupils who have been suspended. Where suspension lasts longer than ten days, parents (and a friend) are invited to a conciliation meeting, the purpose of which is to examine not only the pupil's contribution to the breakdown of relationships with the school but also 'any contributory factors in the school's organization, including teacher attitudes' (ILEA Committee Paper 6092, 1986).

OFF-SITE SUPPORT UNITS

During the 1970s, a major development in educational provision was the growth of off-site units for pupils whose behaviour is held to be beyond the control of the referring schools. As the survey by the ACE (1980) and a recent report on London units (ILEA, 1985) show, the units go under a bewildering variety of names, both nationally and locally, but 'support unit' or 'support centre' is used fairly widely. Off-site units cater mainly, but not entirely, for secondary school children, many of whom have been suspended from school. Besides providing an informal atmosphere and a curriculum centred on basic skills, they attempt to change behaviour through links with the home, tight control of the pupils' activities, a great deal of individual attention and regular group meetings in which the teachers and pupils share perceptions of the problem behaviour.

The number of off-site units in England rose from 23 in 1970 to 239 in 1977 (DES, 1978). In London alone, £1 million was allocated to the 'Disruptive Pupils' programme in 1978/9 (ILEA, 1978). By 1980 the number of units in the 63 per cent of local education authorities who made a return to the ACE was 415 in England and Wales plus a further 23 in Scotland, the Isle of Man and the Channel Islands (ACE, 1980). The same survey showed that the capital had over half the number of units in the UK. The last national survey (Ling et al., 1985) revealed that in 1983 there were 400 off-site units in England and Wales, suggesting that most of the growth had been in the late 1970s. Indeed, the number of units in London doubled between 1978 and 1982, even though the school population in this period fell by 73,000 (ILEA, 1985).

It is important to note that the development of support units has been piecemeal, outside the special school system and without the support of a nationally agreed policy on aims and approach. Ironically, the growth took place at a time when legislation was being passed to provide for the education of handicapped children in ordinary schools (Education Act 1976, s. 10) and the Warnock Committee (DES, 1978) was acknowledging the case for reducing the number of categories of children with special needs and of educating them in the mainstream system. In trying to interpret the trend, Lloyd-Smith (1984a, p. 4) notes the most commonly held view, officially supported by HMI (1978) and the Pack Report on indiscipline in Scottish schools (SED, 1977), that 'contemporary society had produced a generation of pupils among whom a greater proportion behaved in a deviant way'. However, Lloyd-Smith (1984a) goes on to suggest that 'the increase in behaviour problems could partly be due to a reduced willingness among teachers to tolerate "bad" behaviour' (p. 7). According to a recent report of London centres (ILEA, 1985) the development of special behavioural units was a consequence of the 'undertaker syndrome' – get rid of the body at any cost! (para. 2.4) – which in turn was caused by growing pressure from headteachers and teacher unions to do something about a situation 'caused by high staff turnover, shortage of staff, uncertainties in schools following reorganizations and amalgamations, and the ending of corporal punishment' (para. 3.5). Similarly, Whitty (1984, p. 139) observes that 'the sense of urgency evident in many of the proposals produced by local authorities arose from needs of the mainstream schools rather than the educational needs of the pupils extracted from them'.

In spite of their inauspicious beginnings, it seems that the units are generally well perceived by the pupils referred to them, and attendance is much higher than in the feeder schools. When Mortimore et al. (1983) interviewed 162 pupils in all types of behavioural units in London, they found that only 4 per cent complained about their experiences after the transition period. Over half the pupils maintained that they were learning more while a quarter felt that their personal problems were being met and that they were being treated more sympathetically than in school. The high teacher–pupil ratios of around 1 : 6 had enabled unit staff to get to know each pupil well and, in many cases, to develop close links with parents. Leavold (1984) observes how this 'intimate knowledge' not only produces greater opportunity for care, but also exposes pupils to a more intensive form of social control.

None the less, although some pupils clearly do benefit from a complete break with school, the feeling now is that referral to special units is not the best way to deal with most disaffected pupils. This change of view has come about for several reasons. The first of these concerns the *reasons for referring pupils* and the consequences of doing so for them and their schools. The basic issue here is one addressed several times in this book: Is school disaffection at least partly a product of certain features of mainstream schooling? And, if so, could schools themselves not do more to prevent this disaffection and therefore the need for referrals?

Lloyd-Smith (1984b) interviewed thirty-two secondary pupils attending four units in a Midlands education authority. He concluded that the majority suffered from such stress produced by their home circumstances that they were especially vulnerable to the added strains of the school curricula, rules and unsympathetic teacher–pupil relationships. In this study, as in several others, it appeared that many pupils in the units had been victims of 'deviance provocative' teachers, who insist on conformity while demonstrating little understanding of the pupils' personal problems. Lloyd-Smith's (1984b) view is that whilst a minority of referred pupils clearly did need special placement, the majority

> could have survived in conventional situations if their problems had been sensitively recognized and the schools had been able to respond flexibly to their needs. ... Disruption in schools is a problem which could be diminished dramatically if the principle of prevention rather than cure were to guide the schools' responses to it.
>
> (p. 97)

This may appear unsympathetic to the predicaments faced by many teachers, particularly those who work in inner city schools, yet it is a view that in essence emerges in many other reports on the experiences of disaffected pupils (e.g. Raven, 1977; Tattum, 1982; McDermott, 1984; CRE, 1985). One disturbing factor here is the disproportionate number of referred children who are of Afro-Caribbean origin (ILEA, 1981;

Mortimore *et al.*, 1983; CRE, 1985), suggesting the possibility of racial bias. Few would wish to deny that some schools have to contend with a great deal of destructive and provocative behaviour produced by a minority of pupils for whom *some* kind of special provision must be made. It is also no doubt true that some disaffected pupils invoke teacher provocation as an excuse for their behaviour in order to appear innocent victims of injustice. None the less, the consistency and strength of feeling that come through the pupils' comments are impressive. It is also consistent with the finding of Mortimore *et al.* (1983) that few pupils are referred for threatening or violent behaviour, but for conduct that is 'outrageous' or 'rude'. Furthermore, other evidence points to marked variations in the willingness and ability of some schools to contain the problem of disruption, as we noted in the section on suspensions. One head told the Hargreaves Committee (ILEA, 1984) that 'the unit was the place where the school "got rid of its rubbish" ' (para. 3.16.31). Whilst this view is extreme, Bird *et al.* (1981) found not only that there were significant differences in the number of referrals by schools in two outer London boroughs, but that these differences were unrelated to the range of support services available, the number of vacancies in the units or characteristics of the pupils themselves. Rather, the problem seemed to turn on contrasting approaches to the diagnosis of disaffection, different beliefs in the merits of referral versus containment and variations in the means by which a school was able to adapt to individual behavioural needs (e.g. the availability of suitable teachers). Mortimore *et al.* (1983), although 'very impressed' by the units they surveyed and by the teachers who 'enabled pupils with a history of failure and unhappiness to achieve success', recognized that 'off-site units can provide a dumping ground for difficult pupils and schools can be spared the need to take responsibility for disruptive behaviour' (p. 135).

A second kind of problem concerns the *curriculum* available to pupils in off-site units. Golby (1979) has argued that the educational aims of particular groups of pupils must be related to the aims of all pupils. Yet it is impossible to provide units with the range of specialist teaching and resources available in mainstream schools. The bulk of work in many units concerns attainment in English and mathematics. This is appropriate in the light of the pupils' previous lack of progress in the basic skills, but does not provide a balanced curriculum. Some units, however, make arrangements for pupils to take specialist courses on a part-time basis in ordinary schools or colleges of further education.

Thirdly, there is the thorny problem of *reintegration*. The stated aim of almost all units is to return pupils to normal schooling. This is often a phased process, pupils attending their previous school on a part-time basis at first, perhaps only for their favourite subject. However, close liaison between a unit and its feeder schools is clearly a prerequisite for successful reintegration. Studies of individual units (e.g. McDermott, 1984) suggest that teachers are often naturally reluctant to have referred pupils back in their classes, and the pupils themselves sometimes find they are branded on return and have difficulty in catching up with missed work. Return to a hostile context is likely to undo the work of the unit and there are practical difficulties in finding alternative schools. Topping's (1983) analysis of the literature showed how reintegration rates are generally low; and Ling et al. (1985), in a national survey, found that only 35 per cent of unit pupils returned to their original school. Tattum (1982, p. 223) is probably not far off the mark when he comments, 'It is probably true to say that it is easier to get a pupil admitted to a unit than to get him returned to an ordinary school.' Further, once readmitted to school, the problem behaviour often reappears. In one survey covering two northern counties (Daines, 1981), this happened in six out of every ten cases after a period of six or seven weeks. This is not surprising if the original bad behaviour was a response to alienating conditions in the schools.

Finally, largely because of their highly favourable staff–pupil ratios, off-site units are very expensive. From his analysis of different kinds of provision for disaffected pupils, Topping (1983) concluded that off-site units were 'strictly luxury class' in terms of cost-effectiveness. According to the 1980 survey conducted by the ACE, the average per capita cost of educating pupils in special behavioural units was £1,560 (ACE, 1980); this can be compared with £633, which was the equivalent figure for secondary school pupils in 1979–80 (CIPFA, 1981). The important point here is that if restricted resources are directed to the limited number of places in units, large numbers of unreferred pupils who also present behavioural problems are effectively denied support.

In sum, units have generally proved successful in helping pupils with their emotional and behavioural problems, at least in the short term. This is because they offer a complete break from school, increased contacts with parents and a regime in which the pupils feel they matter. None the less, evaluation of the units' success must also take into account the curriculum opportunities given to the pupils, whether more progress is made in learning than would otherwise have been the case, the practical problems of reintegration, the high cost and the possibility that a good deal of the pupils' disaffection could have been avoided in the first place. On these criteria, the viability of off-site units is called into question. Many local authorities are therefore looking at alternative forms of support and provision, and it is to a discussion of some of these that we now turn.

ALTERNATIVES TO OFF-SITE UNITS

On-site units

Units or special classes that are an integral part of the school offer a number of potential advantages over off-site provision. Whilst providing a 'breather' for teachers and 'cooling off' period for pupils, they contrast with off-site units in keeping pupils in the school and thus facilitate liaison between staff in the unit and the main school. Referral and reintegration should be much more straightforward, part-time placement should be a more practical proposition and continued access to the whole range of curriculum opportunities can more easily be ensured. The opportunity is also provided for unit staff to teach in the main part of the school for part of their time, enabling other pupils to benefit from their skills.

Whether these advantages are realized, however, is a different matter. Galloway et al. (1982) found that, in most of the on-site units in Sheffield, little attempt was made to link work with the regular school curriculum. Further, the ease with which pupils can be placed in an on-site unit may itself be a disadvantage if teachers overuse the facility rather than look to their own classroom actions and curriculum provision. The aims of the units must be clear to the pupils and their parents, as well as the teachers, and proper staffing and material sources must be provided to ensure a good measure of success.

School support teams

A radical alternative approach to off-site units involves the use of a peripatetic team to support the work of teachers in schools. On-site or off-site units can still be employed for pupils who need to spend some time away from the main school, but their role is less significant and the numbers of pupils referred can be substantially reduced.

The work of the support team in the Tower Hamlets area of London has been described by Coulby and Harper (1985) and will be taken as illustrative of this approach to disruption. The team comprises twelve teachers (Scale 3), an educational psychologist, a senior educational welfare officer and a clerical officer. Although pupils are not referred to off-site units of the kind described in the previous section, a special class of six pupils, working with one member of the team on a rotation basis, is available for short stays of about two weeks. By working in both the eighty primary schools and the fifteen secondary schools that serve the area, support for pupils who are referred can be continued at transfer.

Pupils who are referred are assessed using the Bristol Social Adjustment Guide and a specially produced checklist of ninety potentially disrupting behaviours. The objective is to pinpoint precisely the behaviours causing concern and to avoid general descriptions. This is because 'the more general ascriptive labels imply something wrong in the child which cannot be changed, whereas the behaviour-specific description points to specific classroom events which are a relatively conventional thing for a teacher to alter' (p. 40). The problem, which at first may have been described in vague terms that focus on faults in the child or deficiencies in his backgrd (e.g. 'disturbed' or 'maladjusted' or 'deprived'), is then carefully restated in precise terms that focus on what the child actually does, how often and when. Through observation in the classroom, a member of the team notes the kind of situation in which the problem is manifest (e.g. the classroom or playground, the day of the week and time), what is happening immediately before the unacceptable behaviour and the reaction of the teacher and other pupils that may be reinforcing the deviant conduct.

As far as possible, the child's home is not brought in to explain behaviour. This is not because parents are considered unimportant, but because it is assumed that school factors that may have precipitated the unacceptable behaviour are more amenable to change. There is also a fear that, by involving the home, a situation where there is already conflict might be worsened. In as many cases as possible, therefore, the focus of intervention is on the relationship between the teacher and the pupil. The programme may involve one or more strategies, such as

(1) working with teachers to improve their skills in dealing with disruptive behaviour;
(2) taking the class in order that the teacher can give more individual attention to the referred pupil and get to know him better;
(3) working with the teacher in the classroom;
(4) working with the pupil by providing remedial help, using behavioural techniques, or helping the pupil to improve his social skills;
(5) working with pupils in groups or even the whole class where the problem is seen as essentially a group one; and
(6) suggesting changes in features of the school organization, such as rules and timetabling.

Moreover, the skills teachers acquire in the course of an intervention programme should be of benefit to all pupils. When it is decided to seek the support of the family (as it is in about one-quarter of the cases), the parents are encouraged to acknowledge and reward the child's good behaviour rather than to indulge in punitive sanctions.

The 'team' approach is seen by Coulby and Harper to have fewer disadvantages than the 'unit' approach. In particular, the problem is treated in the context in which it occurs, and the help given to teachers can have a spill-over effect in the prevention of disruptive behaviour by other pupils. However, the strategy is one that needs painstaking preparation and careful communication within the school. Some teachers regard it as an intrusion into their professional autonomy or an admission of failure. Hence it is vital that time is given to clarifying the role of team members and to removing any mystique that may surround the enterprise.

In the support team approach, disruptive behaviour is not seen as a handicap that needs separate provision; rather it is seen as a special educational need that requires improved provision in mainstream schooling. This is in the spirit of the recommendations made by the Warnock Committee (DES, 1978) and the provisions of the 1981 Education Act. The approach therefore minimizes the chances of stigmatization occurring through categorizing children and placing them in special units, whilst it also enables access to the whole curriculum to be maintained. It is neither a pathological approach, which regards the child as in need of treatment for a 'disease', nor a crude behaviouristic approach, in which children are passively 'shaped' to become more conformist. Rather, it is an approach that recognizes that disruptive behaviour must take account of the way in which children interact with their social environment. By attending to the curriculum, the teaching arrangements and the features of the school organization greater opportunity is being given to the child to gain fulfilment through the development of an interest in learning rather than through the defensive, ego-enhancing routines of disruptive behaviour.

Enlisting parental support

Melton and Long (1986) have described an innovation in King's Lynn, Norfolk, that involves the establishment of behavioural contracts with parents. The scheme is based upon the premise that 'some of the most assertive adolescents have developed a self-centred, controlling attitude to their environment and in personal relationships'. Although 'schools, with their limited sanctions, offer little incentive for pupils to modify their behaviour', the home is much more favourably placed in this respect and can be a powerful determinant of a child's conduct in school. The parents of referred pupils, who may be in primary or secondary schools, are first interviewed by an educational psychologist, support teacher and a senior teacher in the school. The aim here is to define the problem, sort out possible conflicts between home and school and eventually help the parents accept that there is a 'problem' for which they should accept some responsibility and which they can help to solve. The parents are then encouraged to enter into a partnership with the school by making a contract. This involves granting and withholding their child's 'privileges' on the basis of a weekly mark determined by teachers' reports of the pupil's behaviour. For instance, pocket money, freedom to go out, to be with friends and watch television are varied according to this criterion. The pupil's self-reports on his behaviour are also taken seriously to encourage his total involvement.

The scheme is claimed to enjoy a large measure of success, though so far it has not been independently evaluated. In eighteen of the first twenty cases monitored, teachers reported improvement in behaviour. The authors conclude that 'the early resolution of otherwise intractable behaviour problems is promoting positive school attitudes in some of the most difficult children'. Further, the project is highly cost-effective. Whereas an off-site support teacher was taking on only about seven pupils, a project support teacher can supervise as many as twenty-five. It is clear, too, that the scheme scores over off-site units in preserving access to the full range of curriculum activities, as well as helping the pupil to realize improvement in the context in which he was formerly behaving unacceptably.

There are therefore powerful arguments in favour of parental contract schemes. As we saw in Chapter 2, behaviour patterns are, to a large extent, formed as a consequence of control strategies used in the home; and success in off-site units may well be due as much to the special efforts taken to develop links with parents as to work with the pupils directly. There is, of course, the danger that the philosophy will encourage the belief that bad behaviour is all the home's fault and has nothing to do with relationships in the school, learning problems or boredom with the curriculum. It would therefore be extremely important to supplement a parent support scheme with appropriate staff development and support in school, and to ensure that attention is also given to the range of school factors considered in previous chapters, such as teachers' perceptions of disaffection, teacher–pupil relationships, curriculum opportunities, classroom management skills and the use of praise and punishment. Another danger is that, in so far as the scheme relies on the manipulation of privileges, it suffers from the same shortcomings as behaviour modification strategies discussed in Chapter 7, that there is the possibility that behavioural change will be made only because of a desire to win rewards and benefits rather than from any genuine reappraisal of self in relation to others. Finally, there is the danger that, in homes where there is family discord, the child may perceive the restrictions on his life-style as unduly punitive and supplying further evidence of a rejecting environment. Any evaluation of these schemes must therefore be sensitive to these possibilities.

In short, schemes that provide support for the pupils and teachers within the school and enlist the support of parents avoid the main problems that beset off-site units. Needless to say, the schemes are not mutually exclusive. Ideally, a local education authority should ensure support for teachers who are experiencing problems of individual pupil conduct, or who have general difficulties of class control, whilst also facilitating the co-operation of parents and providing a special unit in which pupils can exceptionally be placed for short periods.

The hallmark of a local authority programme for dealing with disruptive behaviour must be its capacity to help all teachers, and not only those directly involved in support units or support teams. Although provision must be made for managing crisis cases, the focus of concern should be on ways in which disaffection and disruption can be prevented. In so far as the special behaviour units, off-site and on-site, have demonstrated some success with pupils who were previously considered 'irremediable', there is room for optimism that teachers in general can learn to adopt the perceptions, approaches and skills of the unit teachers and so reduce the scale of disruptive behaviour in ordinary schools. To this end, the Hargreaves Report (ILEA, 1984) on improving secondary schools recommends that the staff of off-site units should make contributions to in-service courses in classroom management, receive visits from pastoral staff and probationer teachers and be involved in induction courses. A related recommendation is that the experience of working in an off-site unit should be regarded as an important factor by appointment committees considering teachers for promotion. If measures such as these were to be implemented across the country, it is just possible that, in the long run, the extreme behaviour of a minority of disaffected pupils will have indirectly produced benefits for all children in school.

FURTHER READING

Support services

Davis, L. (1985) *Caring for Secondary School Pupils*, Heinemann, London.
(Based on a study of almost 800 pupils in three comprehensive schools, this book reveals many facts – many very depressing – about the quality of care schools and the social services give to pupils with problems.)

Johnson, D. *et al.* (1980) *Secondary Schools and the Welfare Network*, Allen & Unwin, London.
(An account of the pastoral system in schools and links with welfare agencies, educational psychologists, child guidance clinics, etc.)

Support units

Lloyd-Smith, M. (ed.) (1984) *Disrupted Schooling: the Growth of the Special Unit*, John Murray, London.
(A collection of papers dealing with various perspectives and future policy.)
Tattum, D. (1982) *Disruptive Pupils in Schools and Units*, Wiley, Chichester.
(A detailed sociological study of units and of the conditions in schools that lead to referrals.)

Alternatives to off-site units

Coulby, D. and Harper, T. (1985) *Preventing Classroom Disruption*. Croom Helm, London.
(A detailed account of the work in schools by a peripatetic support team in London.)

REFERENCES AND AUTHOR INDEX

Page references are in square brackets at the end of each entry.

Acton, T. A. (1980) Educational criteria of success, *Educational Research*, Vol. 22, pp. 163-9. [36]
Advisory Centre for Education (n.d.) *Suspension* (information sheet). [157]
Advisory Centre for Education (1980) ACE Survey – Disruptive Units, *Where*, 158, pp. 6-7; plus data presented at ACE/NAME Conference on Disruptive Units, 17 May. [157,158,161]
Alexander, P. (1973) Normality, *Philosophy*, Vol. 48, pp. 137-51. [45]
Amidon, E. and Hunter, E. (1966) *Improving Teaching: the Analysis of Classroom Interaction*, Holt, Rinehart & Winston, New York. [85]
Anderson, L. M., Evertson, C. and Brophy, J. (1979) An experimental study of effective teaching in first-grade reading groups, *Elementary School Journal*, Vol. 79, pp. 193-223. [102]
Anderson, L. M., Evertson, C. M. and Emmer, E. T. (1980) Dimensions in classroom management derived from recent research, *Journal of Curriculum Studies*, Vol. 12, pp. 343-56. [93]
Anderson, R., Monoogian, S. T. and Reznick, J. S. (1976) The understanding and enhancing of intrinsic motivation of preschool children, *Journal of Personality and Social Psychology*, Vol. 34, pp. 915-22. [102]
Antcliffe, J. (1986) Power and the teacher, *Values*, Vol. 1, pp. 5-7. [7]
Apple, M. (ed.) (1982) *Education and Power*, Routledge & Kegan Paul, London. [49]
Aronfreed, J. (1976) Moral development from the standpoint of a general psychological theory, in T. Lickona (ed.) *Moral Development and Behavior: Theory, Research and Social Issues*, Holt, Rinehart & Winston, New York. [118]
Assistant Masters and Mistresses Association (1984) *The Reception Class Today*, AMMA, London. [3,5]
Association of Directors of Social Services (1978) *Social Work Services for Children in Schools*, ADSS, Taunton, Somerset. [151]
Association of Educational Psychologists (1983) *Alternatives to Corporal Punishment*, AEP, Durham. [99]

References and Author Index

Ausubel, D. P., Novak, J. D. and Hanesian, H. (1978) *Educational Psychology: a Cognitive View* (2nd edn), Holt, Rinehart & Winston, New York. [50,51,52]

Axelrod, S., Hall, R. V. and Tams, A. (1979) Comparisons of two common seating arrangements, *Academic Therapy*, Vol. 15, pp. 29-36. [95]

Bagley, C. (1982) Achievement, behaviour disorder, and social circumstances in West Indian children, in G. K. Verma and C. Bagley (eds.) *Self-Concept, Achievement and Multicultural Education*, Macmillan, London. [24]

Baldwin, J. (1972) Delinquent schools in Tower Hamlets: a critique, *British Journal of Criminology*, Vol. 12, pp. 399-401. [34]

Baldwin, J. and Wells, H. (1979-83) *Active Tutorial Work*, Books 1-5, Blackwell, Oxford. [144,145,149]

Ball, S. J. (1980) Critical encounters in the classroom and the process of establishment, in P. Woods (ed.) *Pupil Strategies*, Croom Helm, London. [86]

Ball, S. J. (1981) *Beechside Comprehensive*, Cambridge University Press. [63]

Bandura, A. (1977) *Social Learning Theory*, Prentice-Hall, Englewood Cliffs, NJ. [21,120]

Bandura, A., Ross, D. and Ross, S. A. (1961) Transmission of aggression through imitation of aggressive models, *Journal of Abnormal and Social Psychology*, Vol. 63, pp. 575-82. [25]

Barrell, G. (1983) On corporal punishment, *Education Today*, Vol. 33, pp. 5-16. [127]

Bean, P. (1981) *Punishment*, Martin Robertson, Oxford. [136]

Becker, H. S. (1963) *Outsiders: Studies in the Sociology of Deviance*, Collier-Macmillan, New York. [67]

Belson, W. A. (1978) *Television, Violence and the Adolescent Boy*, Saxon House, London. [14,25]

Bennett, S. N., Desforges, C., Cockburn, A. and Wilkinson, B. (1984) *The Quality of Pupil Learning Experiences*, Erlbaum, Hillsdale, NJ. [100]

Berger, M. (1979) Behaviour modification and professional practice: the dangers of a mindless technology, *Bulletin of the British Psychological Society*, Vol. 32, pp. 418-19. [109]

Berger, M. (1982) Applied behaviour analysis in education: a critical assessment and some implications for teachers, *Educational Psychology*, Vol. 2, pp. 289-99. [109]

Berger, M., Yule, W. and Rutter, M. (1975) Attainment and adjustment in two geographical areas: II. The prevalence of specific reading retardation, *British Journal of Psychiatry*, Vol. 126, pp. 510-19. [39]

Berkowitz, L. (1962) *Aggression: a Social Psychological Analysis*, McGraw-Hill, New York. [25]

Berkowitz, L., Parke, R. D., Leyens, J. P., West, S. and Sebastian, R. J. (1978) Experiments on the reactions of juvenile delinquents to filmed violence, in L. A. Herov, H. Berger and D. Shaffer (eds.) *Aggression and Antisocial Behaviour in Childhood and Adolescence*, Pergamon, Oxford. [25,26]

Best, R. and Decker, S. (1985) Pastoral care and welfare: some underlying issues, in P. Ribbins (ed.) *Schooling and Welfare*, Falmer Press, London. [138]

Best, R., Jarvis, C. and Ribbins, P. (1980) *Perspectives on Pastoral Care*, Heinemann, London. [149]

Best, R., Ribbins, P., Jarvis, C. and Oddy, D. (1983) *Education and Care*, Heinemann, London. [139,140]

Beynon, J. (1985) *Initial Encounters in the Secondary School*, Falmer Press, London. [70,88,98]

Bird, C. (1980) Deviant labelling in schools: the pupils' perspective, in P. Woods (ed.) *Pupil Strategies*, Croom Helm, London. [69,70]

Bird, C., Chessum, R., Furlong, J. and Johnson, D. (1981) *Disaffected Pupils*, Brunel University, London. [41,60,160]

Blackburn, K. (1975) *The Tutor*, Heinemann, London. [144]

Board of Education (1905) *Suggestions for the Consideration of Teachers and Others Concerned in the Work of Public Elementary School*, HMSO, London. [54]

Board of Education (1927, 1937) *Handbook of Suggestions for the Consideration of Teachers and Others Concerned in the Work of Public Elementary School*, HMSO, London. [54,55]

Boggiano, A. K. and Ruble, D. N. (1979) Competence and the overjustification effect: a developmental study, *Journal of Personality and Social Psychology*, Vol. 37, pp. 1462-8. [101].

Boggiano, A. K., Ruble, D. N. and Pittman, T. S. (1982) The mastery hypothesis and the overjustification effect, *Social Cognition*, Vol. 1, No. 1, pp. 38-49. [101]

Bohman, M. (1981) The interaction of heredity and childhood environment: some adoption studies, *Journal of Child Psychology and Psychiatry*, Vol. 22, pp. 195-200. [16]

Boseley, S. (1986) Epitaph for Hirofumi, *Times Educational Supplement*, 5 March. [48]

Bowlby, J. (1953) *Child Care and the Growth of Love*, Penguin, Harmondsworth. [17]

Bowlby, J. (1979) *The Making and Breaking of Affectional Bonds*, Tavistock, London. [17]

Bowles, S. and Gintis, H. (1976) *Schooling and Capitalist America*, Routledge & Kegan Paul, London. [48,49]

Boyson, R. (1973) Order and purpose, in B. Turner (ed.) *Discipline in Schools*, Ward Lock Educational, London. [3-4]

British Psychological Society (1980) *Report of a Working Party on Corporal Punishment in Schools*, BPS, Leicester. [127,136]

Bronfenbrenner, U. (1971) *Two Worlds of Childhood: US and USSR*, Allen & Unwin, London. [49-50]

Bronfenbrenner, U. (1976) Who cares for America's children?, in V. C. Vaughan and T. B. Brazelton (eds.) *The Family - Can It Be Saved?*, Year Book Medical Publications, Chicago. [26]

Brophy, J. E. (1981) Teacher praise: a functional analysis, *Review of Educational Research*, Vol. 51, pp. 5-32. [99,100,103,113]

Brophy, J. E. and Evertson, C. M. (1976) *Learning from Teaching*, Allyn & Bacon, Boston. [92,93]

Brophy, J. E., Evertson, C. M., Anderson, L. M., Baum, M. and Crawford, J. (1976) *Student Characteristics and Teaching*, Longman, New York. [102,103]

Brophy, J. E., Evertson, C. M., Anderson, L. M. and Crawford, J. (1981) *Student Characteristics and Teaching*, Longman, New York. [61]

Brown, G. (1982) Comment on article by Dr Kevin Wheldall, 'Applied Behavioural Analysis', Education Section and Review, *British Psychological Society Journal*, Vol. 6, pp. 51-2. [111]

References and Author Index

Bulman, K. (1984) The relationship between the pastoral curriculum, the academic curriculum and the pastoral programme, *Pastoral Care in Education*, Vol. 2, pp. 107-13. [143,144]

Burns, R. B. (1978) The relative effectiveness of various incentives and determinants as judged by pupils and teachers, *Educational Studies*, Vol. 4, pp. 229-43. [103]

Burt, C. and Howard, D. M. (1952) The nature and causes of maladjustment among children of school age, in P. Williams (ed.) (1974) *Behaviour Problems in School*, University of London Press. [33,34]

Burton, R. V. (1976) Honesty and dishonesty, in T. Lickona (ed.) *Moral Development and Behavior: Theory, Research and Social Issues*, Holt, Rinehart & Winston, New York. [118]

Burwood, L. and Brady, C. (1984) Changing and explaining behaviour by reward, *Journal of Philosophy of Education*, Vol. 18, pp. 109-13. [109-10]

Button, L. (1975) *Developmental Group Work with Adolescents*, Hodder & Stoughton, London. [144]

Button, L. (1982/3) *Group Tutoring for the Form Teacher*, Books 1 and 2, Hodder & Stoughton, London. [144,149]

Button, L. (1983) The pastoral curriculum, *Pastoral Care in Education*, Vol. 1, pp. 74-83. [144]

Carnell, C. (1983) Disturbed pupils' perception of the personality characteristics of their teachers, *Maladjustment and Therapeutic Education*, Vol. 1, pp. 22-5. [71,72,74]

Casassus, B. (1986) Death and injury result of hard discipline, *Times Educational Supplement*, 17 January. [125]

Caspari, I. (1976) *Troublesome Children in Class*, Routledge & Kegan Paul, London. [41]

Castle, E. B. (1961) *Ancient Education and Today*, Penguin, Harmondsworth. [46]

Central Advisory Council for Education (England) (1963) *Half Our Future* (The Newsom Report), HMSO, London. [58-9,129]

Central Advisory Council for Education (England) (1967) *Children and Their Primary Schools* (Plowden Report), Vol. 1, HMSO, London. [58,129]

Chartered Institute of Public Finance and Accountancy (1981) *Education Statistics 1979-80 Actuals*, CIPFA, London. [161]

Chazan, M. (1976) The early identification of children with adjustment problems, in K. Wedell and E. C. Raybould (eds.) *The Early Identification of Educationally 'at risk' Children*, Educational Review Occasional Publications No. 6. Birmingham. [27,28]

Chazan, M. and Jackson, S. (1971) Behaviour problems in the infant school, *Journal of Child Psychology and Psychiatry*, Vol. 12, pp. 191-210. [15]

Chazan, M. and Jackson, S. (1974) Behaviour problems in the infant school: change over two years, *Journal of Child Psychology and Psychiatry*, Vol. 15, pp. 33-46. [15]

Chazan, M. and Laing, A. (1982) *The Early Years*, Open University Press, Milton Keynes. [12]

Chazan, M., Laing, A., Jones, J., Harper, G. C. and Bolton, J. (1983) *Helping Young Children with Behaviour Difficulties*, Croom Helm, London. [13,28]

Cheesman, P. L. and Watts, P. E. (1985) *Positive Behaviour Management: a Manual for Teachers*, Croom Helm, London. [110,111,113]

Clegg, A. B. (1962) *Delinquency and Discipline*, Council & Education Press. [125]

Cohen, A. K. (1956) *Delinquent Boys: the Culture of the Gang*. Routledge & Kegan Paul, London. [23]
Cohen, L. and Cohen, A. (1987) *Disruptive Behaviour: a Sourcebook for Teachers*, Harper & Row, London. [10]
Commission for Racial Equality (1985) *Birmingham Local Education Authority and Schools: Referral and Suspension of Pupils*, CRE, London. [155,156,159,160]
Coopersmith, J. (1967) *The Antecedents of Self-esteem*, W. H. Freeman, San Francisco. [22,51]
Corrigan, P. (1979) *Schooling the Smash Street Kids*, Macmillan, London. [49,55,57,78,126-7]
Coulby, D. (1984) The creation of the disruptive pupil, in M. Lloyd-Smith (ed.) *Disrupted Schooling*, Murray, London. [60]
Coulby, D. and Harper, T. (1985) *Preventing Classroom Disruption*, Croom Helm, London. [162,164,167]
Cumming, C. E., Lowe, T., Tulips, J. and Wakeling, C. (1981) *Making the Change: a Study of the Process of the Abolition of Corporal Punishment*, Hodder & Stoughton/Scottish Council for Research in Education, London. [127]
Daines, R. (1981) Withdrawal units and the psychology of problem behaviour, in B. Gillham (ed.) *Problem Behaviour in the Secondary School*, Croom Helm, London. [161]
Daunt, P. E. (1975) *Comprehensive Values*, Heinemann, London. [55]
Davie, R., Butler, N. and Goldstein, H. (1972) *From Birth to Seven*, Longman, London. [15,22,23,29,103]
Davies, B. (1979) Children's perceptions of social interaction in school, *CORE*, Vol. 3, Fiche 11F9. [72,75,88]
Davies, L. (1984) *Pupil Power: Deviance and Gender in School*, Falmer Press, London. [61,77,78]
Davis, L. (1985) *Caring for Secondary School Pupils*, Heinemann, London. [151,166]
Dawson, R. L. (1984) Disturbed pupils' perceptions of their teachers' support and strictness, *Maladjustment and Therapeutic Education*, Vol. 2, pp. 24-7. [71,74,76]
Dearden, R. F. (1984) Behaviour modification: towards an ethical reappraisal, in R. F. Dearden, *Theory and Practice in Education*, Routledge & Kegan Paul, London. [112]
Deci, E. L. (1975) *Intrinsic Motivation*, Plenum, New York. [101]
Delamont, S. (1976) *Interaction in the Classroom*, Methuen, London. [73]
Denscombe, M. (1980) Keeping 'em quiet: the significance of noise for the practical activity of teaching, in P. Woods (ed.) *Teacher Strategies*, Croom Helm, London. [61]
Denscombe, M. (1984) Control, controversy and the comprehensive school, in S. J. Ball (ed.) *Comprehensive Schooling: a Reader*, Falmer Press, London. [6,7]
Denscombe, M. (1985) *Classroom Control: a Sociological Perspective*, Allen & Unwin, London. [52,57,88,139]
Department of Education and Science (1977) *A New Partnership for Our Schools* (Taylor Report), HMSO, London. [154]
Department of Education and Science (1978) *Special Educational Needs* (Warnock Report), HMSO, London. [158]
Department of Education and Science (1983) *Corporal Punishment in Schools: A Consultative Document*, HMSO, London. [128]

Dierenfield, R. (1982) All you need to know about disruption, *Times Educational Supplement*, 29 January. [4]
Docking, J. W. (1982) The impact of control styles on young children in the early years of schooling, *Early Child Development and Care*, Vol. 8, pp. 239-52. [60]
Docking, J. W. (1985) Classroom control strategies and educational outcomes, *Maladjustment and Therapeutic Education*, Vol. 3, pp. 5-12. [53]
Docking, J. W. (1986) The Attribution of Personal Responsibility: A Developmental Study. Unpublished Ph.D. thesis, University of Surrey. [132]
Driscoll, A. and Reynolds, R. (1984) Teachers' self-perceptions and descriptions of students for whom they hold positive attitudes, *Journal of Classroom Interaction*, Vol. 19, pp. 2-8. [61]
Dubanoski, R. A., Inaba, M. and Gerkewic, K. (1983) Corporal punishment in schools: myths, problems and alternatives, *Child Abuse Neglect*, Vol. 7, pp. 277-8. [125]
Dunham, J. (1981) Disruptive pupils and stress, *Educational Research*, Vol. 23, pp. 205-13. [8]
Durkheim, E. (1961) *Moral Education*, Free Press, Glencoe, Ill. [46,47,50]
Dweck, C., Davidson, W., Nelson, S. and Enna, B. (1978) Sex differences in learned helplessness: II. The contingencies of evaluative feedback in the classroom; and III. An experimental analysis, *Developmental Psychology*, Vol. 14, pp. 268-76. [103]
Earls, F. and Richman, N. (1980) Behavior problems in pre-school children of West Indian-born parents: a re-examination of family and social factors, *Journal of Child Psychology and Psychiatry*, Vol. 21, pp. 107-17. [24]
Egglestone, J. (1979) The construction of deviance in school, in L. Barton and L. Barton (eds.) *Schools, Pupils and Deviance*, Nafferton Books, Nafferton. [67]
Elliott, J. (1982) The idea of pastoral curriculum: a reply to T. H. McLaughlin, *Cambridge Journal of Education*, Vol. 12, pp. 53-60. [143]
Emler, N. P. (1983) Moral character, in H. Weinreich-Haste and D. Locke (eds.) *Morality in the Making*, Wiley, Chichester. [16,28,67]
Engfer, A. and Schneewind, K. A. (1982) Causes and consequences of harsh parental punishment: an empirical investigation in a representative sample of 570 German families, *Child Abuse and Neglect*, Vol. 6, pp. 129-39. [19]
Entwistle, H. (1970) *Child-Centred Education*, Methuen, London. [59]
Evans, M. (1967) Punishment in a day school for maladjusted children, *Therapeutic Education*, June, pp. 32-35. [126]
Eysenck, H. J. (1970) *The Structure of Human Personality* (3rd edn), Methuen, London. [119]
Eysenck, H. J. (1975) *The Inequality of Man*, Fontana, London. [16]
Eysenck, H. J. (1977) *Crime and Personality* (3rd edn), Paladin, St Albans. [16]
Eysenck, H. J. (1979) The origins of violence, *Journal of Medical Ethics*, Vol. 5, pp. 105-7. [16]
Eysenck, H. J. and Nias, D. K. B. (1978) *Sex, Violence and the Media*, Temple Smith, London. [25]
Farley, A. C., Kreutter, K. J., Russell, R. R., Blackwell, S., Finkelstein, H. and Hyman, I. A. (1978) The effects of eliminating corporal punishment in schools, *Inequality in Education*, Vol. 23, pp. 57-60. [127]
Farrington, D. P., Biron, L. and Leblanc, M. (1982) Personality and delinquency, in J. Gunn and D. P. Farrington (eds.) *Abnormal Offenders. Delinquency and the Criminal Justice System*, Wiley, Chichester. [16]

Feingold, B. F. (1975) *Why Your Child Is Hyperactive.* Random House, New York. [26]
Ferri, E. (1975) Background and behaviour of children in one-parent families, *Therapeutic Education*, Vol. 3, pp. 6–10. [22]
Feshback, S. and Singer, J. L. (1971) *Television and Aggression.* Jossey-Bass, San Francisco. [25]
Fincham, F. D. (1983) Developmental dimensions in attribution theory, in J. Jaspars, F. D. Fincham and M. Hewstone (eds.) *Attribution Theory and Research: Conceptual, Developmental and Social Dimensions*, Academic Press, London. [132]
Flew, A. (1976) *Sociology, Equality and Education*, Macmillan, London. [67]
Fogelman, K. (1983) *Growing up in Britain*, Macmillan, London. [29]
Foss, B. (1965) Punishment, rewards and the child, *New Society*, Vol. 6, pp. 8–10. [119–20]
Francis, P. (1975) *Beyond Control? A Study of Discipline in the Comprehensive School*, Allen & Unwin, London. [123]
Freedman, J. L. (1975) *Crowding and Behaviour*, W. H. Freeman, San Francisco. [26]
French, D. C. and Waas, G. A. (1985) Behavior problems of peer-neglected and peer-rejected elementary-age children: parent and teacher perspectives, *Child Development*, Vol. 56, pp. 246–52. [18]
Furlong, V. J. (1976) Interaction sets in the classroom: towards a study of pupil knowledge, in M. Stubbs and S. Delamont (eds.) *Explorations in Classroom Observation*, Wiley, Chichester. [73,75]
Furlong, V. J. (1977) Anancy goes to school: a case study of pupils' knowledge of their teachers, in P. Woods and M. Hammersley (eds.) *School Experience*, Croom Helm, London. [73,77]
Furlong, V. J. (1985) *The Deviant Pupil: Sociological Perspectives*, Open University Press, Milton Keynes. [79]
Galloway, D. (1985) *Schools, Pupils and Special Educational Needs*, Croom Helm, London. [153]
Galloway, D., Martin, R. and Wilcox, B. (1985) Persistent absence from school and exclusion from school: the predictive power of school and community variables, *British Education Research Journal*, Vol. 11, pp. 51–9. [155]
Galloway, D., Ball, T., Bloomfield, D. and Seyed, R. (1982) *Schools and Disruptive Pupils*, Longman, London. [31,37,99,140,141,142,153,156,162]
Galton, M. and Wilcocks, J. (1983) *Moving from the Primary School*, Routledge & Kegan Paul, London. [42]
Gannaway, H. (1976) Making sense of school, in M. Stubbs and S. Delamont (eds.) *Explorations in Classroom Observation*, Wiley, Chichester. [71,73,74,75]
Gibson, I. (1978) *The English Vice: Beating, Sex and Shame in Victorian England and After*, Duckworth, London. [55,124,126]
Giles, R. H. (1977) *The West Indian Experience in British Schools*, Heinemann, London. [24,64]
Gillham, B. (1984) School organization and the control of disruptive incidents, in N. Frude and H. Gault (eds.) *Disruptive Behaviour in Schools*, Wiley, Chichester. [97]
Gilmore, C., Mattison, S., Pollack, G. and Stewart, J. (1985) Identification of aggressive behaviour tendencies in junior age children, *Educational Review*, Vol. 37, pp. 53–64. [13]

References and Author Index

Giroux, H. (1981) *Culture and the Process of Schooling*, Falmer Press, London. [49]

Glynn, T. (1982) Antecedent control of behaviour in educational contexts, *Educational Psychology*, Vol. 2, pp. 215-29. [95,96]

Golby, M. (1979) Special units: some educational issues, *Socialism and Education*, Vol. 6, pp. 6-9. [160]

Goldstein, H. (1980) Fifteen thousand hours: a review of the statistical procedures, *Journal of Child Psychology and Psychiatry*, Vol. 21, pp. 363-9. [36]

Gosden, P. H. J. H. (ed.) (1969) *How They Were Taught*, Blackwell, Oxford. [124]

Green, P. A. (1985) Multi-ethnic teaching and pupils' self-concepts, in Swann Report, *Education for All: Report of the Committee of Enquiry into Children from Ethnic Minority Groups*, HMSO, London. [66]

Grunsell, R. (1979) Suspension and the sin bin boom: soft option for schools, *Where*, No. 152, pp. 307-9. [155]

Grunsell, R. (1980) *Beyond Control? Schools and Suspensions*, Writers & Readers/Chamelon, Richmond. [155]

Grunsell, R. (1985) *Finding Answers to Disruption: Discussion Exercises for Secondary Teachers*, School Curriculum Development Committee/Longman, York. [11]

Gunter, B. (1981) Can television teach kindness? *Bulletin of the British Psychological Association*, Vol. 34, pp. 121-4. [26]

Gunter, B. (1984) Television as a facilitator of good behaviour amongst children, *Journal of Moral Education*, Vol. 13, pp. 152-9. [26]

Guthrie, I. D. (1979) The Sociology of Pastoral Care in an Urban School. Unpublished MA dissertation, King's College, London. [138]

Halloran, J. D., Brown, R. C. and Chaney, D. C. (1970) *Television and Delinquency*, Leicester University Press. [14,25]

Hamblin, D. H. (1974) *The Teacher and Counselling*, Blackwell, Oxford. [146]

Hamblin, D. H. (1978) *The Teacher and Pastoral Care*, Blackwell, Oxford. [144,148,149]

Hamilton, D. (1984) First days at school, in S. Delamont (ed.) *Readings on Interaction in the Classroom*, Methuen, London. [87]

Hammersley, M. (1976) The mobilization of pupil attention, in M. Hammersley and P. Woods (eds.) *The Process of Schooling*, Routledge & Kegan Paul/Open University Press, London. [84]

Hannam, C., Smyth, P. and Stephenson, N. (1976) *The First Year of Teaching*, Penguin, Harmondsworth. [3]

Hargreaves, A. (1978) The significance of classroom coping strategies, in L. Barton and R. Meighan (eds.) *Sociological Interpretations of Schooling and Classrooms*, Nafferton Books, Nafferton. [90]

Hargreaves, D. H. (1967) *Social Relations in a Secondary School*, Routledge & Kegan Paul, London. [34,62]

Hargreaves, D. H. (1975) *Interpersonal Relations and Education* (revised student edn), Routledge & Kegan Paul, London. [70,82,83,88,89]

Hargreaves, D. H. (1976) Reactions to labelling, in M. Hammersley and P. Woods (eds.) *The Process of Schooling*, Routledge & Kegan Paul/Open University Press. [67]

Hargreaves, D. H. (1978) What teaching does to teachers, *New Society*, 9 March, pp. 540-2. [8,52]

Hargreaves, D. H. (1981) Schooling for delinquency. In L. Barton and S. Walker (eds.) *Schools, Teachers and Teaching*, Falmer, London. [33]

Hargreaves, D. H. (1982) *The Challenge for the Comprehensive School*, Routledge & Kegan Paul, London. [40-1,42,44,138,139]

Hargreaves, D. H., Hester, S. K. and Mellor, F. J. (1975) *Deviance in Classrooms*, Routledge & Kegan Paul, London. [32,64,68,69,70,79]

Harrop, L. A. (1980a) Behaviour modification in schools: a time for caution, *Bulletin of the British Psychological Society*, Vol. 33, pp. 158-60. [108,109]

Harrop, L. A. (1980b) Recent developments in behaviour modification in the classroom, *Psychology Teaching*, Vol. 8, pp. 29-34. [108]

Haviland, J. M. (1979) Teachers' and students' beliefs about punishment, *Journal of Educational Psychology*, Vol. 71, pp. 563-70. [131]

Heal, K. (1978) Misbehaviour among school children: the role of the school in strategies for prevention, *Policy and Politics*, Vol. 6, pp. 321-32. [37]

Hearn, J. (1985) Progress towards the abolition of corporal punishment, *Forum*, Vol. 27, No. 2, pp. 54-6. [125]

Her Majesty's Inspectorate of Schools (1978) *Behaviour Units: A Survey of Special Units with Behavioural Problems*, Department of Education and Science, London. [158]

Her Majesty's Inspectorate of Schools (1979) *Aspects of Secondary Education in England*, HMSO, London. [4]

Hinde, R. A. and Tamplin, A. (1983) Relations between mother-child interaction and behaviour in preschool, *British Journal of Developmental Psychology*, Vol. 1, pp. 231-57. [18]

Home Office (1985) *Criminal Statistics: England and Wales*, HMSO, London. [5]

Hoffman, M. L. (1970) Conscience, personality and socialization techniques, *Human Development*, Vol. 13, pp. 90-126. [19,121]

Humphries, S. (1981) *Hooligans or Rebels? An Oral History of Working Class Childhood and Youth, 1889-1939*, Blackwell, Oxford. [3,124]

Inner London Education Authority (1978a) *Disruptive Pupils*, Committee Paper 8085. [158]

Inner London Education Authority (1978b) *Survey of Corporal Punishment in ILEA Secondary Schools*. [124,158]

Inner London Education Authority (1981) *Ethnic Census of School Support Centres and Educational Guidance Centres*, RS784/81. [159]

Inner London Education Authority (1983) *Race, Sex and Class: 2. Multi-Ethnic Education in Schools*. [66]

Inner London Education Authority (1984) *Improving Secondary Schools* (Hargreaves Report). [7,37,155,160,166]

Inner London Education Authority (1985a) *Improving Primary Schools* (Thames Report). [42]

Inner London Education Authority (1985b) *Off-Site Support Centres*, Committee Paper 5042. [15,157,158]

Inner London Education Authority (1986a) *The Junior School Project*. ILEA Research and Statistics Branch, London. [4,8,15,23,24,32,33,37,39,40,43,44, 94,97,99,100]

Inner London Education Authority (1986b) *Suspension and Expulsion from Schools*, RS1054/80. [154,155]

Jenkins, R. K. (1973) *Behavior Disorders of Childhood and Adolescence*, Thomas, Springfield, Ill. [19]

References and Author Index

Johnson, D. J. (1985) Pastoral care and welfare networks, in P. Lang and M. Marland (eds.) *New Directions in Pastoral Care*, Blackwell, Oxford. [138]

Johnson, D. J., Ransom, E., Packwood, T., Bowden, K. and Kogan, H. (1980) *Secondary Schools and the Welfare Network*, Allen & Unwin, London. [139,153,166]

Johnson, L. V. and Bany, M. A. (1970) *Classroom Management: Theory and Skill Training*, Collier-Macmillan Canada, Toronto. [83]

Johnston, K. D. and Krovetz, M. L. (1976) Levels of aggression in a traditional and a pluralistic school, *Educational Research*, Vol. 18, pp. 146–51. [42]

Jones, E. E. and Nisbett, R. E. (1971) The actor and the observer: divergent perceptions of the causes of behavior, in E. E. Jones et al. (eds.) *Attribution: Perceiving the Causes of Behavior*, General Learning Press, Morristown, NJ. [61]

Kagan, J. (1979) *The Growth of the Child: Reflections on Human Development*, Harvester, Hassocks. [15]

Kanouse, D. E., Gumpert, P. and Canavan-Gumpert, D. (1981) The semantics of praise, in J. H. Harvey, W. Ickes and R. F. Kidds (eds.) *New Directions in Attribution Research*, Vol. 3, Erlbaum, Hillsdale, NJ. [102]

Kant, I. (trans. 1887) *The Philosophy of Law*, trans. E. Hastie, Clark, Edinburgh. [133]

Kay Shuttleworth, J. P. (1841/1961) *On the Punishment of Pauper Children in Workhouses*, Occasional Papers No. 1, College of St Mark and St John, London. [136]

Kedar-Voivodas, G. and Tannenbaum, A. J. (1979) Teachers' attitudes toward young deviant children, *Journal of Educational Psychology*, Vol. 71, pp. 800–8. [62]

King, R. (1978) *All Things Bright and Beautiful? A Sociological Study of Infant Schools*, Wiley, Chichester. [70]

Kloska, A. and Ramasut, A. (1985) Teacher stress, *Maladjustment and Therapeutic Education*, Vol. 3, pp. 19–26. [6]

Kniveton, B. H. (1973) The effect of rehearsal delay on long-term imitation of filmed aggression, *British Journal of Psychology*, Vol. 64, pp. 259–65. [25]

Kohlberg, L. (1968) The child as moral philosopher, *Psychology Today*, Vol. 2, pp. 25–30. [130,131]

Kounin, J. (1970) *Discipline and Group Management in Classrooms*, Holt, Rinehart & Winston, New York. [81,85,90,92,93,113]

Krumboltz, J. and Thoresen, C. (1969) *Behavioral Counselling*, Holt, Rinehart & Winston, New York. [146]

Kyriacou, C. (1980) Occupational stress among schoolteachers: a research report, *CORE*, Vol. 4, Fiche 11. [6]

Kysel, F., Varlaam, A., Stoll, L. and Sammons, P. (1983) The Child at School – a new behaviour schedule. In ILEA (1986) *The Junior School Project* (Appendix 2), ILEA Research and Statistics Branch, London. [13,38]

Lacey, C. (1970) *Hightown Grammar: the School as a Social System*, Manchester University Press. [51,61,62]

Lake, C. (1985) Preventive approaches to disruption, *Maladjustment and Therapeutic Education*, Vol. 3, pp. 47–52. [94]

Landon, J. (1895) *The Principles and Practice of Teaching and Class Management* (2nd edn), Holden, London. [46]

Laslett, K. and Smith, C. (1984) *Effective Classroom Management*, Croom Helm, London. [98,99]

Lawrence, D. H. (1915) *The Rainbow*, Penguin, Harmondsworth. [1,3]
Lawrence, J., Steed, D. and Young, P. (1977) *Disruptive Behaviour in a Secondary School*, Goldsmiths College, University of London. [43,142]
Lawrence, J., Steed, D. and Young, P. (1984a) *Disruptive Children – Disruptive Schools?*, Croom Helm, London. [97,141,142]
Lawrence, J., Steed, D. and Young, P. (1984b) European voices on disruptive behaviour in schools: definitions, concern, and types of behaviour, *British Journal of Educational Studies*, Vol. 32, pp. 4–17. [4]
Leach, D. (1977) Teachers' perceptions and 'problem' pupils, *Educational Review*, Vol. 29, pp. 188–203. [60]
Leavold, J. (1984) A sanctuary for disruptive pupils, in M. Lloyd-Smith (ed.) *Disrupted Schooling*, Murray, London. [159]
Lefkowitz, M. M. (1977) *Growing up to Be Violent*, Pergamon, New York. [18,23]
Leigh, M. (1978) Group counselling in practice, in H. J. Blackham (ed.) *Education for Personal Autonomy*, Bedford Square Press, London. [148]
Lepper, M. R. (1983) Extrinsic reward and intrinsic motivation: implications for classroom practice, in J. M. Levine and M. C. Wang (eds.) *Teacher and Student Perceptions: Implications for Learning*, Erlbaum, Hillsdale, NJ. [101,113]
Lepper, M. R. and Gilovich, T. (1981) The multiple functions of reward: a social-developmental perspective, in S. S. Brehm, S. M. Kassin and F. X. Gibbons (eds.) *Developmental Psychology: Theory and Research*, Oxford University Press, New York. [101]
Lepper, M. R., Green, D. and Nisbett, R. E. (1973) Undermining children's intrinsic interest with extrinsic reward, *Journal of Personality and Social Psychology*, Vol. 28, pp. 129–37. [100–1]
Light, P. (1979) *The Development of Social Sensitivity*, Cambridge University Press. [121]
Ling, R. (1984) A suspended sentence: the role of the LEA in the removal of disruptive pupils from school, in J. F. Schostak and T. Logan (eds.) *Pupil Experience*, Croom Helm, London. [155,157]
Ling, R., Davies, G., Brannigan, C., Cooper, M. and Weston, B. (1985) A survey of off-site special units in England and Wales, *CORE*, Vol. 9, Fiche 4/5. [158,161]
Livingstone, S. (1975) Implications of corporal punishment, *New Behaviour*, Vol. 25. [126]
Lloyd-Smith, M. (1984a) The growth of special units for disaffected pupils, in M. Lloyd-Smith (ed.) *Disrupted Schooling*, John Murray, London. [158,167]
Lloyd-Smith, M. (1984b) Disaffected pupils in special units, in M. Lloyd-Smith (ed.) *Disrupted Schooling*, Murray, London. [60,159,167]
Lowenstein, L. F. (1972) *Violence in Schools and its Treatment*, National Association of Schoolmasters, Hemel Hempstead. [3,5]
Lowenstein, L. F. (1975) *Disruptive Behaviour in Schools*, National Association of Schoolmasters, Hemel Hempstead. [5]
McCann, E. (1978) Children's perceptions of corporal punishment, *Educational Studies*, Vol. 4, pp. 167–72. [126]
McDermott, J. (1984) A disruptive pupil unit: referral and integration, in M. Lloyd-Smith (ed.) *Disrupted Schooling*, Murray, London. [159,161]
McGee, R., Silva, P. A. and Williams, S. (1984) Behaviour problems in a population of seven-year-old children: prevalence, stability and types of disorder – research report, *Journal of Child Psychiatry and Psychology*, Vol. 25, pp. 251–9. [13,15,39]

McLaughlin, T. H. (1982) The idea of a pastoral curriculum, *Cambridge Journal of Education,* Vol. 12, pp. 34-52. [143]

Macmillan, K. (1977) *Education Welfare: Strategy and Structure,* Longman, London. [151]

Macmillan, K. (1980) The education welfare officer: past, present and future, in M. Craft, J. Raynor and L. Cohen (eds.) *Linking Home and School* (3rd edn), Harper & Row, London. [151]

McMichael, P. (1981) Behavioural judgements: a comparison of two teacher rating scales, *Educational Studies,* Vol. 7, pp. 61-72. [13]

McPhail, P., Ungoed Thomas, J. R. and Chapman, H. (1972) *Moral Education in the Secondary School,* Longman, London. [71,72,73]

Manning, M. and Slukin, A. M. (1984) The function of aggression in the pre-school and primary years, in N. Frude and H. Gault (eds.) *Disruptive Behaviour in Schools,* Wiley, Chichester. [84,98]

Manning, M., Heron, J. and Marshall, T. (1978) Styles of hostility and social interactions at nursery, at school and at home, in L. A. Hersov and M. Berger (eds.) *Aggression and Anti-Social Behaviour in Childhood and Adolescence,* Pergamon, Oxford. [28]

Marland, M. (1974) *Pastoral Care,* Heinemann, London. [138,149]

Marland, M. (1980) The pastoral curriculum, in R. Best, C. Jarvis and P. Ribbins (eds.) *Perspectives on Pastoral Care,* Heinemann, London. [143]

Marsh, P. (1979) Review of Belson (1978), op. cit., *Educational Research,* Vol. 21, pp. 230-1. [14]

Marsh, P., Rosser, E. and Harré, R. (1978) *The Rules of Disorder,* Routledge & Kegan Paul, London. [74]

Marshall, J. D. (1984) John Wilson on the necessity of punishment, *Journal of Philosophy of Education,* Vol. 18, pp. 97-104. [130]

Maurer, A. (1974) Corporal punishment, *American Psychologist,* Vol. 29, pp. 614-24. [126]

Measor, L. and Woods, P. E. (1984) *Changing Schools: Pupil Perspectives on Transfer to a Comprehensive,* Open University Press, Milton Keynes. [42]

Melton, K. and Long, M. (1986) Alias Smith and Jones, *Times Educational Supplement,* 11 April. [43,164-5]

Merrett, F. E. (1981) Studies in behaviour modification in British settings, *Educational Psychology,* Vol. 1, pp. 13-38. [106]

Merrett, F. E. (1985) *Encouragement Works Better than Punishment,* Positive Products, Birmingham. [105,106,114]

Merrett, F. E. and Wheldall, K. (1978) Playing the game: a behavioural approach to classroom management in the junior school, *Educational Review,* Vol. 30, pp. 41-50. [107]

Merrett, F. E. and Wheldall, K. (1984) Classroom behaviour problems which junior school teachers find most troublesome, *Educational Studies,* Vol. 10, pp. 87-92. [6]

Merrett, F. E. and Wheldall, K. (1986) Observing pupils and teachers in classrooms (OPTIC): behavioural observation schedule for use in schools, *Educational Psychology,* Vol. 6, pp. 57-70. [107]

Miller, W. B. (1958) Lower class culture as a generating milieu of gang delinquency, *Journal of Social Issues,* Vol. 14, pp. 5-19. [23]

Milner, D. (1984) The development of ethnic attitudes, in H. Tajfel (ed.) *The Social Dimension,* Vol. 1, Cambridge University Press. [66]

Mitchell, S. and Shepherd, M. (1966) A comparative study of children's behaviour at home and at school, *British Journal of Educational Psychology*, Vol. 36, pp. 248-54. [13]

Moore, T. (1966) Difficulties of the ordinary child in adjusting to primary school, *Journal of Child Psychology and Psychiatry*, Vol. 7, pp. 17-38. [42]

Morine-Dershimer, G. (1982) Pupil perceptions of teacher praise, *Elementary School Journal*, Vol. 82, pp. 421-35. [102]

Mortimore, P., Davies, J., Varlaam, A. and West, A. (1983) *Behaviour Problems in Schools*, Croom Helm, London. [23,32,158,160]

Musgrave, P. W. (1977) Corporal punishment in some English elementary schools, 1900-39, *Research in Education*, Vol. 17, pp. 1-11. [124]

Nash, P. (1966) *Authority and Freedom in Education*, Wiley, New York. [56,110,117]

Nash, R. (1973) *Classrooms Observed*, Routledge & Kegan Paul, London. [51]

Nash, R. (1976a) Pupil expectations of their teachers, in. M. Stubbs and S. Delamont (eds.) *Explorations in Classroom Observation*, Wiley, Chichester. [71,72]

Nash, R. (1976b) *Teacher Expectations and Pupil Learning*, Routledge & Kegan Paul, London. [75,89]

National Association of Schoolmasters/Union of Women Teachers (n.d.) *The Retreat from Authority*, NAS/UWT, Birmingham. [47]

National Association of Schoolmasters/Union of Women Teachers (1981) *Discipline or Disorder in Schools: a Disturbing Choice*, NAS/UWT, Birmingham. [31]

National Association of Schoolmasters/Union of Women Teachers (1985) *Pupil Violence and Disorder in School*, NAS/UWT, Birmingham. [3,4,5]

National Institute of Mental Health (1982) *Television and Behaviour*, US Department of Health and Human Service, Washington, DC. [25]

National Union of Teachers (1976) *Discipline in Schools*, NUT, London. [48]

National Union of Teachers (1983, 1984) *Corporal Punishment: the Case for Alternatives*, NUT, London. [127,128]

Neill, A. S. (1960) *Summerhill: A Radical Approach to Child Rearing*, Hart, New York. [50]

Neill, R. St J. (1986) Children's reported responses to teachers' non-verbal signals: a pilot study, *Journal of Education for Teaching*, Vol. 12, pp. 53-63. [86]

Nelson-Jones, R. (1982) *The Theory and Practice of Counselling Psychology*, Holt, Rinehart & Winston, New York. [146]

Newell, P. (ed.) (1972) *A Last Resort? Corporal Punishment in Schools*, Penguin, Harmondsworth. [124]

Newell, P. (ed.) (1979) *Corporal Punishment in Schools: Abolition Handbook*, Society of Teachers Opposed to Physical Punishment, Croydon. [124]

Newell, P. (1984) Suffer little children, *Times Educational Supplement*, 30 November. [124,125]

Newson, J. and Newson, E. (1963) *Patterns of Infant Care in an Urban Community*, Allen & Unwin, London. [23]

Newson, J. and Newson, E. (1968) *Four Years Old in an Urban Community*, Allen & Unwin, London. [126]

Newson, J. and Newson, E. (1976) *Seven Years Old in the Home Environment*, Allen & Unwin, London. [126]

Ng, Y. Y. J. (1982) The effects of various seating arrangements on a group of ESN(M) children with behavioural problems, *CORE*, Vol. 6, Fiche 1/2. [95-6]

O'Hagan, F. J. and Edmunds, S. G. (1982) Pupils' attitudes towards teachers strategies for controlling disruptive behaviour, *British Journal of Educational Psychology*, Vol. 5, pp. 331-40. [122]

O'Hagan, F. J. and Swanson, W. I. (1983) Teachers' views regarding the role of the educational psychologist in schools, *Research in Education*, Vol. 29, pp. 29-40. [152]

O'Leary, K. D. and O'Leary, S. G. (1977) *Classroom Management: the Successful Use of Behaviour Modification* (2nd edn), Pergamon, New York. [108]

O'Leary, K. D., Kaufman, K. F., Kass, R. E. and Drabman, R. S. (1970) The effects of loud and soft reprimands on the behaviour of disruptive students, *Exceptional Children*, Vol. 37, pp. 144-5. [120]

Otty, N. (1972) *Learner Teacher*, Penguin, Harmondsworth (Reprinted 1983 by Bristol Classical Press). [53,54]

Page, G. T. and Thomas, J. B. (eds.) (1977) *International Dictionary of Education*, Kogan Page, London. [52]

Parke, R. D. and Deur, J. L. (1972) Schedule of punishment and inhibition of aggression in children, *Developmental Psychology*, Vol. 7, pp. 231-4. [116]

Partington, J. A. and Hinchliffe, G. (1979) Some aspects of classroom management, *British Journal of Teacher Education*, Vol. 5, pp. 231-41. [94]

Patterson, Littman, R. and Bricker, W. (1967) Assertive behavior in children: a step towards a theory of aggression, *Monographs of the Society for Research in Child Development*, Vol. 32, No. 113. [21]

Peters, R. S. (1966) *Ethics and Education*, Allen & Unwin, London. [59,116,129]

Phillips, A. and Whitfield, R. (1980) *Report of Pilot Survey of Secondary School Teachers' Working Conditions*, University of Aston Department of Educational Enquiry, Birmingham. [8]

Piaget, J. (1932) *The Moral Judgement of the Child*, Routledge & Kegan Paul, London. [130-1]

Piaget, J. (1953) *The Origins of Intelligence in the Child*, Routledge & Kegan Paul, London. [20]

Pik, R. (1981) Confrontation situations and teacher-support systems, in B. Gillham (ed.) *Problem Behaviour in the Secondary School*, Croom Helm, London. [136]

Plamenatz, J. (1967) Responsibility and punishment, in P. Laslett and W. C. Runciman (eds.) *Philosophy, Politics and Society: Third Series*, Blackwell, Oxford. [132]

Pollard, A. (1982) A model of classroom coping strategies, *British Journal of Sociology of Education*, Vol. 3, pp. 19-37. [90]

Pollard, A. (1984) Coping strategies and the multiplications of differentiation in infant classrooms, *British Journal of Educational Research*, Vol. 10, pp. 33-48. [90]

Poteet, J. A. (1974) *Behaviour Modification: a Practical Guide for Teachers*, Unibooks, London. [110]

Power, M. J., Alderson, M. K., Phillipson, C. M., Schoenberg, E. and Morris, J. M. (1967) Delinquent schools, *New Society*, 19 October. [34]

Pring, R. (1981) Behaviour modification: some reservations, in P. Gurney (ed.) *Behaviour Modification in Education*, University of Exeter. [112]

Professional Association of Teachers (1985) *Corporal Punishment and Alternative Sanctions*, PAT, Derby. [3]

Purkey, S. and Smith, M. (1983) Effective schools: a review, *Elementary Schools Journal*, Vol. 83, pp. 427-52. [33]
Quicke, J. C. (1978) Rogerian Psychology and 'non-directive' counselling in schools, *Educational Research*, Vol. 20, pp. 192-200. [146]
Ralphs Report (1973) *The Role and Training of Education Welfare Officers*, Report of the Local Government Training Board, HMSO, London. [151]
Rampton Report (1981) *West Indian Children in our Schools*, Interim Report of Inquiry into the Education of Children from Ethnic Minority Groups, HMSO, London. [155]
Raven, J. (1977) School rejection and its amelioration, *Educational Research*, Vol. 20, pp. 3-9. [40,159]
Raymond, J. (1985) *Implementing Pastoral Care in Schools*, Croom Helm, London. [139,149]
Rawls, J. (1954) Two concepts of rules, in H. B. Acton (ed.) *The Philosophy of Punishment*, Macmillan, London. [122]
Redl, F. (1966) *When We Deal with Children*, Free Press, New York. [82]
Reynolds, D. (1976) The Delinquent School, in M. Hammersley and P. Woods (eds.) *The Process of Schooling*, Routledge & Kegan Paul/Open University Press, London. [32,33,34,44,117,118]
Reynolds, D. (1982) The search for effective schools, *School Organization*, Vol. 2, pp. 215-37. [33,34,43]
Reynolds, D. (1985) *Studying School Effectiveness*, Falmer Press, London. [33,43,44]
Reynolds, D. and Murgatroyd, D. S. (1977) The sociology of schooling and the absent pupil: the school as a factor in the generation of truancy, in H. C. M. Carroll (ed.) *Absenteeism in South Wales: Studies of Pupils, Their Homes and Their Secondary Schools*, Faculty of Education, University of Swansea. [125]
Reynolds, D. and Sullivan, M. (1979) Bringing schools back in, in L. Barton and R. Meighan (eds.) *Schools, Pupils and Deviance*, Nafferton Books, Nafferton. [47-8,63]
Ribbins, P. (ed.) (1985) *Schooling and Welfare*, Falmer Press, London. [149]
Richardson, E. (1967) *The Environment of Learning*, Nelson, London. [86,87]
Riley, D. and Shaw, M. (1985) *Parental Supervision and Juvenile Delinquency*, HMSO, London. [19,23,51]
Ritchie, J. and Ritchie, J. (1981) *Spare the Rod*, Allen & Unwin, Sydney. [126]
Roberts, J. I. (1971) *Scene of the Battle: Group Behavior in the Urban Classrooms*, Anchor Books, New York. [82,83,93]
Robertson, J. (1981) *Effective Classroom Control*, Hodder & Stoughton, London. [98]
Robinson, M. (1978) *Schools and Social Work*, Routledge & Kegan Paul, London. [147]
Rogers, C. R. (1942) *Counselling and Psychotherapy*, Houghton-Mifflin, Boston. [146]
Rogers, C. R. (1951) *Client-centered Therapy*, Houghton-Mifflin, Boston. [22,146]
Rose, G. and Marshall, A. (1975) *School Counselling and Social Work*, Wiley, Chichester. [151]
Rosenbaum, M. (1986) Vote on corporal punishment, *ACE Bulletin*, Vol. 12, p. 2. [128]

Rosenfield, P., Lambert, N. M. and Black, A. (1985) Desk arrangement effects on pupil classroom behavior, *Journal of Educational Psychology*, Vol. 77, pp. 101-8. [96]
Rosser, E. and Harré, R. (1976) The meaning of trouble, in M. Hammersley and P. Woods (eds.) *The Process of Schooling*, Routledge & Kegan Paul/Open University, London. [76]
Royce, R. J. (1984) School-based punishment, *Journal of Philosophy of Education*, Vol. 18, pp. 85-95. [134]
Russell, B. (1932) *Education and the Social Order*, Allen & Unwin, London. [50]
Russell, C. and Russell, W. M. S. (1979) The natural history of violence, *Journal of Medical Ethics*, Vol. 5, pp. 108-17. [26]
Rutter, M. (1967) A children's behaviour questionnaire for completion by teachers, *Journal of Child Psychology and Psychiatry*, Vol. 8, pp. 1-11. [13]
Rutter, M. (1970) Sex differences in children's responses to family stress, in E. J. Anthony and C. Koupernik (eds.) *The Child and his Family*, Wiley, New York. [15]
Rutter, M. (1975) *Helping Troubled Children*, Penguin, Harmondsworth. [15,19,51]
Rutter, M. (1979) Maternal deprivation, 1972-78: new findings, new concepts, new approaches, *Child Development*, Vol. 50, pp. 283-305. [16]
Rutter, M. (1981) *Maternal Deprivation Reassessed* (2nd edn), Penguin, Harmondsworth. [17]
Rutter, M. (1983) School effects in pupils' progress - findings and policy implementation, *Child Development*, Vol. 54, pp. 1-29. [33]
Rutter, M. and Giller, H. (1983) *Juvenile Delinquency: Trends and Perspectives*, Penguin, Harmondsworth. [19,23]
Rutter, M. and Madge, N. (1976) *Cycles of Disadvantage*, Heinemann, London. [16]
Rutter, M., Tizard, J. and Whitmore, K. (1970) *Education, Health and Behaviour*, Longman, London. [39]
Rutter, M., Yule, W., Berger, M., Yule, B., Morton, J. and Bagley, C. (1974) Children of West Indian immigrants: I. Rates of behavioural deviance and of psychiatric disorder, *Journal of Child Psychology and Psychiatry*, Vol. 15, pp. 241-62. [24]
Rutter, M., Yule, B., Morton, J. and Bagley, C. (1975) Children of West Indian immigrants: III. Home circumstances and family patterns, *Journal of Child Psychology and Psychiatry*, Vol. 16, pp. 105-23. [24]
Rutter, M., Maughan, B., Mortimore, P. and Ouston, J. (1979) *Fifteen Thousand Hours: Secondary Schools and their Effects on Children*, Open Books, London. [4,8,32,33,35,36,39,44,96,99,120,125,140]
Ryan, B. A. (1979) A case against behavior modification in the 'ordinary' classroom, *Journal of School Psychology*, Vol. 17, pp. 131-6. [111,112]
Saunders, M. (1979) *Class Control and Behaviour Problems*, McGraw-Hill, London. [98]
Schostak, J. F. (1983) *Maladjusted Schooling: Deviance, Social Control and Individuality in Secondary Schooling*, Falmer Press, London. [79,138,139]
Scottish Education Department (1977) *Truancy and Indiscipline in Schools* (Pack Report), HMSO, London. [6,52,158]

184 Control and Discipline in Schools: Perspectives and Approaches

Seebohm Report (1968) *Report of the Committee on Local and Allied Personal Social Services,* HMSO, London. [151]
Sharp, A. (1981) The significance of classroom dissent, *Scottish Educational Review,* Vol. 13, pp. 141–51. [78–9]
Sharp, R. and Green, A. (1975) *Education and Social Control: A Study in Progressive Primary Education,* Routledge & Kegan Paul, London. [50,62]
Sherzter, B. and Stone, S. C. (1974) *Fundamentals of Counselling,* Houghton-Mifflin, Boston. [145]
Shipman, M. D. (1971) *Education and Modernization,* Faber, London. [48]
Short, G. (1983) Rampton revisited: a study of racial stereotypes in the primary school, *Durham and Newcastle Review,* Vol. 10, pp. 82–6. [64]
Silberman, C. E. (1973) *Crisis in the Classroom: the Remaking of American Education,* Wildwood House, London. [52]
Skinner, A., Platts, H. and Hill, B. (1983) *Disaffection from School: Issues and Inter-agency Responses,* National Youth Bureau, Leicester. [152,153]
Skinner, B. F. (1953) *Science and Human Behavior,* Macmillan, New York. [104]
Skinner, B. F. (1968) *The Technology of Teaching,* Appleton-Century-Crofts, New York. [119]
Skinner, B. F. (1973) *Beyond Freedom and Dignity,* Penguin, Harmondsworth. [21,104,119,126,133]
Smith, R. (1985) *Freedom and Discipline,* Allen & Unwin, London. [57,134]
Society of Education Officers (1979) *The Education Welfare Service,* SEO, London. [151]
Sollenberger, R. T. (1968) Chinese-American child-rearing practices and juvenile delinquency, *Journal of Social Psychology,* Vol. 74, pp. 13–23. [26]
Sparks, A. D., Thornburg, K. R., Ispa, J. M. and Gray, M. M. (1984) Prosocial behaviours of young children related to parental childrearing attitudes, *Early Child Development and Care,* Vol. 15, pp. 291–8. [19]
Stagles, B. (1985) What teachers like about Active Tutorial Work, *Pastoral Care in Education,* Vol. 3, pp. 13–24. [145]
Stebbins, R. (1980) The role of humour in teaching: strategy and self-expression, in P. Woods (ed.) *Teacher Strategies,* Croom Helm, London. [75]
Steed, D. (1985) Disruptive pupils, disruptive schools: which is the chicken, which is the egg?, *Educational Research,* Vol. 27, pp. 3–8. [6,7]
Stenhouse, L. (1975) *An Introduction to Curriculum Research and Development,* Heinemann, London. [52]
Stillman, A. and Maychall, K. (1984) *School to School,* NFER/Nelson, Windsor. [43]
Stott, D. H. (1966) *Studies of Troublesome Children,* Tavistock, London. [15]
Stott, D. H. (1974) *The Social Adjustment of Children,* Hodder & Stoughton, London. [13]
Stott, D. H. (1979) The Bristol Social Adjustment Guides, *Therapeutic Education,* Vol. 7, pp. 34–44. [13]
Stott, D. H. (1981) Behaviour disturbance and failure to learn: a study of cause and effect, *Educational Research,* Vol. 23, pp. 163–72. [39]
Swann Report (1985) *Education for All,* Report of the Committee of Inquiry into the Education of Children from Ethnic Minority Groups, HMSO, London. [24,65]

Swann, W. B. and Pittman, T. S. (1977) Initiating play activity of children: the moderating influence of verbal cues on intrinsic motivation, *Child Development*, Vol. 48, pp. 1128-32. [102]

Tall, G. (1985) An evaluation of the introduction of Active Tutorial Work on a Birmingham Comprehensive School, *Pastoral Care in Education*, Vol. 3, pp. 24-9. [145]

Tannenbaum, P. H. (1980) Entertainment as vicarious emotional experience, in P. H. Tannenbaum (ed.) *The Entertainment Functions of Television*, Erlbaum, Hillsdale, NJ. [25]

Tattum, D. (1982) *Disruptive Pupils in Schools and Units*, Wiley, Chichester. [76,138,159,161,167]

Tattum, D. (1984) Disruptive pupils: system rejects? in J. F. Schostak and T. Logan (eds.) *Pupil Experience*, Croom Helm, London. [72,78]

Tattum, D. (1985) Disrupted pupil behaviour: a sociological perspective, *Maladjustment and Therapeutic Education*, Vol. 3, pp. 12-18. [60]

Taylor, M. J. (1983) *Caught Between: A Review of Research into the Education of Pupils of West Indian Origin* (revised edn), NFER/Nelson, Windsor. [24,64]

Taylor, M. J. and Hegarty, S. (1985) *The Best of Both Worlds ... ?: A Review of Research into the Education of Pupils of South Asian Origin*, NFER/Nelson, Windsor. [64]

Thacker, J. (1985) Extending developmental group work to junior/middle schools: an Exeter project, *Pastoral Care in Education*, Vol. 3, pp. 4-31. [144]

Thompson, B. (1975) Secondary school pupils: attitudes to school and teachers, *Educational Research*, Vol. 18, pp. 62-72. [76]

Tizard, B. (ed.) (1980) *Fifteen Thousand Hours: a Discussion*, University of London Institute of Education. [36]

Topping, K. J. (1978) Consumer confusion and professional conflict in educational psychology, *Bulletin of the British Psychological Society*, Vol. 31, pp. 265-7. [151-2]

Topping, K. J. (1983) *Educational Systems for Disruptive Adolescents*, Croom Helm, London. [28,161]

Tutt, N. (1983) Maladjustment - a sociological perspective, *Maladjustment and Therapeutic Education*, Vol. 1, pp. 7-14. [13]

Tyler, L. (1970) The counsellor's identity, *The Counsellor*, Vol. 5, pp. 2-5. [145]

University of Exeter (1980) *The Rutter Research*, University of Exeter School of Education. [36]

Wall, W. D. (1973) The problem child in schools, *London Educational Review*, Vol. 2, pp. 3-21. [20]

Walker, R. and Goodson, I. (1977) Humour in the classroom, in P. Woods and M. Hammersley (eds.) *School Experience*, Croom Helm, London. [75]

Waller, W. (1932) *The Sociology of Teaching*, Wiley, New York. [88]

Wedge, P. and Prosser, H. (1973) *Born to Fail?*, Arrow Books/National Children's Bureau, London. [31]

Weiss, B. (1982) Food additives and environmental chemicals as sources of childhood behavior disorders, *Journal of the American Academy of Child Psychiatry*, Vol. 21, pp. 144-52. [26]

Wells, H., Baldwin, J. and Smith, A. (eds.) (1983) *Active Tutorial Work: Sixteen to Nineteen*, Blackwell, Oxford. [144]

Werthman, C. (1963) Delinquents in school: test of the legitimacy of authority, in B. R. Cosin *et al.* (eds.) *School and Society,* Routledge & Kegan Paul/Open University Press, London. [76]
West, D. J. (1982) *Delinquency: its Roots, Careers and Prospects,* Heinemann, London. [14,15,18,29,37]
Wheldall, K. and Merrett, F. E. (1984) *Positive Teaching: the Behavioural Approach,* Allen & Unwin, London. [114]
Wheldall, K., Morris, M., Vaughan, P. and Ng, Y. Y. (1981) Rows versus tables: an example of the use of behavioural ecology in two classes of eleven-year-old children, *Educational Psychology,* Vol. 1, pp. 171-84. [95]
Whitty, G. (1984) Special units in a changing climate: agencies of change or control?, in M. Lloyd-Smith (ed.) *Disrupted Schooling: the Growth of the Special Unit,* Murray, London. [158]
Williams, N. and Williams, S. (1970) *The Moral Development of Children,* Macmillan, London. [110]
Williamson, D. (1980) Pastoral care or 'pastoralization', in R. Best, C. Jarvis and P. Ribbins (eds.) *Perspectives on Pastoral Care,* Heinemann, London. [138]
Willis, P. E. (1977) *Learning to Labour: How Working Class Kids Get Working Class Jobs,* Saxon House, Farnborough. [24,29,49,78]
Willis, P. E. (1983) Cultural production and theories of reproduction, in L. Barton and S. Walker (eds.) *Race, Class and Education,* Croom Helm, London. [29]
Wilson, J. (1977) *Philosophy and Practical Education,* Routledge & Kegan Paul, London. [129]
Wilson, J. (1984) A reply to James Marshall, *Journal of Philosophy of Education,* Vol. 18, pp. 105-7. [129,130]
Wilson, P. S. (1971) *Interest and Discipline in Education,* Routledge & Kegan Paul, London. [55,56,133-4,136]
Wilson, P. S. (1974) Perspectives on punishment – reply to Pamela Moore, *Proceedings of the Philosophy of Education Society of Great Britain,* Vol. 8, pp. 103-34. [133,134]
Wiseman, S. (1964) *Education and Environment,* Manchester University Press. [125]
Wolff, S. (1967) The contribution of obstetric complications to the etiology of behavior disorders in childhood, *Journal of Child Psychology and Psychiatry,* Vol. 8, pp. 57-66. [15]
Woods, P. (1975) Showing them up in secondary school, in G. Chanan and S. Delamont (eds.) *Frontiers of Classroom Research,* NFER, Windsor. [120]
Woods, P. (1976a) Pupils' view of schools, *Educational Review,* Vol. 28, pp. 126-37. [73]
Woods, P. (1976b) Having a laugh: an antidote to schooling, in M. Hammersley and P. Woods (eds.) *The Process of Schooling,* Routledge & Kegan Paul/Open University, London. [75]
Woods, P. (1979) *The Divided School,* Routledge & Kegan Paul, London. [73,90]
Woods, P. (1980) *Pupil Strategies,* Croom Helm, London. [32]
Wragg, E. C. (1978) A suitable case for initiation, *Times Educational Supplement,* 15 September. [93]
Wragg, E. C. (1981) *Class Management and Control,* Macmillan, London. [94]
Wragg, E. C. (ed.) (1984) *Classroom Teaching Skills,* Croom Helm, London. [98]

Wragg, E. C. and Dooley, P. A. (1984) Class management during teaching practice, in E. C. Wragg (ed.) *Class Management and Control,* Macmillan, London. [94]

Wragg, E. C. and Wood, E. K. (1984a) Teachers' first encounters with their classes, in E. C. Wragg (ed.) *Class Management and Control,* Macmillan, London. [86,98]

Wragg, E. C. and Wood, E. K. (1984b) Pupil appraisals of teaching, in E. C. Wragg (ed.) *Class Management and Control,* Macmillan, London. [71,72,75,98]

Wright, C. (1985a) Opportunities of children of West Indian origin: I. Learning environment or battleground; and (1985b) II. Who succeeds at school – and who decides?, *Multicultural Teaching,* Vol. 4, pp. 11–22. [65,78,80]

Wright, D. (1971) *The Psychology of Moral Behaviour,* Penguin, Harmondsworth. [120]

Wright, D. (1972) The punishment of children: a review of experimental studies, *Journal of Moral Education,* Vol. 7, pp. 199–205. [132]

Youngman, M. B. (1982) Behaviour as an indicator of pupils' academic performance, *Aspects of Education,* Vol. 27, pp. 129–46. [40]

Yule, W., Urbanowicz, M., Lansdown, R. and Millar, I. B. (1984) Teachers' ratings of children's behaviour in relation to blood lead levels, *British Journal of Developmental Psychology,* Vol. 2, pp. 295–305. [26]

SUBJECT INDEX

Acts of Parliament: Education (1944) 155; Education (1976) 153; Education (1981) 153, 164; Education No. 2 (1986) 123, 128, 154-5, 156-7
adjustment to schooling 41-3
adopted children 16
Advisory Centre for Education 157, 158, 161
aggression: adult influences 19, 23, 51, 120, 122; assessment of 38; and corporal punishment 126; deterrence of 116-17; perceptions of 13; school influences 42; sex differences 15; social class differences 23; and TV 24-6
anomie 50
assessment of behaviour: *see* behaviour
Assisted Places Scheme 124
Assistant Masters and Mistresses Association 3, 5
attachment bonds 17-18
attention-seeking 20, 78-9, 105, 119, 126
authority, concept of 47, 110

BATpack 106, 108
behaviour: assessment of 13, 27-8, 79, 105, 152; definition problems 13, 31-2, 36, 60; *see also* aggression; behaviour problems; conduct disorders; delinquency; group behaviour; maladjustment; pupils, teachers' images of
behaviour modification: educational value 111-13; ethics of 110-11; in ordinary classrooms 106-8; programmes 27, 105-8; technical problems 108-9; theory of 104, 109-11
behaviour problems, causes of: factors in the child 14-17, 31, 32; home influences 17-23, 31; implications for teachers 27-9; and physical environment 26-7; school influences 9, 30 ff., 106, 108; societal influences 23-6

body language 85-6, 103
boredom 78-9, 165
Bristol Social Adjustment Guides 13, 163

Campell & Cosans v. the UK 127-8
capitalism and discipline 48-9
causes of behaviour problems: see behaviour problems
character-training 54, 55
'Child at School' schedule 13, 38
child guidance clinics 153-4
child-rearing practices 18-22; see also parental influences
Children's Behaviour Questionnaire 13
classroom management skills 7, 30, 39, 90-4; see also behaviour modification; first encounters
cognitive-developmental theory 14, 20, 27
Commission for Racial Equality 155-6, 159, 160
conduct disorders 15, 19
conscience, development of 121
contracts with pupils and parents 105, 164-6
control, concept of 10, 51-3, 54; see also discipline
corporal punishment: see under punishment
counselling 145-8
cultural and subcultural factors: and sex differences 15; working-class 23-4, 27, 49, 55, 78, 126
curriculum opportunities 30, 40-1, 55-6, 138, 160, 165

delinquency: and corporal punishment 125; identifying causes of 14; parental influences 15, 18, 19, 51; personality factors 16; school influences 34, 35, 37
detention 123
discipline: concept of 9-10, 45 ff., 140; educative value 53-6; managerial value 10, 51-3, 54; and pastoral care 139-41; and personal needs 50-1; and societal needs 46-50
disruptive behaviour: see behaviour
disruptive pupils: see pupils, teachers' images of

educational psychologists 152-3, 162, 164
Educational Welfare Service 150-2
ethnic minority groups 24, 64-6, 78, 80, 155-6, 159-60
ethos of schools 36, 38
European Court of Human Rights 127-8
exclusion: see suspension and exclusion
expectations of 'good' teaching 71-6
expulsion 155; see also suspension and exclusion
extroversion and introversion: see personality factors

fairness, pupils' perceptions of 76-9
first encounters 1-3, 86-90
food additives 26-7
form tutor, role of 142, 144-5, 148

group behaviour 49-50, 81-4, 92
guilt and punishment 118

Hargreaves Report 7, 37, 155, 160, 166

heads and senior staff: and counsellors 147; and educational psychologists 152; leadership role 36, 38; support to teachers 53-4, 141-2; and suspensions 154, 156
hereditary factors 15-16
home influences: see behaviour problems; parental influences; parent-teacher relationships
house points 123
humour in classrooms 75, 84-5

intervention in 'at risk' cases 27
intrinsic interest and discipline 55-6, 100-2, 111

Japan, discipline in 48, 125
judgements: of pupils by teachers 50, 60 ff.; of teachers by pupils 55, 71 ff.; see also labelling; pupils, teachers' images of

labelling and labelling theory 14, 22, 27, 33, 67-71, 79
Law of Effect 105
lead levels in blood 26
learning difficulties 39-40
learning theory 14, 20-1, 22, 27; see also behaviour modification

maladjustment: causal factors 15; and cognitive developmental theory 20; definition problems 13, 163; and labelling 28, 67; and learning problems 39-40; school influences 33-4
management skills: see classroom management skills
mixed ability groups 93

NAS/UWT 3, 4, 5

National Association for Pastoral Care in Education 137
National Child Development Study 22
Newsom Report 58-9, 129
noise in classrooms 52, 61
non-verbal communication 85-6, 103
NUT 48, 127, 128

obedience 46, 54-5, 56
one-parent families 22-3
overcrowding 26
over-justification effect 100-1

parent-teacher relationships 34-5, 38, 43-4; and behavioural contracts 164-6; and School Psychological Service 123, 152; and support units 157, 159
parental influences 18-23, 31, 43, 51, 121, 151, 159, 164
pastoral care: concept of 137-9; counselling 145-8; and discipline 139-41; pastoral curriculum 142-5; and 'trouble-shooting' 141-2
perceptions of behaviour: see behaviour; pupils, teachers' images of
peripatetic support teams: see support teams
permissiveness 18, 47
personality factors 16, 28
Plowden Report 58
Poundswick High School 6, 156
praise 36, 49, 99-100, 102-3
Professional Association of Teachers 3
progressive schools 50, 62
psychiatric social worker 153

psychodynamic theory 14, 17, 22, 27, 121
psychotherapy 153-4
punishment: children's views 71-6 passim, 122, 126-7; corporal punishment 2, 34, 36, 123-9, 158; educational value 129-36; effects and effectiveness of 19, 20-1, 63, 75, 82, 105, 116-21; moral significance of 19, 121, 130-4; and personality factors 19, 119; and social control 48, 51, 115-23; research problems 117
pupils, teachers' images of 7, 29, 35, 51, 61 ff., 108, 152

racism: see ethnic minorities
Ralphs Report 151
Rampton Report 155
referrals: to senior staff 141; to support units 159-60
relationships: see teacher-pupil relationships
report, placing pupils on 123
reprimanding 39, 83-4, 112, 120
research problems 5-6, 12-14, 31-3, 36, 117
respect: for persons 59, 76, 79; for teachers 47, 48, 55
rewards 20, 38, 48, 49, 99-102, 110, 163: see also behaviour modification
'ripple' effect 85
rules 45, 46-7, 48, 53, 56, 129-30, 133, 159

sarcasm and ridicule 51, 84, 120
school effectiveness studies 8-9, 33-9
school ethos 36, 38

school influences 8-9, 30 ff.
School Psychological Service 152-3
seating arrangements 95-6
Seebohm Report 151
self-concept 21-2, 51
self-control 51, 52, 57
self theory 14, 21-2
sex differences 15, 61, 103
size of class and school 34, 38, 39
social class influences: see cultural and subcultural factors
social learning theory 14, 21, 27, 120-1
societal influences 23-6, 46-7, 158; see also cultural and subcultural influences
Spartan education 46
special needs 153, 158, 164
STOPP 127
strain theory 33
streaming 34, 62-3
stress: and counselling 147; and home conditions 151, 159; and impairment 15; and punishment 19; in teachers 6-7; and temperamental differences 16; and transition to school 41-3
subcultural theory 14
support for teachers 8, 52, 152, 153, 162-4, 166
support teams, peripatetic 162-4
support units: alternatives to 162-6; cost 161; curriculum in 160; development of 158; off-site 157-62; on-site 162; pupils' views 159; referral problems 159-60; reintegration problems 160; sex ratio in 15; statistics 158;
surveys of discipline problems 3-6, 124

suspension and exclusion 37, 154–7
Swann Report 24, 65
Swansea Behaviour Checklist 13, 28
'systemic' approach 9

Taylor Report 154
Teacher Education Project 93–4
teacher–pupil relationships 1–3, 53–6, 59–60, 111, 148, 159, 163; see also judgements of pupils by teachers; judgements of teachers by pupils; expectations of 'good teaching'; fairness; pupils, teachers' images of
teachers, pupils' expectations of good 71–6
teaching practice 86, 88, 94
television, influence of 14, 24–6
Thomas Report 42

'time out' 123
token economy 105
transition from home to school 41–2
transition from primary to secondary school 42–3

USA, school discipline in 48–9, 125
USSR, school discipline in 49–50

verbal communication 84–5, 102
violence in schools 3–6, 35; see also aggression

Warnock Report 158, 164
welfare services 150–2
whole-school policy 96–8
withdrawal units 123; see also support units
withdrawal of privileges 123, 165